52
NEW YORK
Weekends

52
NEW YORK
Weekends

Michael A. Schuman
Illustrated by Dale Swensson

Country Roads Press
CASTINE • MAINE

52 New York Weekends
© 1994 by Michael A. Schuman. All rights reserved.

Published by Country Roads Press
P.O. Box 286, Lower Main Street
Castine, Maine 04421

Text and cover design by Studio 3, Ellsworth, Maine.
Cover photograph courtesy of the South Street Seaport Museum,
    New York City.
Illustrations by Dale Swensson.
Typesetting by Typeworks, Belfast, Maine.

ISBN 1-56626-056-6

Library of Congress Cataloging-in-Publication Data

Schuman, Michael
    52 New York weekends / Michael A. Schuman ; Dale Swensson,
    illustrator.
        p.   cm.
    Includes index.
    ISBN 1-56626-056-6 : $9.95
    1. New York (State)–Tours.   I. Title.   II. Title: Fifty-two
New York weekends.
F117.3.S375   1994
917.4704'43–dc20   93-40587
                                                            CIP

Printed in the United States of America.
10 9 8 7 6 5 4 3 2 1

*For David and Fay Schuman
and Patti Jensen Schuman
with love and admiration,
without whom this book
would never have come to be.*

CANADA

St. Lawrence River

Lake Champlain

Lake Ontario

VERMONT

18   16   35, 46, 47
   20   9
3, 21 30, 31 33
              42, 43
23, 37   8
50 ● Rochester 6, 34
26
11, 38 19 15 ● Syracuse Albany ●
4   36   13, 24
Buffalo   NEW YORK   25   1
Lake Erie
   27
32   49   48   28

MASS.

CONN.

Hudson River

New York City

0   100
   MILES

PENNSYLVANIA   NEW JERSEY   Long Island

29
   4, 5

41, 45   40, 2
51, 52   14, 10   7, 22
12

LONG ISLAND

Contents

Spring

Summer

Fall

Winter

Introduction

New York state is likely the most misunderstood state in the nation. You don't have to be from California to think that the state's borders begin in Staten Island and end in Westchester County. There are people that live much closer who associate the Empire State with New York City and little else.

Certainly the Big Apple is one of the greatest cities in the world and worth many visits. But New York is a state filled with diversity, and you would be hard-pressed to find more within any other state's borders.

The Hudson is one of America's most storied rivers. It rolls past handsome estates, past bluffs that hug it like an apron, past pastoral farms, past cities. Its valley is rich with heritage.

The Adirondacks region offers miles and miles of wilderness, with a vastness as grand as the peaks of these alps in this, the Methuselah of mountain ranges.

The Finger Lakes and their surrounding hills and valleys serve up limitless recreation and views that change and impress at every turn.

Leatherstocking country – Cooperstown and the rest – looks more like New England than parts of New England.

So how could I narrow down the list to present the best in a single book? It was hard work, but fun. I traversed the entire state, investigating the many places where one can spend his or her free time. And I found these places fit into five major categories.

Colonial heritage. Colonists from all over Europe came to New York: the Dutch, the English, the Huguenots from France. More Revolutionary War battles were fought on New York state soil than in all of New England. When the war was over, George Washington was inaugurated as president of the United States on the site of Federal Hall in Manhattan.

Beauty. New York state has the best in mountains, rivers,

waterfalls, lakes, caverns, gorges, *and* the seashore. What more can an outdoors person want?

Work and play. New Yorkers have earned their wages on whaling ships and on farms, in resounding mills and on the floor of the stock exchange, by manufacturing glass and by selling herbs. And they spend their valuable leisure time in so many ways: tasting the wine, sailing the waters, shopping at reborn markets, and relaxing at the old ball game.

Famous personalities. New Yorkers have made their marks on the world in all fields. They have been presidents, authors, inventors, reformers, and of course, there is the lady in the harbor.

Castles and mansions. The wealthy and the eccentric had a passion for building Corinthian castles in the most beautiful settings. These are truly the homes of New York state's rich and famous.

To make this book handy for travelers planning weekend or day trips, I have organized it by season. This does not mean that the attractions in each section can be visited only at that particular time of year. For example, the Buffalo and Erie County Historical Society and the New York State Museum in Albany are open year-round. But I thought it would be convenient to list these sites as wintertime trips, knowing that New Yorkers sometimes hunger for sightseeing activities in the cold weather months, while emphasizing outdoor activities in the warmer weather.

I used three basic criteria in selecting places to be included. First, each must offer insight into an aspect of New York state's character. Second, I wanted to touch as many of New York state's geographic corners as possible. Third, I included only quality attractions, only those I would recommend to a friend.

I visited and personally researched every place featured in this book. I didn't just breeze through them in ten minutes.

I took every tour, screened every film and slide show, and spoke with curators, rangers, and other staff personnel to gain the detailed and special information visitors should know.

Please keep in mind two factors as you read on. While every detail has been verified at press time, changes in operating procedures and schedules can always occur. I deliberately omitted specific hours and costs, since these change often. Instead, I tell you generally when an attraction is open and whether or not admission is charged. For specific information about hours, costs, or the exact days of special events, it is recommended that you call or write in advance.

Also, just about all the attractions discussed – even those keeping year-round hours – shut down on Thanksgiving, Christmas, and New Year's Day. If you plan a special trip on any of those days, again please call ahead.

Finally, a note about the overnight accommodations mentioned in this book. For the most part they were not personally visited, and their inclusion does not represent a recommendation. However, the information was compiled from reliable sources, and hopefully it will be a convenience for travelers in this expansive state.

I am certain that whether you are making your first or 101st visit to any of these special places, you will find them to be wholly enjoyable and reflective of a special part of New York state's character.

To simplify road designations, I've used the following abbreviations: I=Interstate, US=U.S. Route or Highway, State= State Route or Highway.

Happy traveling!

Philipsburg Manor

1 The Roosevelts and Vanderbilts
Hyde Park

Franklin and Eleanor Roosevelt had common goals but, for much of their married lives, separate houses. Franklin had the lavish and heavy Victorian big house while Eleanor preferred the informal stucco home she named Val-Kill. Both are open to the public today in Hyde Park.

No member of the public would have been permitted to see the crude little wheelchair in FDR's dressing room at the Hyde Park big house. Not while he was alive. The president was concerned that, should his handicap be seen by the public, his image as a strong and able leader would suffer.

Today, when visitors parade by the second-floor dressing room and see the wheelchair, they don't recall FDR as a weakling or an incapacitated man. Most still think of the only four-time presidential election winner as the leader who steered his country through a depression and a world war, who soothed us with words of comfort over the radio, and who embodied the spirit of a nation trying to land on its feet. All the wheelchair does is humanize the legendary statesman.

Amid the dark and heavy late-Victorian opulence throughout the house are hints of FDR's personality. His chair at the oak dining room table is turned back slightly in order that his wheelchair could be accommodated.

1

Two high-backed leather chairs by the library fireplace were gifts he received during his two terms as governor of New York, and he often sat in one while giving his famous fireside chats. The cozy room down the hall, known as the snuggery, was the domain of Franklin's mother, Sara, who was often found sitting at the desk paying bills or writing to friends.

It is said by those who knew the Roosevelt family that Sara Roosevelt's domination of the big house didn't stop at the snuggery. As a result, Eleanor spent much of her time in Hyde Park at Val-Kill. Even when she came here with her husband as president and first lady, she rarely stayed overnight at the mansion.

Her second-floor bedroom is cold and empty. When you peer into the small, sparsely furnished room, you see a single bed, a wicker chair, a dresser, and a lonely writing table. It is not the room of a person who felt at home.

Not so for Franklin's room. He selected it because of its sweeping view of the Hudson River and of the distant Catskill Mountains. Pencil sketches of his mother and daughter are on the wall, and a picture of his well-known Scotty, Fala, hangs above his bedroom fireplace.

The president usually began his day holding court with his staff and advisers while still in bed. Within easy reach are two telephones, one on the nightstand and one on the wall; the wall phone was secretly coded with a direct line to the White House and was used many times during World War II.

Some of FDR's reading material during his brief fourth term still rests on a desk by a far window in his bedroom. The subjects reflect his concerns for the future. There is a biography of Italian dictator Benito Mussolini, a *Time* magazine dated March 5, 1945, a Bible, and a book titled *Agenda for a Post-War World*.

Like the big house, the museum of the Franklin D. Roosevelt Library next door helps visitors understand a complex man. Various items help tell his story.

The despised Scottish suit–kilts and all–that Sara made Franklin wear as a child is displayed near a tongue-in-cheek election poster for the editorial staff of the Harvard University newspaper; both are evidence of his privileged background. The crutches and cane he used, emblems of his struggle against polio, are supplemented by his 1936 Ford Phaeton convertible equipped with special manual controls.

The hard times of the 1930s are interpreted by photos of breadlines, National Recovery Administration posters with the famous blue eagle, and the first page of the 1933 inaugural speech containing the words "The only thing we have to fear is fear itself" circled in bright red.

The rough draft of another famous speech, the one given on December 8, 1941, is displayed; in the speech the president asked Congress for a declaration of war following the Japanese attack on Pearl Harbor. The first and most famous line, which reads, "a date which will live in infamy," originally said, "a date which will live in world history." You can see where the bland "world history" is crossed out and replaced with the direct and hard-hitting "infamy."

To learn more about Eleanor, spend some time in her specially designed library wing or take a look inside her home, Val-Kill. One would not expect to find a former first lady of the United States living in a converted factory off a dirt road in the woods. But of course, Eleanor Roosevelt was not a typical first lady.

To many, she was better known as a diplomat and a humanitarian than as the official White House hostess from 1933 to 1945. And it was her verve and energy that made her the most active, independent, and widely known first lady in the world.

Eleanor's Hyde Park home is a metaphor for Eleanor's self-image, plain as cardboard on the outside but warm and comfortable inside. Eleanor saw herself as awkward and homely, while

3

the majority of Americans viewed her as a person of inner beauty and compassion that was truly uncommon.

The piano in the Val-Kill living room is emblematic of her care and concern for others. She couldn't play, but her children and grandchildren could, and she kept it there for their use. And like most grandmothers, she went out of the way to accommodate them, offering freshly baked cookies or reading aloud Rudyard Kipling tales as they relaxed on the flower-print chairs in the living room.

But her thoughtfulness toward others extended far beyond close family members. Her home's five guest rooms were commonly occupied, and it wasn't unusual for her to put baked treats, flowers, or a book or magazine in a room for a special guest.

There were many: John F. Kennedy, Soviet Premier Nikita Khrushchev, and Yugoslavia's Marshal Tito to name a few. Although she was an otherwise perfect hostess, she rarely cooked and freely admitted her weakness in that department. When the tour takes you into the dining room, you hear about the time she cooked her guests a dinner of macaroni, potatoes, and creamed chicken topped off with pancakes and syrup.

Her preference for the informal life is especially apparent when you enter the screened-in porch upstairs. It was Eleanor's favorite place to sleep in summer—where she could enjoy the fresh night air and the sounds of the crickets and the distant silhouetted views of the Catskill Mountains—and looks more like the bunk where your counselor at Camp Waxahachie slept rather than a bedroom for the first lady of the United States.

That is appropriate though. This was a first lady who would rather pass up a formal party to sit in a wicker chair on her porch while family and friends cooked hot dogs in a fireplace or relaxed on the lawn enjoying nothing but the view and the sunshine. The atmosphere was such that respected personalities – Britain's Winston Churchill, for one – thought nothing of dropping formalities to take a soothing swim in the outdoor pool before grabbing a hot dog for lunch.

Such a casual lifestyle was hardly that of the man who had lived just up the road from the Roosevelts, Frederick W. Vanderbilt. An introductory ten-minute slide show and a series of exhibits inform you that Frederick was a painfully shy man but that his introversion was surpassed only by his altruism. For example, after noticing laborers on a job with no protective hand covering, he ordered and paid for gloves for all. In another instance, he and his wife, Louise, threw a special dinner for hardworking but poorly paid paperboys.

Vanderbilt, however, like the rest of his family, spared no expense in building his own summer palace. Whereas his brother William, in Newport, went in for marble, Frederick had a passion for tapestries, and you will see them throughout his three-story mansion.

Guests were greeted in the main hall, where you see your first tapestry. It hangs above the fireplace and depicts the coat of arms of the Medici family of Florence, Italy. Another, in the south foyer on the first floor, brings the Trojan War to life and was crafted in sixteenth-century Brussels. Still more tapestries are opposite this one in the north foyer and upstairs, blanketing Frederick's bedroom walls.

Like most wealthy Americans of the day, Frederick and Louise emphasized French decor with a shading of Italian styles. And like other Vanderbilts, Frederick built a home that members of European royalty would find as lavish as the throne rooms in their own palaces.

The lush rococo style of the reception room, also called

the gold room, bathes it with an elegance that's a hallmark of continental luxury. Gold leaf decorates the wood-paneled walls, and the Louis XV furniture fits in perfectly. This room was meant to convey the feeling of a mid-eighteenth-century French salon and it succeeds.

Upstairs, Louise had a white-and-gold railing built around the bedroom – after all, that is the way it was done at Versailles. We learned that this room was modeled after a French queen's bedroom of the Louis XV period. The queen would have had a railing surrounding her bed, since it was a custom for ladies of nobility to hold receptions in the morning while still in bed. Eager tradesmen, standing outside the railing, would present flowers, ribbons, gloves, and other goods to her while Her Majesty's friends sat inside the rail on folding stools or cushions.

Genuine royalty made their presence felt here. The Duke of Marlborough was entertained in the living room, also called the drawing room, which occupied enough space for a small orchestra to provide live entertainment. It was the setting for innumerable fetes and formal dances.

How did the other half live? You are given a peek as you finish your tour. "We came in like the upper crust and we leave like the servants," our guide said as he led us down a spiral staircase into the basement.

Actually, servants lived well in the Vanderbilt mansion. Their dining room table is set with Royal Copenhagen china, and although the kitchen appears small for such a palace, we were told that a visitor from the nearby Culinary Institute of America said that he could fix a meal for a hundred people in it with little problem.

We were led outdoors by way of the hired hands' quarters but were invited to walk the mansion grounds on a high bank above the river, enjoying a view that a millionaire could appreciate.

Location: FDR's big house, properly called Franklin D. Roosevelt National Historic Site, is on US 9, about a mile south of the center of Hyde Park. The FDR Presidential Library and Museum is on the grounds of the home. Val-Kill is two miles east of the FDR home, and the Vanderbilt Mansion is on US 9, two miles north of the entrance to FDR's home.

Admission is charged for the FDR house, the presidential library, and the Vanderbilt Mansion. Admission is free to Val-Kill.

Hours: The library/museum is open daily year-round. FDR's home and the Vanderbilt Mansion are open daily April through October and Thursday through Monday, the rest of the year. Val-Kill is open daily May through October; Saturday and Sunday, March-April and November-December; closed January and February.

Allow an hour to see each of the four sites; you might want to allow another half hour to an hour to walk the grounds of the Vanderbilt Mansion.

Information: Roosevelt-Vanderbilt National Historic Sites, 519 Albany Post Road, Hyde Park, NY 12538, 914-229-9115. Franklin D. Roosevelt Library and Museum, 511 Albany Post Road, Hyde Park, NY 12538, 914-229-8114.

Events: January 30, Franklin Roosevelt's birthday, graveside ceremony, West Point color guard, Army firing team; mid-June, antique auto show at Vanderbilt Mansion; summer, lawn concerts at Vanderbilt Mansion; October 11, Eleanor Roosevelt's birthday, graveside ceremony, talks, exhibits; early December through January 1, Christmas at Hyde Park, Val-Kill, and the Vanderbilts, accurate re-creations of both Roosevelt homes as they were decorated during the holidays and typical Gilded Age decorations at the Vanderbilt Mansion.

Note: Combination admission tickets are available to the FDR home and presidential library. Picnics are permitted on the Vanderbilt grounds. Up to seventy-five people can be

7

accommodated on one tour of the Vanderbilt Mansion, which means that at busy times you may have to sacrifice some personal attention. On summer weekends, tours are offered every twenty minutes; at other times they are every half hour.

If you are staying overnight: Dutch Patroon Motel, US 9 (half a mile north of the FDR home), Hyde Park, 914-229-7141; The Roosevelt Inn, US 9 (a mile north of the FDR home), Hyde Park, 914-229-2443; Super 8 Motel, US 9, Hyde Park, 914-229-0088; Beekman Arms, US 9 (at junction with State 308), Rhinebeck, 914-876-7077.

When in the area: There are lots of other attractions nearby. Another Gilded Age palace, Mills Mansion State Historic Site (pages 69–73), is five minutes north in Staatsburg. The Huguenot Street stone houses (pages 145–149), dating to the seventeenth century, are to the west in New Paltz, while airplanes from the days of Lindbergh and Earhart take to the air on weekends at Old Rhinebeck Aerodrome (pages 141–144) fifteen minutes north in Rhinebeck. If visiting presidential homes stirs your patriotic blood, keep in mind that West Point is half an hour south.

2 Long Island's Vanderbilt Museum
Centerport

The view from the Northport Porch at the Centerport, Long Island, Vanderbilt Museum mansion is to many worth the price of admission alone. In the foreground is the patio. Look past the patio and you see the calm waters of Northport Harbor. Beyond is bountiful Long Island Sound, and when it is extraordinarily clear, Norwalk, Connecticut, ten miles away, is visible.

The Vanderbilts, whether in Newport or up at Hyde Park or here on Long Island, had a way of incorporating aquatic views into their properties. But you get lots more for the admission price at Centerport's Vanderbilt Museum than a look at the lodgings and seaside scenery.

Here visitors explore what could stand on its own as a formidable natural history museum. William Kissam Vanderbilt II, adventurer, conservationist, and builder of this twenty-four-room residence he called Eagle's Nest, started a collection of animal and marine specimens that he willed with his home to the public. In addition, this mansion comes with a bonus—the Vanderbilt Museum Planetarium, constructed in 1971 on the site of the family tennis courts.

It is the mansion that initially draws the curious, and as far as houses of the rich and famous go, this one doesn't disappoint. But don't expect the palatial splendor and architectural braggadocio of the estates in Newport and Hyde Park. This is a low-key mansion, showy but livable. It will impress but won't overwhelm.

Owner William Kissam Vanderbilt II was the great-grandson of Commodore Cornelius Vanderbilt, the railroad and shipping magnate who founded the family fortune. The lush Vanderbilt mansions open to the public elsewhere were the homes of various members of the third generation; that includes Marble House in Newport, built in 1892 at the cost of $11 million and the summer "cottage" of William's father. (Perhaps by the fourth generation, with wealth no longer new, it was no longer necessary to lavishly impress.)

But don't worry, there are still plenty of treasures from throughout the world to admire within the white stucco walls and under the red tile roof of this three-story Spanish Revival abode. The list includes the limestone-and-marble fifteenth-century sitting room fireplace from Portugal depicting knights of the Crusades. Also from Portugal are the brown-and-turquoise floor tiles in the dining room. Sitting upon those tiles are seventeenth-century Flemish carved walnut chairs, a sacristy cabinet, and a sixteenth-century wooden monastery side table. The ceiling of hand-carved, painted Florida cypress adds to the medieval feel.

Mr. Vanderbilt's master bedroom is dominated by French Empire-style pieces with a bust of Napoleon on the desk and the seal of Napoleon embossed on the front of the bed. It is a touch of the Far East though – a nineteenth-century Chinese screen – that aesthetically blocks the bathroom from the casual visitor's view at the entrance to the room.

The lengthy list of lavishness is not to imply that all you see is centuries-old. The organ room is appropriately named for the 2,000-pipe Aeolian Duo-Art organ that Vanderbilt installed in the 1920s. You will notice other evidence of the twentieth century as your guide conducts you through Eagle's Nest: a wicker toilet seat cover and hamper in a bathroom and art deco closets in a dressing room.

While on the tour keep your eyes out for maritime decorations signaling William Vanderbilt's great love for all things nautical. Try to spot the scallop shell replicas on the front door, the shell moldings around the master bedroom ceiling, and the wood carvings of sea horses, snails, and scallops on the stairway columns of the courtyard's bell tower.

That will warm you up for sightings of the real things. Following the mansion tour you are left on your own to take your time and inspect the museum exhibits. You'll come face-to-face with vividly plumed birds – seemingly representing every shade and tint in the spectrum – and grotesque marine life that could only have been hauled up from the depths of the ocean.

There is a red macaw from Brazil, a green festive parrot from the upper Amazon River, and a sharp, light blue–capped fly-catcher from the Fiji Islands. The plumage of Count Rossi's Bird of Paradise looks amazingly similar to a spiked orange punk haircut, while the long, flowing white feathers of the Greater Bird of Paradise, from Papua New Guinea, resemble the powdered wig of a colonial merchant.

Shells and sea creatures take up eight rows on each wall in the next gallery. Clams, sponges, sea urchins, crayfish, and starfish in innumerable varieties are displayed, all specimens collected while William journeyed on three voyages, from 1926 to 1932, on which he visited all the world's seas and oceans. To make the most of his opportunities at sea he took with him an artist and curator, a taxidermist, a photographer, and a doctor. His yacht, *Alva*, named for his mother and built in Germany in 1930, was designed solely for his hobby of collecting marine life.

On the opposite side of the estate is the Vanderbilt Museum Planetarium, one of the largest in the United States. It has the capabilities of showing the appearance of the sky with the sun, moon, planets, and stars in their proper places from any location on earth, during any time of year, and from the beginnings of time onward into the future. Its "skyshows," open to the public, are changed three or four times a year with talks on astronomy and related fields planned periodically.

Location: To reach the Vanderbilt Museum, take the Long Island Expressway (I-495) to exit 51N (Deer Park Avenue) and follow

11

Deer Park Avenue (State 231) north for six miles; turn right onto Broadway and continue past State 25A where Broadway becomes Little Neck Road. The museum and mansion is at 180 Little Neck Road.

Admission is charged.

Hours: Year-round, Tuesday through Sunday. Call for planetarium schedule.

Allow an hour to ninety minutes to take the guided tour of the mansion and see the museums.

Information: Vanderbilt Museum, 180 Little Neck Road, Centerport, NY 11721, 516-262-7800. During the school year: for planetarium information, call 516-262-STAR (for a taped message), and for laser show information, call 516-262-8888. For planetarium or laser show information in summer, call 516-262-7800.

Events: Numerous special events take place annually. A partial list includes: spring concerts in the library (a room not seen on the standard mansion tour); courtyard concerts in summer; yacht race in fall; lectures throughout the year; carol sing in December.

Note: Buy tickets in the reception center, to the left as you walk from the parking lot to the mansion. There is a limit of twenty persons per tour. Picnic tables are by the main gate in front of the parking lot.

If you are staying overnight: Howard Johnson Motor Lodge, 270 West Jericho Turnpike (State 25), Huntington Station, 516-421-3900; Ramada Inn, 8030 Jericho Turnpike (State 25), Woodbury, (516) 921-8500; Holiday Inn, 215 Sunnyside Boulevard (Long Island Expressway [I-495], exit 46), Plainview, 516-349-7400. Please note that lodging is extremely expensive on Long Island.

When in the area: Theodore Roosevelt's home, the celebrated

Sagamore Hill, which some have called the country's first Summer White House, is just east in Oyster Bay (pages 263–269). Old Bethpage Village Restoration (pages 52–57) is an archetypal nineteenth-century village to the south in Old Bethpage.

3 Sainte Marie Among the Iroquois
Syracuse

"This is GNN, the Global News Network and now, at the top of the hour, here are the lead stories for June 21, 1657.

"In England, efforts to structure a successful new form of government continue to encounter difficulties since the beheading of King Charles I almost ten years ago. Last month Oliver Cromwell, who led the civil war against Charles, refused Parliament's request to become the new king. Efforts to draft a new constitution continue . . .

"Switching to Quebec, center of the struggling colony that the French have planted along the St. Lawrence River, leaders have expressed cautious optimism regarding their efforts to forge a long-lasting, peaceful relationship with their former Iroquois enemies."

Such is the beginning of the news broadcast on the seventeenth century's version of CNN, as heard on a TV monitor in the visitors center at Sainte Marie Among the Iroquois, the combination re-created village and museum near the shores of Onondaga Lake in Syracuse. The time is 1657, and present-day Syracuse is endless wilderness, infinite stretches of woods and meadow, the home of the Onondaga Nation, part of the great Iroquois Confederacy. At the time you are visiting, the Jesuits from the Quebec settlement in New France have come to live among the native Iroquois.

"Imagine what it was like three hundred and fifty years ago," says park spokesman Bob Geraci. "Try not to put white hats or black hats on anybody's heads. There is no right or wrong here. It is just two very different cultures that have come together."

The living-history settlement, says Geraci, is based on a similar one in Midland, Ontario, called Sainte Marie Among the Hurons, and is located very near the site of the original settlement. This American version opened in 1991, replacing what

Syracusans had known for years as "the French fort" in Onondaga Lake Park, a sort of ersatz re-creation of a stockade, which,
Geraci says, "was a place to pretend you were Davy Crockett
fighting the Indians."

Sainte Marie Among the Iroquois is in effect two attractions:
the visitors center, which is a hands-on museum giving visitors
from the twentieth century background about the time and
place portrayed here, and the actual village. You will need the
background obtained in the visitors center to be able to converse with the village residents, who, like the residents of Fort
Stanwix National Monument (pages 113–117), offer first-person
interpretation. They play the roles of actual settlers here and are
stuck in the year 1657. They cannot discuss anything that took
place at a later time.

One's time is best spent equally between the two parts,
for the settlement itself is small, currently consisting of three
buildings and an open yard with a wooden cross. (A dormitory is being constructed.) The attractions of Sainte Marie are
the village residents as much as the structures, all of which
were created from scratch to replace what was the crumbling
French fort.

Exhibits in the visitors center, all state-of-the-art, explain a
bit about the Onondaga people of yesterday and today, their
relationship with the forest and the animals, as well as the
French in the seventeenth century in the motherland and in the
New World.

In a mounted display you read, "To the Onondagas, the
forest was more than just a bountiful resource for food, shelter,
tools and medicine. Natives also possessed a spiritual bond to
the woods. To them, this was a place where every animal and
plant had unique spirits, habits, needs and uses . . . The Iroquois also believed that animals were not inferior species and
looked upon them as spiritual equals who had their own souls.

15

Certain animals were chosen as traditional names for Iroquois clans."

Another display, headed "What is sugar to one people is bitter wormwood to the other," features a quote from a Jesuit named Paul Le Jeune, who in 1658 said, "The world is full of variety and change . . . If one were mounted on a tower high enough to survey all the Nations of the earth, he would find it very hard, amid such strange varieties to say who are wrong and who are right."

It is in the mission village that you meet the people you read about in the visitors center. In the refectory we made the acquaintance of Joseph Boursier, a Jesuit brother, and Rene Oure, a *donné*, or domestic helper, here not for the religion but for the free food and shelter given in exchange for his work. Rene was busy at the hearth cooking up a batch of sagamite, a concoction of cornmeal, berries, herbs, and maybe an eel or two from the nearby lake for added flavor, while Joseph, in gray bonnet, linen chemise, and short linen breeches called *hauts-de-chausses*, was sitting at a table taking inventory with a quill pen.

While somewhat crudely constructed, the refectory is a surprisingly handsome building considering the lack of machinery and resources of that day. Inside is a pleasant clutter of rough-hewn tools, muskets, a lumpy bed, and a barrel covered with a cloth where resident soldiers relaxed with a game of cards away from the watchful eye of the brothers.

"Rest yourself, you need not stand," Joseph said to us (in English, not French—the language aspect of reality is suspended so that twentieth-century Americans can communicate with seventeenth-century Frenchmen) as we entered the refectory and proceeded to sit across the table from him. He then allowed the children in our group to help out with the inventory by trying their hand at writing with a quill pen.

Joseph ran down the list: "Ten candles, five bars of iron, six bars of soap, no cows. We could not bring cows with us since we had to travel by canoe. Pigs and chickens were the only animals we brought with us."

As the kids are busy writing, Joseph marvels, "So many young ones literate. This is so rare in France. Your families must be wealthy."

The ink, he explained, is made from a dye brought from France, also used to dye clothes. The Iroquois, he added, have been most helpful, providing corn, beans, and tobacco in addition to permitting the French to use their lake, filled with salmon, trout, and eel. "The eel are so plentiful, you can cross the lake on the back of them," Joseph marveled.

He then asked a couple of adult twentieth-century visitors to lend a hand grinding corn with a mortar and pestle and sweeping the floor with a makeshift broom, little more than wrapped twigs bound to a stick. At other times, adults or children may be given an opportunity to help out baking bread, try playing a seventeenth-century game, making a Native American corn bracelet, or even sampling a taste of New France cuisine, circa 1657, such as beaver, rabbit, or sagamite.

In the workshop (call it an "atelier" and you'll pass as an expert), blacksmith Louis Gaubert was crafting a gambrel but stopped his chores to discuss the birch bark canoe hanging overhead, similar to the one the men rode here, and handed out a piece of the thin bark for us to touch. It was important, he said, that canoes be light, since the men would have to carry them at times of unpassable water.

We also met Charles Boivin, master builder and architect of the mission, who had served in a similar capacity at Sainte Marie Among the Hurons until that village was decimated by sickness and war. While sharpening his tools, Charles told us that it took seven weeks to travel the 400 miles from Quebec to the present site.

Unless you are here for a special event, you probably won't meet Native Americans except through the GNN News on the video terminal in the visitors center. An Onondaga man being interviewed by a reporter on video said of the French missionaries, "I found these bearded men very ugly at first with hair sticking out from their face where only smooth skin should be, but over time I came to tolerate it. Their ways are very strange but I do not fear them."

The Native American continued, "I know that some in our village say that those who wear the black robes are sorcerers. When they lived among the Hurons, many thousands died, especially after the French priests poured water on their heads. That is why some of the priests were killed . . . to protect our people."

It was a dangerous situation for all involved, but danger was a way of life here for many a couple of centuries later too. Those who worked in the salt houses of the nineteenth century are offered tribute in the Salt Museum, across the street in Onondaga Lake Park. The museum, made from timbers from abandoned salt houses, sits on the site of an 1856 salt manufactory. The land surrounding Onondaga Lake was pure salt marshland, and the salt industry built Syracuse, which understandably became known as the Salt City.

A re-created salt block in the museum incorporates the chimney of the original salt manufacturing structure. As you pore over the accompanying copy, you read that working in a salt factory was as close as possible to what a present-day worker might call a "job from hell." Workers labored in ninety-degree heat and brutal humidity up to twelve hours a day, seven days a week. The possibility of being seriously injured or killed on the job was real and ranged from being sprayed by a scalding splash of brine to falling into a kettle filled with boiling brine. Ouch!

About 5,000 people were employed in the salt and related industries, including lumbering, wagonmaking, and coopering. A reconstructed cooper's shop has ringlets of wood piled on the wall, and planes, axes, and shaved and unshaved logs are tossed about like yesterday's newspaper. There is also a clunky drilling rig, used to tap brine around the southern end of Lake Onondaga, and room for regularly scheduled temporary exhibitions, not all related to the salt industry. We saw one called "Bringing Up Baby" showcasing the progress of pregnancy and baby care and play for the last century.

Location: To reach Sainte Marie Among the Iroquois in Syracuse, from the New York State Thruway (I-90), exit 38, take a right onto State 57 to the museum; entrance is on the left. From I-81 heading south, exit 23, take a left onto Hiawatha Boulevard, then left again onto Park Street; bear left onto Onondaga Lake Parkway (State 370W); entrance is on the right. From I-81 heading north, exit 24 in Liverpool, take Onondaga Lake Parkway (State 370W) to the site entrance on the right.

Admission is charged to Sainte Marie Among the Iroquois, and there is a nominal charge to the Salt Museum.

Hours: Sainte Marie Among the Iroquois is open daily except Monday, May through December, and daily except Monday and Tuesday the rest of the year. The Salt Museum is open daily, May through October, afternoons only on Sunday.

Allow an hour and a half to two hours at Sainte Marie Among the Iroquois (preferably forty-five minutes to an hour in both the visitors center and the village) and half an hour to the Salt Museum.

Information: Onondaga County Department of Parks and Recreation, P.O. Box 146, Liverpool, NY 13088, 315-453-6767.

Events: There are many. A partial list at Sainte Marie includes: Easter, Latin mass in village church; late May or June, Canoe

Festival, canoes handcrafted on the grounds, speakers; mid-August, Resupply: A French-Native Cultural Celebration, historic re-creation of second trip by French, demonstrations of musketry and fencing; October, A Gathering of the Iroquois, Native American food, crafts, children's games, music, dance, and lectures; December, Symbols of Christmas, self-guided lantern tours, holiday play, visit from Pere Noel (French Santa Claus). Special hands-on activities are scheduled for Wednesdays in summer and Sundays the rest of the year.

At the Salt Museum: Salt City 4th of July, crafts, old-time children's games, ice cream, music.

Note: Picnic tables are on the Sainte Marie grounds and at Onondaga Lake Park. The park is also used for numerous other recreational activities like boating, walking, roller blading, and tram tours in the warm weather months.

If you are staying overnight: Ramada Inn, 1305 Buckley Road (I-90, exit 36, then west), Syracuse, 315-457-8670; Arborgate Inn, 430 Electronics Parkway (at I-90, exit 37), Liverpool, 315-453-6330; Motel 6, 6577 Court Street Road, East Syracuse, 315-433-1300; John Milton Inn, Carrier Circle, Syracuse, 315-463-8555; Howard Johnson Lodge, Carrier Circle, Syracuse, 315-437-2711.

When in the area: In downtown Syracuse is the Erie Canal Museum (pages 122–124), in an original 1850 canal weighlock building, the only surviving building of its kind. About forty-five minutes east are Erie Canal Village (pages 118–121) and Fort Stanwix National Monument (pages 113–117) in Rome.

4 Sleepy Hollow Country
Tarrytown and Croton-on-Hudson

"He was the Bill Cosby of his day," said Geri Heisser, site manager of Sunnyside, Washington Irving's gabled riverside home in Tarrytown, a property of Historic Hudson Valley, the group administering several historic homes and other properties in the lower Hudson Valley.

"By the time he moved here he was a well-known celebrity," she continued. "He was fifty-two, famous and respected as much in Europe as here. The United States was not respected for literature until Washington Irving came along."

Irving first became known in 1809, when he published his satirical *History of New York,* for which he created his well-known character Diedrich Knickerbocker. (He didn't borrow the word "knickerbocker." He created it.) Short stories like the celebrated "Rip Van Winkle" and "The Legend of Sleepy Hollow" followed. There were also sizable serious volumes like *The Life of Columbus*. There had also been years of public service as a diplomat at American posts in Madrid and London.

While Irving's career was firmly established when he purchased Sunnyside in 1835, his dream house was not. It was just a small stone cottage until the proud new owner added Dutch stepped gables, weather vanes, and various Gothic and Romanesque architectural features. Irving later referred to his finished home as "a little old-fashioned stone mansion all made up of gable ends and as full of angles and corners as an old cocked hat."

There was one factor Irving didn't take into account when he bought the house: the growing railroad industry. But could he ever have known that track would be laid on the land between his home and the Hudson River? Said Irving later, in a Cosbyesque piece of cynicism, "If there was a Garden of Eden on the earth today, a train would run right through it." The

railroad is still there. Commuting suburbanites roll past Sunnyside daily en route to and from fashionable Westchester County
homes and midtown Manhattan offices.

If Irving were alive today, he likely would be taking the same
train, since Sunnyside was as modern and innovative for its time
as solar homes are for late-twentieth-century residents. In the
Sunnyside kitchen is a cast-iron cooking stove, a sparkling new
convenience in 1850s America, when the open hearth was still
the rule in most homes.

Washington Irving's Sunnyside in Tarrytown, "a little old-fashioned
stone mansion all made up of gable ends and as full of angles and
corners as an old cocked hat"

The pantry has a wooden drying rack, one of the first kitchen area space savers. Other state-of-the-art marvels in Sunnyside include a chest lined with zinc (sort of an ancestor of the icebox) and a bathtub—at a time when even the White House couldn't claim one. But the most progressive of all Washington's innovations was the hot-water boiler and running water fed from the Sunnyside pond through a gravity-flow system.

After the kitchen and pantry most visitors like Irving's study best. It's a snug little workplace loaded with books. Ironically, it is in this room where you hear that Irving was not a good student. He hated school and loved good times, but he also loved the arts.

The study is the best-documented room in Sunnyside because many artists who visited Irving kept a visual record of it. The desk was a gift from his publisher, George P. Putnam, and a common first reaction from visitors is that the drawers are on the wrong side. Actually, the drawers that you face are fake; real drawers are on the side you can't see. In the rear of the study is the red divan on which Irving often slept.

Irving never married, but he didn't live alone. Nieces Catherine and Sarah Irving resided with him and served as hostesses while brother Ebenezer slept upstairs in a pallid little room reflecting his conservative tastes.

On the other hand, the author's bedroom tells of a colorful extrovert. While Ebenezer slept on a plain rope mattress, his more famous brother, when not asleep in his study, rested his weary bones on a lofty Sheraton tester bed with a bold and bright Jacquard double-leaf coverlet.

On a bedroom table is an engraved likeness that haunted Irving until his death. He had once been engaged to a woman named Matilda Hoffman, daughter of a former attorney general, but she died of tuberculosis before they married. Irving kept the engraving next to his bed throughout his life and it was here when he died in 1859.

Two other Historic Hudson Valley properties take visitors back to Dutch colonial New York. Our guide welcomed us into the main house at Philipsburg Manor, Upper Mills, a colonial home and mill complex in North Tarrytown, by saying, "You've heard of the family room, the living room, the dining room, and the play room? Well, you're in it."

The time portrayed at Philipsburg Manor is the period when this modern commuter-land was sparsely settled, and even the busy borough of Brooklyn to the south was little more than cows and sheep and an occasional farm. This was a time when conditions were spartan even for a wealthy family like that of Frederick Philipse, who came here in the 1650s as Gov. Peter Stuyvesant's carpenter but later built up a great fortune that included this twenty-acre parcel of land on which he operated a gristmill and a granary. Reconstructions of both are here today.

Visitors cross on the reconstructed dam over the millpond on their way from the reception center to the main attractions here: the manor house, the gristmill, the granary, and the New World Dutch barn.

In the white stone manor house the floors are bare, the windows have no curtains, and as you can tell from your guide's opening remarks, a single room had many purposes. The multipurpose room is the first stop. Its walls are whitewashed, since it was commonly believed that light colors promoted good health. The centerpiece is a Dutch draw-top table covered with a colorful carpet.

A Dutch kas, or cabinet, dominates the parlor, and the upper kitchen has shelves lined with delftware and pewter serving dishes. Anyone heading upstairs had to pass through the upper kitchen, so it was natural for the family to put its best possessions on display here.

Despite its name, the upper kitchen was mainly a showplace, used often for dining and only occasionally for cooking. Most meal preparation took place down in the lower kitchen with its stone floor that served as insurance against fires caused by flying sparks.

The spicy scents of apples filled the air when we visited as staff members garbed in mop hats, shawls, blue aprons, and wooden shoes baked apple puffs. One woman rolled dough on a wooden table while another tended apples simmering in wine and a six-pack of spices in a Dutch oven, a squatty little pot with legs. After one whiff of the hot, tangy aroma there were many requests from our tour group for recipes.

The Philipsburg Manor tour ends with a look inside the dairy, an underground chamber with milk containers from Holland, and the mill house. Visit when things are in gear and you can watch corn or another grain being ground while a staff member explains the processes involved in operating the machinery.

The explanation of milling, mechanics and all, is less complex than the roots of the Van Cortlandt family, whose manor and ferry houses are in Croton-on-Hudson, a few miles north of Philipsburg Manor, where they guard the confluence of the Hudson and Croton rivers.

Here you are given another look at early New York life, and you will hear the background on the family's generations and marriages – and more generations and more marriages – as you stand outside the sturdy home on a path paved with oyster shells. In brief, the first Van Cortlandt arrived in New Amsterdam in 1638, and over the decades his descendants married into such prestigious families as the Schuylers, Livingstons, and Philipses.

The manor house, which has occupied this site for over 200 years, has been restored to reflect its appearance from 1790 to 1814. The upper half is built in the Palladian style, the bottom half like a hunting lodge.

Our guide entered the house through the rear while we climbed up the outdoor staircase in the front. The guide was there to greet us, peering over the bottom half of a split Dutch door, telling us that the closed bottom door was a device to keep children in and animals out while the open upper door allowed a breeze to sweep inside.

We were given a mini-course in furniture design. We saw Chippendale chairs with their ball-and-claw feet and Queen Anne chairs with typical rounded backs. But for all the show-pieces, we saw reminders of the lack of comforts, even for a wealthy family like the Van Cortlandts. We stepped over a door-mat made of corn husks while entering the kitchen. Upstairs in a bedroom is a Chippendale toilet chair, elegantly styled but with a practical chamber pot underneath. Behind the manor is the outdoor necessary house, certainly necessary but definitely unpleasant on numbing January mornings.

The tour leaves the manor and follows the brick path known as "the long walk" (although it's really a short walk) to the ferry house. In this tavern travelers could have a few drinks, some conversation, and a view of the rushing Croton River be-fore taking a ferry across the river or a stagecoach on the Albany Post Road.

Stagecoach operators delivering the mail often stopped here, evidenced by the bullwhip resting by a barroom table. That room's raison d'etre is symbolized by gin and Madeira bottles, while five rows of the Van Cortlandt family's pewter ware—tankards, plates, and mugs—line the shelves of the sprawling hutch.

Take a look at the posted signs outside the ferry house before you leave. They were travelers' best friends, whether relating reports of runaway slaves (slavery was common in New York state, and the Van Cortlandts had about a dozen slaves) or giving the latest Albany stagecoach schedule. According to the posted timetable, the trip from Croton-on-Hudson to Albany took two and a half days.

Location: Sunnyside is west of US 9 on West Sunnyside Lane, one mile south of the Tappan Zee Bridge and one mile south on the New York State Thruway (I-87), exit 9. Philipsburg Manor, Upper Mills, is on US 9, two miles north of I-87, exit 9, and the Tappan Zee Bridge. Van Cortlandt Manor is one-quarter mile south of the Croton Point Avenue exit off US 9. It is nine miles north of I-87, exit 9, and the Tappan Zee Bridge.

Admission is charged to all Historic Hudson Valley properties.

Hours: All three are open March through December, daily except Tuesday; January and February, weekends only.

Allow forty-five minutes for the Sunnyside tour and up to a couple of hours if you wish to walk the grounds. Allow an hour to an hour and fifteen minutes for the Philipsburg Manor tour and an hour for the tour of Van Cortlandt Manor.

Information: Historic Hudson Valley, 150 White Plains Road, Tarrytown, NY 10591, 914-631-8200.

Events: Sunnyside: August, Storytelling Festival; late October, Legend of Sleepy Hollow Weekend, puppets, storytellers; Thanksgiving at Sunnyside; late December, candlelight tours. Philipsburg Manor, Upper Mills: mid-May, Pinkster Celebration, Dutch colonial spring festival with music, country dancing, children's games; early December, candlelight tours. Van Cortlandt Manor:

early and mid October, Marketplace, handcrafts, apples, ciders, pumpkins for sale; mid-October, Autumn Crafts and Tasks, demonstrations of farm and horse labor in preparation for eighteenth-century winter, handcrafts.

Note: Buy admission tickets for Sunnyside in the reception center before you reach the house. Discounted tickets for Sunnyside; Philipsburg Manor, Upper Mills; and Van Cortlandt Manor are available. All three Historic Hudson Valley properties maintain picnic tables and all three have quality gift stores. At Philipsburg Manor, Upper Mills, you can buy cornmeal or grains made at the mill. A joint ticket for neighboring Lyndhurst (see pages 29–32) is also available.

The newest site run by Historic Hudson Valley is a magnificent property noted for both its historic and aesthetic significance. Kykuit (pronounced "Kye-cut," Dutch for "lookout") was the country villa of John D. and several other Rockefellers. Built between 1907 and 1913 in the elegant beaux-arts style, the mansion is full of antiques, Oriental porcelains, Chinese ceramics, and the works of modern artists Pablo Picasso, Robert Motherwell, Alexander Calder, and Andy Warhol, among others. The garden consists of roses, annuals, perennials, rhododendron, garden pavilions, grottoes, fountains, and modern sculpture. Kykuit is open by appointment only. Call Historic Hudson Valley, 914-631-8200, as far in advance as possible for reservations.

If you are staying overnight: Westchester Marriott Hotel, 670 White Plains Road (State 119, I-287, exit 1), Tarrytown, 914-631-2200; Days Inn, 200 Tarrytown Road (State 119, I-287, exit 1), Elmsford, 914-592-5680; Ramada Inn, 540 Sawmill River Road (State 9A, about a mile and a half north of State 119), 914-592-3300; Courtyard by Marriott, 631 Midland Avenue (I-95, exit 22N) or I-95 (exit 21S), Rye, 914-921-1110.

When in the area: The Gould Mansion, Lyndhurst (pages 29–32), a Hudson River Gothic–style classic, is also in Tarrytown.

5 Lyndhurst
Tarrytown

George Washington rejected the notion that he become the first king of America, and so our country is without official royalty. That is probably why we create unofficial royalty – commercial and political royalty, people with power and money. That goes whether they earned it the hard way or the old-fashioned way . . . through an inheritance.

Like British royalty, American royalty has long resided in palaces and castles. Of all those built alongside the Hudson River, Lyndhurst in Tarrytown is credited as the earliest and is regarded as the first of the many mansions classified as Hudson River Gothic. As the architectural label hints, Lyndhurst, with its Gothic trademarks of arched doors and windows, finials, bosses, and ribbed and vaulted ceilings, looks the part of a royal family's castle. As icing on the structural cake, it sports turrets, lushly landscaped grounds, and a tower.

Which American "royalty" lived here? First there was a politician, former New York City Mayor William Paulding, who commissioned Andrew Jackson Davis in 1838 to design the mansion. The grounds were designed based on the progressive ideas of Andrew Jackson Downing, recognized as the country's first professional landscape architect. Paulding called his home Knoll, and it was a humble one, small but perfect as a retirement home for the ex-mayor who lived here until 1864.

But when the next owner, wealthy New York City merchant George Merritt, moved in with his wife and six children, it was obvious the place needed to be enlarged. So Merritt called back Davis, who raised the roofline and added a wing, a porte cochere, and the striking tower, giving the place its distinct, castle-like feel.

It was the final owner, the famous (and, in some minds, infamous) Jay Gould, railroad magnate and Wall Street speculator, who best fit the role of American commercial royalty. His improvements on the mansion, by then called Lyndhurst, were relatively minor.

A painting of Jay Gould hanging in the vestibule is a metaphor for his perceived stature. Gould stood only five feet two inches, but his posture and the positioning of his chair in the painting make him look taller. Surely the man who in 1884 controlled Western Union Telegraph, the New York El, and the Erie Railroad could hardly be perceived as small. He was worth nearly $72 million when he died in 1892.

Until 1961, when the home was willed to the National Trust for Historic Preservation, Lyndhurst never left the Gould family's possession. Daughter Helen took charge of Lyndhurst after her father's death, and after Helen died in 1938, her sister, Anna, Duchess of Talleyrand-Perigord (at last, some genuine royalty!) returned from France to live her last years here.

In the late nineteenth century, long before swimming pools and Porsches, the wealthy had other ways to broadcast their status, and you will encounter them as you walk through Lyndhurst. For one thing, there's the cork floor in the kitchen. For another, there is the disguised pine wood in the dining room. The lowly pine has been dressed up to fool your eyes, and to the eyes of most visitors, it succeeds. The marble columns in the dining room really are pine; the rosewood and oak ceilings there are also pine.

You will find this pattern throughout Lyndhurst. Our guide, Juliette, pointed out wooden doors in the porte cochere painted to appear bronze. In the vestibule, plaster walls have been painted to resemble yellow marble, and plaster ceilings to resemble white marble. The purpose of disguising common wood to make it look valuable was not, as we first thought, for Lyndhurst's owners to fake out guests. On the contrary, said Juliette, status-conscious people went to this trouble to show that they could afford to hire artists who could make the ordinary appear expensive.

An abundance of stained glass – some Tiffany, some Bohemian – is an additional hallmark of the time. But the stained glass dining room alcove windows are energy efficient as well. The window on the right is red, to help heat the room in the morning; the window on the left is blue, to cool the room in the afternoon.

Other highlights of Lyndhurst? There's the library that has tiered bookshelves, a clever method of displaying as many books as possible. It also has two doors, one that opens into the music room and another that opens into a blank wall, created for the sake of symmetry.

The art gallery, which was a library before the Merritts enlarged the house, is the only room with a true Gothic ceiling. Here is the Goulds' art collection, some forty paintings lining the walls. The most famous is *First Caress* by William Adolphe Bouguereau, created in 1866. Look above the framed art to see the faces of classical writers and philosophers like Voltaire, Shakespeare, Dante, and Rousseau carved into the walls.

You end the tour where there is no art or stained glass or any other trademark of the nineteenth-century rich and famous. Step into the butler's pantry and you have a servant's-eye view of the dining room. But there is a touch of the high class here too. The floor is made of cork, making it less likely to be damaged and cushioning the tired feet of the butler and head footman.

Downstairs was a scullery, the workplace for the unassuming scullery maid, often a girl from the slums, who with a little old-fashioned luck and pluck, could work her way up to the respectable position of head housekeeper. A royal head housekeeper, no doubt.

Location: Lyndhurst is on US 9, about half a mile south of the New York State Thruway (I-87) at the Tappan Zee Bridge.

Admission is charged.

Hours: May through October, Tuesday through Sunday; November through April, weekends.

Allow forty-five minutes for the tour and up to two hours if you walk the expansive grounds.

Information: Lyndhurst, 635 South Broadway, Tarrytown, NY 10591, 914-631-0046.

Events: There are several, including: May, chamber music concerts; May and September, craft shows; June, Rose Day; July, Sunset Serenades Concert Series; September, Westchester Dog Show; October, tag sale and auction; December, candlelight tours.

Note: There are picnic tables on the grounds. The gift shop in the carriage house has a fine selection of Victorian-style items. In addition, light lunches are available in the carriage house. The carriage house is a showplace for special exhibits relating to Lyndhurst or those who lived here. People with an interest in horticulture should plan some time to walk the grounds, especially in summer when the rose and fern gardens are in bloom.

If you are staying overnight: Westchester Marriott Hotel, 670 White Plains Road (State 119, I-287, exit 1), Tarrytown, 914-631-2200; Days Inn, 200 Tarrytown Road (State 119, I-287, exit 1), Elmsford, 914-592-5680; Ramada Inn, 540 Sawmill River Road (State 9A, about a mile and a half north of State 119), 914-592-3300; Courtyard by Marriott, 631 Midland Avenue (I-95, exit 22 N) or I-95 (exit 21 S), Rye, 914-921-1110.

When in the area: The properties of Historic Hudson Valley — Sunnyside (Washington Irving's home); Philipsburg Manor, Upper Mills; Van Cortlandt Manor; and Kykuit (home of John D. Rockefeller) (pages 21–28) — are in the vicinity.

6 American Museum of Fire Fighting
Hudson

Some say experience is the best teacher. That being the case, there is no better person than Charlie Duggan to lead you on a tour of the American Museum of Fire Fighting in Hudson. Charlie is a veteran firefighter, a resident of the adjacent Volunteer Firemen's Home of the state of New York, and the senior tour guide at the museum.

You may not have Charlie Duggan to show you around, but it is likely you will have someone like him. All guides are residents of the firemen's home. And, like many old-timers, there are guides who feel that modern methods can't match the quality of the past.

But they aren't even talking about their own youth. They are referring to a time long past, long before the days of manning the red engines. We look at a brilliantly carved, high-carriage, piano-style fire engine built in 1851. Our guide tells us that it was crafted by a piano maker, so it is no coincidence that the chassis looks like a baby grand.

He points out its four panels, each adorned with a hand-painted portrait done by Joseph H. Johnson, an artisan known among fire-fighting buffs for his decorations of fire engines. The likenesses depict Chief Engineer of New York Alfred Carson and three better-known Americans: Henry Clay, George Washington, and Thomas Jefferson; this engine was owned by New York's Jefferson Engine Company.

It is shown that, despite the beauty of these depictions, one of them is flawed. Sure enough, looking closely at Jefferson's image, we see that the third president is wearing two left shoes. Other than as a reference to possible poor dancing ability, it is not known why that is. But if your guide should try to catch you on that painting, you'll be ready.

The piano-style fire engine is displayed in a hall devoted

solely to fire-fighting apparatus built prior to the twentieth century. The museum also has equipment from the steam and motorized ages, through the late 1920s.

One of the most modern acquisitions is a long, lanky hook-and-ladder made by Elmira's La France Fire Engine Company, which churned out fire-fighting vehicles for decades. This one served from 1916 to 1956 in Oyster Bay, Long Island.

But the claim of many veterans that they don't make them like they used to holds true when you spot an earlier hook-and-ladder, also a New York state product, built by Rumsey & Company in Seneca Falls. Its lengthy body belies its light weight—so light in fact that it was meant to be pulled by manpower and only later was altered so it could be pulled by horses. Hand-painted floral patterns on the chassis, ladders, and tools make this another beauty.

The oldest machines are usually the most ornate. A double-deck end-stroke machine built in 1846 in Philadelphia resembles a circus calliope more than a fire-fighting machine. The sides of the panel box serve as canvases for more of Joseph H. Johnson's works: George Washington crossing the Delaware, the rescue of Captain John Smith by Pocahontas, and a female allegorical figure, the Genius of Freedom. There are painted depictions of eagles on the ornate wooden carvings on the machine's sides and classy brass sunbursts on its wheel hubs.

It is surprising that this much art exists in such an unlikely place, and we see why veteran firefighters are understandably proud. But the one fire-fighting machine that made our guide beam the most is the one you will see when you first set foot in the museum.

The Newsham Engine was built in London in 1725, when good King George I was ruling England and George Washington wasn't yet born. The Newsham is the oldest piece of fire-fighting machinery in the museum and claimed to be the oldest in existence anywhere in the United States. This contraption of wooden wheels and leather pipes was one of two carried across the Atlantic on the ship *Beaver,* which arrived in New York in 1731; it would enjoy a long and active life, serving the people of Manhattan for 154 years.

Engineer Richard Newsham's invention is now regarded as America's first successful mobile fire-fighting machine. But its mobility came with limitations; because both axles were fixed, it was necessary to lift the machine, solid wooden wheels and all, to make any turns.

While comprising the bulk of the museum collection, fire-fighting machines are not all you see. A wooden statue freezes in time the most thrilling yet threatening moment in a firefighter's life. It depicts a fire chief, circa 1850, in blue coat and white hat, raising a trumpet to his mouth with one hand and thrusting the other into the air as if to urge on his cohorts.

This hand-carved relic of folk art is proof that beautiful design in the firefighter's sphere was not limited to machinery. We were told that the statue stood atop a firemen's association building in the Coney Island section of Brooklyn for more than seventy-five years before being brought here for eternal protection and rest. The figure was modeled after a real person, Jameson Cox, chief engineer of the New York Fire Department in the 1820s.

Our guide concluded the tour by letting us know of one case in which equipment changed for the worse only to return to its original design. As we looked over the collection of old leather hats, we were told that they were initially designed to protect the wearer from head injury, guard the face from torrid heat, and shed water from the back of the neck. Leather eventually was replaced by inexpensive plastic, but in time it was shown that plastic didn't protect the head or resist heat like leather. So in some cases they have gone back to leather and – our guide smiled – are once more making them like they used to.

Location: From the New York State Thruway (I-87), exit 21, take State 23 east, cross the Rip Van Winkle Bridge, and turn left onto State 9G (South Third Street) heading north into Hudson. Turn right onto State Street, then left onto Carroll Street, which leads into Harry Howard Avenue. Bear right after Underhill Pond and the museum will be on the left, less than a mile away. From the Taconic State Parkway, take the State 23B exit and head west into Hudson on State 23. Turn right onto US 9, left onto Joslen Boulevard, left again onto Harry Howard Avenue and follow it to the museum.

Admission is free.

Hours: April through October, daily except Monday.

Allow forty-five minutes to an hour and a half.

Information: American Museum of Fire Fighting, 125 Harry Howard Avenue, Hudson, NY 12534, 518-828-7695.

Note: Enter through the arched gateway facing Harry Howard Avenue, follow the driveway, and bear left. The museum is in the brick building, farthest to the left, separate from the rest of the Volunteer Firemen's Home complex.

If you are staying overnight: HoJo Inn, 2764 State 32 (off I-87, exit 20), Saugerties, 914-246-9511; Super 8 Motel, 2790 State 32 (off I-87, exit 20), Saugerties, 914-246-1565; Red Ranch Motel, 4555 State 32 (nine miles north of I-87, exit 20), Catskill, 914-678-3380; Carl's Rip van Winkle Motor Lodge, State 23B (off I-87, exit 21), Catskill, 914-943-3303.

When in the area: Painter Frederic Church's Persian-style mansion, Olana (pages 195–200), is high on a nearby hill. President Martin Van Buren's home, Lindenwald (pages 42–46), is about twenty miles north in Kinderhook.

7 Long Island Maritime Museum
West Sayville

In the early 1900s, the *Suffolk County News* reported a major local story: Captain Joseph Weeks set a regional record of opening seventy-five gallons of oysters in just three days while employed in William Rudolph's oyster house. That oyster house is still in Suffolk County, on display at the Long Island Maritime Museum in West Sayville, and it looks as if Captain Weeks or some other hard-handed oyster handler has just walked out.

The purpose of this museum is to protect and preserve the maritime heritage of Long Island – all of Long Island, Nassau and Suffolk counties. The museum's main building, once the carriage house of a large estate, harbors seafarer's artifacts on a variety of subjects. In the Penney Boathouse craftsmen restore old boats and build new ones. They are usually there on weekends and are pleased to talk with onlookers, whether you are a veteran mariner or a novice who can't tell a sloop from a schooner. The Bayman's Cottage, decorated in 1890s style, shows where a typical oyster worker returned after a long day's work culling oysters.

And of course there are the boats. In the water are the Long Island-built schooner *Priscilla* (1888) and the sloop *Modesty* (1923) along with the tugboat *Charlotte*. Another thirty to fifty small vessels are housed in the Small Craft Facility located on the eastern part of the museum.

When you enter the little but practical William Rudolph Oyster House, you get a close look at the gritty world of the Great South Bay oystermen who from the late 1800s to the 1940s culled and packed oysters in structures like this. The thirty-mile-long bay, with its warm waters and suitable salt content, was regarded as the best oyster breeding ground north of Chesapeake Bay, and it produced renowned Blue Point oysters.

The workbench is covered with mountains of oyster shells

and a few other isolated sea creatures that snuck themselves into the last load, including whelk eggs and a starfish, the oyster's mortal enemy. The bench also displays the tools of the oysterman: opening knives, a culling iron, a crackling block and hammer, and rubber mitts, or finger stalls. It was a neat trick to speedily open an oyster while at the same time not damage its meat or slice off one's finger. Look above the bench and you will see the skylights that provided workers with their only illumination. The pay in 1910? A dollar a day.

Displays inside afford vital information about the Long Island oyster industry and the lot of its workers, from the tools they used to the boats they sailed (and later motorized). "Nostalgia for sail had little influence on bay men," reads one exhibit. "When the small gasoline engine was perfected for small boats before World War I, most bay men eagerly installed them in their sailboats."

Tucked in the corner of the oyster house is the oyster shipper's office, a semblance of order in a cluttered building. The oak desk is filled with lots of slots and pecks of pigeonholes, and the wooden filing cabinet next to it has brass fittings.

You can also see evidence of other past ways of life when eyeing the small craft collection. Several craft were the work of Gil Smith, who was born on Long Island in 1843 and who built boats well into his nineties. A museum brochure says that Smith was to boats what Chippendale was to furniture, a master craftsman in his time.

Smith's original catboats were narrower and shallower than similar New England fishing boats. In New England's rougher waters boats were big and tubby. Since the waters of the Great South Bay are generally about six feet deep, Smith designed his catboats to skim across the water.

In time, wealthy boat owners learned that Gil Smith's catboats, built for subsistence farmers and fishermen, were speedier than existing similar-size vessels built specifically for sport. They then asked him to make catboats for racing, and examples of both working and racing catboats are in the collection, the working catboats being bigger in the beam and deeper to hold as many shellfish as one could stuff in them.

For men spending months, not just hours, at sea, extra time gave them a chance to practice crafts like knot tying, and the intricate strand braids, knob knots, and decorative rope work on view are some of the results. Mounted on the wall nearby are ships' figureheads, additional examples of seamen's art, from vessels that ran aground on or near Long Island.

The museum library contains files of shipwrecks and

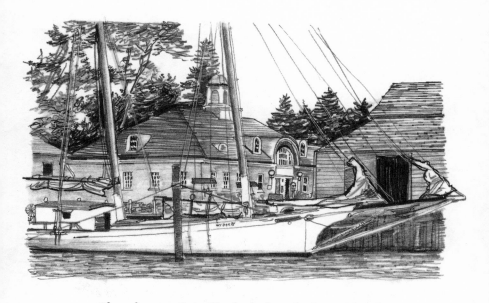

The schooner Priscilla *docked at the Long Island Maritime Museum, West Sayville*

groundings off the Long Island shore dating from 1657, many on record here in the forms of photographs and written descriptions. A corresponding map designates the locations of many of these accidents. You needn't be a maritime historian to be impressed by nature's raw power, the cause for many of the disasters.

An eighteenth-century flintlock pistol and a once-sunken chest are other artifacts taken from downed ships, while a megaphone straight from the days of Rudy Vallee (though intended for more serious purposes than Vallee's crooning) and a handsome blue uniform, symbols of the United States Lifesaving Service, also fill space in the main building.

Location: The Long Island Maritime Museum is at 86 West Avenue, located off State 27A (Montauk Highway) east of the center of West Sayville. It is on the eastern perimeter of the West Sayville Golf Course.

Admission is charged.

Hours: Year-round, Wednesday through Sunday, afternoons only on weekends.

Allow one to two hours.

Information: Long Island Maritime Museum, Box 144, West Sayville, NY 11796, 516-854-4974.

If you are staying overnight: Holiday Inn, 3845 Veterans Memorial Highway (just over four miles southeast of Long Island Expressway [I-495], exit 57), Ronkonkoma, 516-585-9500; Econo-Lodge, 3055 Veterans Memorial Highway (off I-495, exit 57), 516-588-6800; Best Western Strathmore, 1730 North Ocean Avenue (off I-495, exit 63), 516-758-2900; Summit Motor Inn, 501 East Main Street (State 27A), Bay Shore, 516-666-6000. Note that lodging is very expensive on Long Island. Even here in central Long Island you will be hard-pressed to find a double room priced under $80 a night. If you are en route to another location, consider staying elsewhere.

When in the area: To mix seaside recreation and maritime history, consider visiting Fire Island National Seashore (pages 126–132).

8 Martin Van Buren Country
Kinderhook

The packaging of candidates and selling of their images is nothing new. It predates TV, radio, the age of the professional politico, and the era of mass journalism.

In 1940, President Martin Van Buren, a native of Kinderhook, ran for a second term against the contrived but, for that age, very slick campaign of Whig challenger William Henry Harrison, who was portrayed by the Whigs as a man of the people, born in a log cabin and a drinker of hard cider. They cursed Van Buren as a high-living, champagne-drinking aristocrat. In 1840, the country was suffering through its first significant depression and Van Buren was accused of living in the lap of luxury while the common man suffered.

In truth, Harrison was the scion of a prosperous Virginia family; an ancestor signed the Declaration of Independence. Harrison was born at Berkeley, a grand Virginia plantation, and at the time of the campaign was living very much at ease on a comfortable Ohio farm.

It was true that Van Buren enjoyed a sip of champagne and had his share of the good life. But he came from a basic background, the son of a Kinderhook tavernkeeper who supplemented his income as a farmer. And Van Buren was a true Jacksonian Democrat; he was, in fact, Andrew Jackson's hand-picked successor.

Van Buren lost the election overwhelmingly and went down in history as a one-term failure. After his death in 1862, he became an obscure figure. His Kinderhook home, Lindenwald, had no historic significance; it was just another home in the upper Hudson Valley.

The twentieth century has been kinder to Martin Van Buren. The 1982 presidential rating survey of nearly 1,000 historians conducted by Pennsylvania State Professor Robert Murray rated

Van Buren twentieth among thirty-seven presidents, in the middle of the "average" category. Many historians agree that the depression was something Van Buren inherited rather than caused. He was an easy scapegoat.

Even so, it wasn't until 1987 that Lindenwald was open to the public on a full-time basis. A National Park System property, Martin Van Buren National Historic Site is the place to hear more about the 1840 campaign, learn what today's experts know that Van Buren's contemporaries didn't, and see one of the Hudson Valley's most eclectic, eye-pleasing early homes.

"Lindenwald," said Ranger Marion Berntson, "was to be Martin Van Buren's retirement home, but retirement came earlier than expected."

In 1839, the president picked out the neglected Georgian home built in 1797 on land that had belonged to a distant relative several generations back. To Van Buren, purchasing it symbolized a restoration of family holdings, and soon after the deal was closed, he began massive alterations to make it his retirement estate. It is thought that he had hopes of turning Lindenwald into another Mount Vernon or Monticello.

One of his first actions was to demolish an entrance hall stairway and turn the hall into a large room for dining and entertaining. Van Buren wallpapered it with a French hunting scene, Landscape of the Hunt. The original paper still hangs on the room's long walls. On its short walls are accurate reproductions of the paper, which allow you to see what the colors looked like when Van Buren was master of the house.

Alterations took place over several years, but the most radical were orchestrated by Van Buren's youngest son, Smith Thompson Van Buren, who moved into Lindenwald at his father's suggestion. Smith hired architect Richard Upjohn, designer of Manhattan's Trinity Church, to do the work.

While the former president had told his son he could alter

the home to accommodate his tastes, Van Buren was leery about the scope of the changes. Still, he kept his sense of humor about it and said, "The idea of seeing in life, the changes which my heir would be sure to make after I am gone, amuses me." By the time all was complete, the house little resembled the simple Georgian home Van Buren had purchased; it had become the merry mix of Renaissance, Italianate, Romanesque, and Gothic Revival styles you see today. It also was one of the most modern houses in its time.

Van Buren's then brand-new coal-burning kitchen stove is still there. (Slaving over a hot stove was a literal thing; the stove is small.) So are the flush toilet with its Wedgwood porcelain bowl, and Van Buren's most boastful modern touch, the zinc-lined bathtub. Lindenwald was also one of the first homes to be equipped with running water. If you ever visit Calvin Coolidge's boyhood home in Vermont, you will see the crude two-hole wooden privy, used until the early 1930s. Keep in mind that Van Buren's plumbing was installed in the 1840s.

To maintain the ex-president's "simple, elegant life-style," extra help in the form of servants was needed. Van Buren had four – a cook, a parlor maid, a waitress, and a laundress, all Irish women. Van Buren appreciated their work and treated them well – for the time. They were given only half a day off a week, a work schedule more reflective of the day than Van Buren's attitude. They lived in wallpapered rooms and ate meals off British Amoy china, similar to Dutch Delft, in their own sitting room, very plush for servants in the 1840s.

The additions to Lindenwald gave the servants a huge house to care for, thirty-six rooms in all. From the outside the most noticeable feature is the four-and-a-half-story tower, purely ornamental. It's the magnet that initially draws visitors' eyes when they first set foot on the grounds.

The library is anything but ornamental. It is a room blessed with wonderful natural lighting, and the view enabled the president to watch his grandchildren play on the estate lawn. Political cartoons deck the library walls as they did when Van Buren lived here. One depicts Van Buren as a red fox losing his tail as he is about to go down in political defeat; he was given the nickname "The Red Fox" for his red hair. He was also called "The Little Magician" for his short physical stature (he was five feet six inches tall) and ability to maneuver politically or, in the eyes of political enemies, be conveniently noncommittal.

When not playing politics, Van Buren was often playing cards. A favorite game was whist, a forerunner of bridge, and the parlor card table is set up for it. Looking down on the table are photographic reproductions of Thomas Jefferson and Andrew Jackson, statesmen that Van Buren greatly admired.

Upstairs are more decorated rooms. Van Buren's bedroom, where he died at age seventy-nine, is filled with original possessions, including his sleigh bed and shaving stand.

Van Buren died in 1862. The first president born an American citizen, Van Buren was disheartened in his last year by the onset of the Civil War. But overall he enjoyed his last twenty-one years, which were spent at Lindenwald, saying in his will, ". . . but for the last and happiest years of my life, a farmer in my native town." Martin Van Buren is buried in Kinderhook Cemetery on Albany Avenue (County 21) in Kinderhook.

Location: Martin Van Buren National Historic Site is on Old Post Road, just off State 9H, southeast of the town of Kinderhook. *Admission* is charged for adults, free for seniors and children.
Hours: Mid-April through October, daily; November into early December, Wednesday through Sunday.

Allow forty-five minutes to an hour for the guided tour and an extra half hour if you wish to walk the grounds.

Information: Martin Van Buren National Historic Site, P.O. Box 545, Kinderhook, NY 12106, 518-758-9689.

Events: June, Columbia County Coaching Society carriage show, nineteenth-century carriages and drivers in performances; summer, picnic on lawn, afternoon concerts, nature walk.

Note: Parking is available on Old Post Road in front of the mansion. Each tour is limited to fifteen people.

If you are staying overnight: Blue Spruce Motel, US 9, Kinderhook, 518-758-9711; Chatham TraveLodge, State 295, Chatham, 518-392-2266; Kinderhook Bed & Breakfast (four-room B&B in 1855 Greek Revival-style home), 16 Chatham Street (in the village square), Kinderhook, 518-758-1850.

When in the area: Half an hour north is the state capital, Albany, with its New York State Museum (pages 246–250) and Schuyler Mansion State Historic Site (pages 251–254). A half hour south is Olana (pages 195–200), the Persian-style mansion home of artist Frederic Church, and the American Museum of Fire Fighting in Hudson (pages 33–36).

9 Saratoga National Historical Park
Stillwater

When Gen. John "Gentleman Johnny" Burgoyne surrendered to the colonists at Saratoga in October 1777, it was enough to make one American supporter break out in song. He wrote an anthem, forty-six verses long, to commemorate the event. A sample verse, number 29, went like this:

> *Our brave soldiers all with powderhorn and ball*
> *Each man with a gun on his shoulder.*
> *With courage so stout directly turn'd out*
> *No men in New England were bolder.*

The victory was as vital as it was sweet. Most historians believe that if the colonists had lost at Saratoga, they never would have secured needed help from France, and without that aid they would have ultimately lost the Revolution. In addition, the battle lifted the sagging spirits of the colonists, who had seen themselves as David up against a towering Goliath. Following Burgoyne's surrender one colonist said, "Rebellion, which a twelve-month ago was a contemptible pygmy, is now in appearance a giant."

The British had been hoping to control the Hudson River, cutting off New England from the rest of the colonies. They planned for Burgoyne's forces to meet with those of two other generals in Albany. Burgoyne was moving his army south from Montreal. As a diversion, Col. Barry St. Leger was to start from present-day Oswego on Lake Ontario and penetrate the upper Mohawk Valley, while Sir William Howe planned to march north from New York City to join his forces with Burgoyne's.

The plan was approved by the British Crown and orders were sent from London to Burgoyne. However, orders never reached Howe, and he decided to move his forces to the colonial capital in Philadelphia. St. Leger, meanwhile, held Fort Stanwix in present-day Rome (see pages 113–117) under siege, only to retreat back toward Canada after hearing that Gen. Benedict Arnold, still on the side of the colonies at that time, was bringing a substantial force to the fort.

Burgoyne and his men were left on their own. They met the colonists under Gen. Horatio Gates at Freeman's Farm on September 19. The British were staved off, but three weeks later, on October 7, they attacked again only to be beaten back once more. The British suffered 1,000 casualties, more than twice as many as the Americans, and the next day they retreated north. The American army swelled in size as more militiamen joined Gates; they surrounded Burgoyne's troops, causing him to surrender on October 17.

To keep yourself from surrendering in confusion, plan to make the park visitors center your first stop. Here you can pick up a park brochure with a map of the nine-mile-long battlefield auto-tour route.

The visitors center is also the place to take a close look at the battle and get a feel for life as a colonial soldier. *Checkmate on the Hudson* is the twenty-one-minute film that re-creates the battle through the use of visual and aural effects, including regiments of toy soldiers, a chess board, and a tense drumroll. There are two theaters, so even in the busiest times long waits are rare.

While *Checkmate on the Hudson* interprets the strategy and political implications of the battle, the visitors center museum shows you the human side of eighteenth-century warfare. On view are soldiers' eating implements, including a wooden bowl, two-pronged forks, a rusty old butter knife, a squat, little camp stove, and colonial-era toothbrushes. In addition, you'll learn trivia facts, some of which are extraordinary: for example, the Continental Army was not segregated by race–that would not happen again until the Korean War in the 1950s.

To offer news for those in the military and at home, broadsides were posted on faded clapboard barns and city building walls throughout the colonies. An example is the song celebrating Burgoyne's surrender quoted at the start of this section.

To see where that surrender took place, head for the auto-tour route, which includes ten stops where important incidents in the battle took place. There are audiotapes, each lasting one to three minutes, at most of the stops.

Perhaps the most popular point to pause is site #7, the Breymann Redoubt. Gen. Benedict Arnold was injured in the leg here in an incident immortalized by the "boot monument," a favorite photo spot. Arnold, of course, survived. Had he died from the wound he would have gone down in history as one of America's finest generals and patriots.

Expect to confront militiamen or camp followers in the flesh if you visit in summer. Living-history reenactments are often scheduled at site #2, the Nielson Farm, which American generals used as headquarters. Catch these colonial characters in their acts and you can learn everything from methods of making meals in an army encampment to the rigors of a military drill. You can even show your patriotism by putting your John Hancock on the muster roll at the Officer's Marquee on Company Street.

You used to be able to take your Saratoga visit to great heights by walking the 190 steps to the top of Saratoga Monument in Schuylerville, eight miles from the battlefield. At present, though, the monument is in need of extensive interior renovation and is closed to the public. Still, you can look at and admire the 155-foot-high monument, built from 1877 to 1883 and standing on land once occupied by a portion of Burgoyne's October 1777 camp.

Near the monument and also part of the National Historical Park is the Schuyler House, built in three weeks as the home of

Gen. Philip Schuyler, who preceded Horatio Gates as the commander of American forces. Schuyler once described his wilderness retreat in this manner: "My hobby horse has long been a country life; I dismounted once with reluctance and now saddle him again with a very considerable share of satisfaction, and hope to canter him on to the end of the journey of life."

The two-story frame building was actually Schuyler's third home here; the others were destroyed during the French and Indian Wars and by Burgoyne. But this one survived marauders, and there are three pieces inside that belonged to the general: a Chippendale drop-leaf dining room table, a linen press in an upstairs vestibule, and a dresser in the master bedroom.

Location: From I-87 (the Northway), take exit 12 onto State 67 toward Mechanicville; then take State 32 north and follow the signs to the park.

To reach Schuylerville, site of the Schuyler House and the Saratoga Monument, follow the signs for US 4 from the visitors center parking lot and take US 4 north for eight miles. The Schuyler House is on US 4 on the right side, just before you cross Fish Creek and head into town. To reach the monument, follow US 4 into town, where it becomes Broad Street. Take a left onto Burgoyne Street; the monument is on the left between Gates Street and Cemetery Avenue.

Admission is charged May through October.

Hours: Visitors center: year-round, daily. Auto-tour route: April through November, weather permitting; the road is not plowed, so it's not unusual for a late spring or early fall snowstorm to close it. Schuyler House is open mid-June to Labor Day.

Allow three hours to explore the entire park if you are a casual visitor. Park rangers recommend forty-five minutes to see the film and visitors center, an hour and a half to drive the auto-tour route, and up to half an hour to tour the Schuyler House. Allow ten to twenty minutes if you wish to take a stroll around the monument. Anyone with more than a casual interest in the battle could spend three to four hours on the auto-tour route alone and should plan a full day to see the entire park.

Information: Saratoga National Historical Park, 648 Route 32, Stillwater, NY 12170, 518-664-9821.

Events: Lectures, slide programs, and living-history demonstrations such as encampments are offered periodically during the summer.

Note: There are two picnic areas in the park. One with grills is by the visitors center parking lot; one with no grills is by site #10 on the auto-tour road. Some small hiking trails, which become cross-country ski trails in winter, are also in the park.

If you are staying overnight: Burgoyne Motor Inn, 220 North Broad Street, Schuylerville, 518-695-3282; Empress Motel, 177 Broadway, Schuylerville, 518-695-3231; Kings Ransom Farm B&B, 178 King Road, Schuylerville, 518-695-6876. Also see the lodging listed under Saratoga Springs attractions the Canfield Casino and the National Museum of Racing and Hall of Fame.

When in the area: In the city of Saratoga Springs are the National Museum of Racing and Hall of Fame (pages 275–278) and the Canfield Casino (pages 270–274), where the reminders of Saratoga's Victorian glory are on display. Grant Cottage State Historic Site (pages 201–206), just to the north in Wilton, is the hilltop home where the dying president and Civil War general spent his last days writing his memoirs.

10 Old Bethpage Village Restoration
Old Bethpage

There was a time when a shopping spree on Long Island meant the purchase of a bundle of rags and linseed oil from John B. Luyster's general store and an order for a felt hat from hatmaker Lewis Ritch. Long before the development of plastic, Long Islanders were already shopping on credit. In fact, almost all business at Luyster's store was conducted on a credit basis, and the desk on which the accountant kept the books can still be seen when you visit the store at Old Bethpage Village in Old Bethpage. Today the Luyster store's costumed clerks sell a variety of historic reproductions and other items.

Luyster's store joins sixteen other structures relocated to the re-created nineteenth-century village. When you leave the modern reception center and walk along the dusty road of clamshells and dirt, you enter Long Island a generation before the Civil War.

You can buy something to eat in the village, but you can't use twentieth-century currency. You exchange that in the reception center for nineteenth-century paper scrip. The going rate when we last visited was 75 cents from the twentieth century for six Old Bethpage cents. But the trade-off is just fine; six cents bought then what 75 cents buys today.

Your shopping spree at Old Bethpage Village will be limited to old-time goodies like root beer, apple cider, pretzels, and penny candy, which you can buy at the store of Luyster's closest competitor, John M. Layton, or at the center of Old Bethpage social activity, the Noon Tavern. Most of us have no use for rags and linseed oil anyway.

As we paid for our snacks—wintergreen and cherry candy sticks for a penny each—we learned that the money we were using was legal tender in Old Bethpage only. Each community's bank printed its own paper money.

What else is found on Layton's shelves? His stock runs from school slates to sausage grinders and everything a nineteenth-century farmer could ever need. Long Island's economy was still primarily agricultural during this period.

The Powell Farm, a residence and working farm, is the only original part of Old Bethpage Village. Even though the industrial revolution was finding its way into Long Island in the 1840s, farming was still the bread and butter, so to speak, for most families' existence. Pumpkin pies were baking and batter for a pound cake was being mixed when we entered the Powell kitchen. In 1850 the Powell clan included children, grand-parents, and hired hands for a total of fifteen persons under one roof—food preparation was an endless job.

And there were hungry animals to feed too. A hired hand using some bulky wooden implement we had never seen before was slicing beets and greens from one of the four major kitchen gardens to be fed to the resident cows in the Powell family barn. Nearby are a smokehouse and an outhouse and apple and pear orchards. Many of the meals are concocted from products grown or raised on the farm, and the women working in the kitchen stick to nineteenth-century recipes.

When you leave the farm, walk as the Powells did down the main road to the village center to see signs of other commerce that made Old Bethpage thrive. Enter the Lewis Ritch hat shop where, with a hefty supply of felt, a set of wooden crown molds, and about four days of labor, Ritch could fashion a stylish felt hat for village farmers.

A handmade hat lasted ten to fifteen years, and since hat-makers could rush out no more than two hats a week, craftsmen like Ritch ran other businesses on the side to supplement their income. Ritch, for instance, also had a farm and cordwood cut-ting business.

For another example of time-consuming work, visit the

broom maker. In the 1840s some broom parts, such as the dowels and strings, were made in factories. But brooms were still handmade, and we were told by the resident artisan that a good worker could turn out up to thirty brooms a day. At six cents a broom he would sweep up with $1.80 for a day's work, not a bad income at that time. But little did he know he would be an obsolete man in ten years when brooms would be routinely made in factories.

An innkeeper, however, never needs to worry about becoming useless. His job will continue as long as people need to eat and rest. The Noon Inn, conveniently situated at the main crossroads in Old Bethpage Village, was constructed about 1840 and restored to a period about ten years later. It provided sustenance and sleep for weary Long Island travelers for many years at the

A yoke of oxen from the farm at the
Old Bethpage Village Restoration, Old Bethpage

crossroads of Newbridge and Prospect avenues in East Meadow, ten miles west.

It also served as a meeting place for locals. The barroom, with its bottles and decanters stacked behind the wooden counter and its patriotic prints posted on the walls, was the center of action. It is here that you can buy cider and pretzels with your scrip, and there are tables and benches upstairs where you can relax. Upstairs is the ballroom where townwide social activities took place. There are also two guest bedrooms, since local law mandated that any establishment serving alcohol must provide sleeping quarters.

Most families, like the Noons, lived in the building in which they did business. And as the private homes at Old Bethpage reveal their owners' professions, they also afford hints to their backgrounds. For example, the Powell homestead, with its few contemporary furnishings mixed with modest colonial furniture handed down through generations, is typical of its owner's Quaker heritage.

The Dutch roots of wealthy farmers Martin and Minne Schenck are symbolized by the hidden bed box, the huge stone jambless fireplace, and the split Dutch door, effects more commonly seen in the Hudson Valley. The Schenck House, the first restored building visitors approach from the reception center, is considered the oldest Dutch farmhouse in Nassau County and one of the oldest in the country. The home was in the Schenck family for over 200 years.

Farmers such as the Schencks made their living from the land, but other Long Islanders thrived on different natural commodities. Joseph Conklin's small one-and-a-half-story home is filled with fishing, eeling, crabbing, and clamming implements, reminders of his life's work at sea. The tiny kitchen with its rough-hewn table is representative of his moderate income.

John Layton, on the other hand, did splendidly with his

general store, as demonstrated by his residence in the same building. It is decorated in early Victorian style with due respect to the fads of the day, including flowers dipped in beeswax and a framed newspaper print chronicling "The Life and Age of Woman, Stages of a Woman's Life from Infancy to the Brink of the Grave." It is at age thirty, the print maintains, that "Woman may be considered at the zenith of her intellectual and physical powers."

But don't think about that too long. Not everything written 140 years ago was accurate, for this was also a time when any well-read Old Bethpage resident would urge you to stay home at night. People were convinced at the time that night air caused tuberculosis.

Location: From I-495 (the Long Island Expressway) take exit 48 or from the Northern State Parkway, exit 39; head south from either onto Round Swamp Road and follow the signs to the village entrance.

Admission is charged.

Hours: Year-round, Wednesday through Sunday.

Allow three to five hours for the village.

Information: Old Bethpage Village Restoration, Round Swamp Road, Old Bethpage, NY 11804, 516-572-8400.

Events: There are many and they are celebrated at all times of the year. The biggest is the Long Island Fair in mid-fall. A brief sampling of others includes: May, Spring Festival, crafts, music, sheep shearing; July 4, Independence Day celebration circa 1851; summer, nineteenth-century-style baseball; September, military musters; fall, early food preparations; November, Thanksgiving meal preparations; December, weekend evening Christmas program.

Note: Before leaving the reception center, be sure to see the twenty-minute film that sets the tone for your visit. Also, picnic tables are on the grounds.

If you are staying overnight: Holiday Inn, 215 Sunnyside Boulevard (north of I-495, exit 46), Plainview, 516-349-7400; Plainview Plaza Hotel, 150 Sunnyside Boulevard (off I-495, exit 46), Plainview, 516-349-9100; Comfort Inn, 333 South Service Road (I-495, exit 48), Plainview, 516-694-6500. Note that lodging is very expensive on Long Island. If you are en route to another location, consider staying elsewhere.

When in the area: The handsome homes of Theodore Roosevelt (pages 263–269) and William Kissam Vanderbilt II (pages 9–13) are open to the public in Oyster Bay and Centerport, respectively.

11 Naval and Servicemen's Park
Buffalo

Don't let Buffalo's location fool you. This inland city on the shore of Lake Erie boasts a maritime park that would fit just fine in any location along a saltwater shore.

All branches of the armed forces are represented at Buffalo & Erie County Naval & Servicemen's Park, situated on a six-acre waterfront site. However, the three navy ships will occupy the most time of visitors. The guided missile cruiser USS *Little Rock* is herculean – 610 feet long – and filled with collections and exhibits offering a look at the life led by the 1,400 men who lived aboard it during the thirty years it was in active use. Contrast it with the World War II submarine USS *Croaker*, which truly fits the cliched image of the sardine can under water. Then step on board the USS *The Sullivans*, the destroyer named for the legendary brothers who gave their lives together during World War II.

The submarine *Croaker* saw action during World War II. Commissioned on April 21, 1944, it left Groton, Connecticut, for Pearl Harbor. *Croaker* went on to sink eleven Japanese vessels in six patrols before it left Subic Bay in the South China Sea for the United States in August 1945.

Claustrophobics beware. Space is tight, exceedingly tight. Your fat cousin Fred would have to squeeze sideways through some of the passageways. But there is an old navy saying that there is room for everything aboard a submarine except for a mistake.

The crew of seven officers and seventy-four enlisted men shared two showers, which were used sparingly. To conserve water, the men on board were not permitted to shower until their first three weeks of duty had expired. The shower stalls did not go to waste when unoccupied. Spare room was at a premium, so the crew would stack potatoes or other nonperishable foodstuffs in the two shower stalls.

To serve eighty-one crewmen, meals were prepared around the clock, making *Croaker* like an amphibious all-night diner. Two tables sat six crewmen in the after battery, also used as the mess hall. And there was "soup down," when cold cuts, pastries, and soup were served to men just going on or off duty.

The entire mess area—cupboards, benches, and sinks—is a metallic gray-green in color. For men stationed here months or possibly years at a stretch, this bland shade was easy on weary eyes that could suffer if exposed to bold or bright colors.

In the control room, the basic hows and whys of submarine hydraulics are explained. When air replaced water in the ballast tank, the sub rose. It descended when water replaced air. The nerve center of the underwater vessel is an instrument panel alive with red lights. Since the board provided the only bright colors on the sub, it was affectionately dubbed the Christmas tree.

In both the forward and after torpedo rooms, 3,600-pound torpedoes lie dormant, symbols of the many "fish" *Croaker* expended in the South Pacific. Leisure-time activities helped break the tension. Backgammon and checker boards are inlaid into mess area tables, and more than fifty men would crowd into the cozy quarters to watch a movie to take their minds off war. There was no screen; the film was projected directly onto the gray-green metallic wall.

Compared to a submarine, the *Little Rock* is palatial, but try explaining that to men who berthed in metal cots one practically atop the other. A total of 1,100 enlisted navy men, 150 officers, and 150 marines sailed at any given time on this cruiser.

The *Little Rock* was launched on August 27, 1944, as a light cruiser and was converted to a guided missile cruiser in 1957.

The ship made four voyages to the Mediterranean and two to the North Atlantic, and it served as flagship for the Second and Sixth fleets. You can see where admirals coordinated fleet operations in the war room and where they marked ships' locations on the plexiglass plotting board in the pilothouse. The man making the notations stood on the reverse so as not to be in anyone's way, just as we've seen in so many war movies.

In a way, the *Little Rock* was a floating village, with many of the services you would find in any community on terra firma. There is a barbershop used exclusively by officers, where old razors and a container of Old Spice rest as reminders of the many men who shaved at the small sink, the sort you'd find on a commercial airplane today. There is a post office and a laundry area, where white pants belonging to a sailor named R. F. Gilman are still waiting to be picked up. There is the dental compartment and rooms you'd find in any hospital: an operating room and a recovery room. A dentist and doctors were on board.

While you wouldn't find a missile magazine or a missile-warhead handling room in any land-based town, these were instrumental in the ship's reason for being. Everything here, our guide said, is here for a reason. The deck is wood, not metal, because bullets would embed themselves in wood but dangerously ricochet on a metal floor. And what children think are telephone booths are actually storage areas for lifesaving equipment like life jackets and helmets.

Several rooms that formerly served as officers' or enlisted men's sleeping areas have been converted into exhibit rooms, each focusing on a theme like the Vietnam War, the Korean War, or the Destroyer Escort Sailors Association. And in one room is a copy of the *Stars and Stripes,* the newspaper of the armed forces, dated August 14, 1945. The headline is the simple word "PEACE," accompanied by an illustration of a spear poking through a Japanese flag. The article's lead reads, "The Pacific War ended Tuesday, 1,347 days after the sneak attack on Pearl Harbor."

For the five Sullivan brothers from Waterloo, Iowa, the end came too late. The brothers enlisted together on January 3, 1942 – less than a month after Pearl Harbor – and insisted that they be stationed together, despite a naval wartime policy stating that family members be barred from serving on the same ship.

Joseph, Francis, Albert, George, and Madison Sullivan were on board the USS *Juneau* in the Pacific in November 1942 when it was hit by torpedoes from a Japanese submarine. The ship had been severely hit earlier in a battle off Guadalcanal, and to the crippled ship this second blow was fatal. George survived the attack, but died while awaiting rescue. Our guide said that rumor has it that the ghost of George can be seen aboard the ship, searching in vain for his lost brothers.

Word of the deaths crushed the nation. The brothers' parents, Mr. and Mrs. Thomas F. Sullivan, actively promoted the sale of war bonds, and their younger sister, Genevieve, enlisted in the navy. Mrs. Sullivan wrote an article titled "I Lost Five Sons" to help others cope with the loss of family members in the war, and the family approved the making of a movie, *The Fighting Sullivans*. The mother also sponsored and christened a Fletcher Class destroyer named for her sons, and she along with many family members was present for its launching in San Francisco on April 4, 1943.

This ship is docked permanently in Buffalo today. Shamrocks on the smokestack and engines, and elsewhere, offer tribute to the brothers through their Irish heritage while photos and a posted commentary tell their tale. The ship saw action in much of the South Pacific, and its war duties included rescuing many downed pilots and survivors of ship attacks. *The Sullivans* proved its worth by recovering 166 survivors from the aircraft carrier *Bunker Hill* after it was hit by kamikaze aircraft in 1945 and 118 men from the *Houston* in 1944, which had been hit by Japanese planes.

Stroll through the tight corridors of *The Sullivans* today for a taste of life on board during World War II. Strains of the classic 1940s hit song "You Made Me Love You" waft through the air, only to be interrupted by a piercing voice calling out commands beginning with the chilling words "Now hear this!"

Written on the window of the radar room are the words "In God We Trust, All Else We Track" while on the fantail is something a bit more foreboding – the antisubmarine warfare weapons called hedgehogs that fired twenty-four explosive canisters in a circular or elliptical pattern around a submarine.

The most popular place on the ship? Our guide said it was the bakery near the mess hall, where the scent of fresh bread lured the hungry here at 4 A.M.

Also on the park grounds are an army M-41 tank, an air force F-101 Fighter Interceptor jet, a navy Fury jet, and a marine armored personnel carrier. A collection of ship's models crafted by artist James Gillis can be seen in the museum, where two videos, on the park and the *Croaker* specifically, are shown regularly.

Location: The waterside park is on Buffalo Place at the foot of Main and Pearl streets, behind Buffalo Memorial Auditorium. From the south, take I-190, Church Street exit, right onto Lower Terrace (first intersection) and right again onto Pearl Street. From the north, take I-190, Niagara Street exit, right onto Niagara and right onto South Elmwood, which turns into Lower Terrace after the Church Street intersection.
Admission is charged.
Hours: Daily, April through October; weekends in November.

Allow two to three hours.

Information: Buffalo & Erie County Naval & Servicemen's Park, 1 Naval Park Cove, Buffalo, NY 14202, 716-847-1773.

Note: There are several picnic tables on the grounds and a kiosk where light meals are sold.

If you are staying overnight: Best Western Downtown, 510 Delaware Avenue (State 384), Buffalo, 716-886-8333; Holiday Inn–Downtown, 620 Delaware Avenue (State 384), Buffalo, 716-886-2121; University Manor Motel, 3612 Main Street (State 5), Buffalo, 716-837-3344; Lancaster Motor Inn, 6685 Transit Road (State 78, just north of I-90, exit 49), Williamsville, 716-634-6560; Motel 6, 4400 Maple Road (off I-290, exit 5B), Amherst, 716-834-2231.

When in the area: The remaining vestiges of Buffalo's 1901 world's fair, which introduced the marvel of electricity to the world, are found at the Buffalo and Erie County Historical Society and the Theodore Roosevelt Inaugural National Historic Site (pages 255–258) north of downtown. A bit farther north is legendary Niagara Falls (pages 150–155).

12 Historic Richmond Town
Staten Island

"There was an expression heard often on Staten Island," we were told by a resident craftsperson at Historic Richmond Town. "The rich man has a canopy over his bed. The poor man has a canopy under his bed." The canopy under the bed, an expression used regionally, referred to a chamber pot. In Staten Island it was likely made from redware, a type of pottery commonly used here.

You will be told other similar tales of long-ago days in Staten Island when you visit Historic Richmond Town, a burgeoning living-history museum on ninety-six acres in the island's Greenbelt area. The Richmond Town staff refers to the complex as "New York City's only historic village," and that point is well taken. Walk in lower Manhattan or Queens or Brooklyn and there is virtually no vestige of the colonial heritage of the city other than a few isolated historic buildings rubbing elbows with steel-and-glass skyscrapers, row houses, and commercial blocks. But Staten Islanders had foresight. As far back as the 1920s, members of the Staten Island Historical Society began acquiring historic buildings with an eye toward preservation.

The original village of Richmond first took root in the 1690s as a minor crossroads on an island dotted with farms and country estates. Its name then was Cocclestown, and the Historic Richmond Town staff is fortunate enough to still have the Voorlezer's House as a link to those earliest days on the island.

"Voorlezer" is not a family name. It was the title of the Reformed Dutch Church's lay minister and teacher, who lived here from the time the structure was built (about 1695) until 1700. The house stands as the oldest surviving elementary school in the country and the oldest building on its original site in Historic Richmond Town.

Cocclestown eventually became Richmond Town, and the

village grew to finally become the seat of county government. Representing this period of growth are the Guyon-Lake-Tysen House, a sizable Dutch colonial farmhouse, and the Treasure House. The Treasure House is the second oldest building here. It dates to the turn of the eighteenth century, with several later additions, and it got its name from a story that a bundle of gold coins concealed by the British during the American Revolution was uncovered during a renovation in 1860. The Treasure House is now under renovation and is closed to the public for the time being.

On the other hand, if you enter the Guyon-Lake-Tysen House in peak season, you will probably see the early American lady of the house engaged in weaving at the loom upstairs or concocting the midday meal downstairs in the kitchen's brick oven. Our guide said there was a simple way for a cook to tell whether the bricks were hot enough for baking. She would put her arm inside the oven and count to ten. If the hairs on her arm were not singed, the oven was not yet ready. It often took an hour and a half of preheating for the oven to reach the proper cooking temperature.

The Guyon-Lake-Tysen House had several face-lifts in the nineteenth century. The kitchen was added about 1820 and dormers about twenty years later. So it is not inappropriate that the upstairs bedrooms depict different periods. For example, the 1815 room is heavy on Shaker-style boxes. Across the hall is the 1815–1830 Classical Revival room with a sleigh bed and a heavily carved chest of drawers. The late-nineteenth-century bedroom is garnished with a grain-painted "cottage" bedroom suite.

Staten Islanders are lucky that the Guyon-Lake-Tysen House has lasted the centuries, considering that the island was occupied by the British during the Revolutionary War and that many of its earliest buildings, including the early Dutch Church, where the voorlezer gave his sermons, were destroyed during the occupation.

In summer craftspeople plying their trades in many of the buildings make this a thriving living-history village. Depending on the timing of your visit, plan to run into the resident tinsmith (in a former store representing the period around 1860), the basket maker (in a circa 1810–20 Dutch home), and the furniture maker (in a 1966 adaptation of an 1835 building), all hard at work and eager to talk about their jobs.

Come in the lengthy off-season, when most of the buildings are empty, and you will be given a guided tour, usually into five buildings. In addition to the Guyon-Lake-Tysen House, our tour also included the Bennett House, a Greek Revival residence with a considerable collection of toys, dolls, and games, and the Stephens/Black General Store, a combination mercantile outlet and post office.

What could one buy in a Victorian-era general store? Containers for edible treats like National Biscuit Company Water Crackers and Runkel Brothers Breakfast Cocoa establish the Stephens/Black General Store setting to be about 1860 to 1875, although there are stocked items that would have been sold into the early twentieth century. A well-rounded combination of consumer items – lanterns, oil heater wicks and lamps, dress-making materials, and bird cages – supplement the food. Off and on, the store also served as a post office, and Staten Island residents' post boxes still line the right side of the store.

Some envision the Big Apple as a concrete carpet topped with buildings stacked one atop the other on every square inch of real estate. But in this part of New York City, Historic Richmond Town rests on 100 acres of open land. Presently, Historic Richmond Town consists of twenty-seven historic buildings, eleven of which are on their original sites and twelve of which have interiors regularly open to the public. In time more will be opened.

Location: Historic Richmond Town is at the intersection of Richmond Road, Clarke Avenue, and Arthur Kill Road, adjacent to LaTourette Park in the Greenbelt area in the center of Staten Island. From Brooklyn, take the Verrazano-Narrows Bridge, follow the New Jersey West route, and take the Richmond Road/ Clove Road exit; at the second light turn left onto Richmond Road, and after about five miles turn left onto St. Patrick's Place and follow the signs. From the Bayonne Bridge, exit at the Goethals Bridge sign, bear right, and take the first exit (Richmond Avenue); turn right onto Richmond Avenue, then left onto Arthur Kill Road; at the third traffic light, turn right onto Clarke Avenue and follow the signs. From Elizabeth, New Jersey, take the Goethals Bridge onto I-278 (the Staten Island Expressway), exit onto Richmond Avenue; head south and turn left onto Arthur Kill Road; at the third light, turn right onto Clarke Avenue and follow the signs. From the Staten Island Ferry, take Bay Street south about two miles, then turn right onto Vanderbilt Avenue; at the fourth signal bear left onto Richmond Road, and after about five miles, turn left onto St. Patrick's Place and follow the signs.

Admission is charged.

Hours: Year-round, Wednesday through Friday; Saturday and Sunday afternoons; the restoration is in full operation in July and August.

Allow an hour to an hour and a half.

Information: Staten Island Historical Society, 441 Clarke Avenue, Staten Island, NY 10306, 718-351-1611.

Events: A few of the many are: Late August, Richmond County

Fair; mid-October, Old Home Day, eighteenth- and nineteenth-century crafts and domestic activities demonstrations; early December, Christmas in Historic Richmond Town.

Note: Tours start in the visitors center in the courthouse. A snack bar and picnic table are on the grounds.

If you are staying overnight: The following are all located on Staten Island: Staten Island Hotel, 1415 Richmond Avenue, 718-698-5000; Cosmopolitan Motel, 1274 Hyland Boulevard, 718-979-7000; Midland Motel, 630-632 Midland Avenue, 718-987-8322; Hartshore House (B&B), 88 Henderson Avenue, 718-273-8105; Victorian Bed & Breakfast, 92 Taylor Street, 718-273-9861.

When in the area: The sites of Manhattan are just a ferry ride away. These include the New York Stock Exchange and Federal Hall National Memorial (pages 238–245), Theodore Roosevelt's birthplace (pages 263–269), and South Street Seaport (pages 304–310). And don't forget the lady in the harbor and Ellis Island (pages 295–303).

13 Mills Mansion State Historic Site
Staatsburg

If you live in a typical suburban American raised ranch or split-level house, it is safe to say that your house could comfortably fit inside the dining room of the Mills Mansion in Staatsburg. You will likely hear that fact as you proceed on the guided tour through this emblem of Gilded Age wealth and style just north of Hyde Park. It is a comparison declared in order to help visitors realize the sheer size of the place where Ogden and Ruth Mills had their evening meals, since the words fifty by thirty feet may not by themselves get the point across.

The dining room rug is thirty-five feet long, and when eighteen leaves are added, the table extends as long as the rug. When you tour you will probably see the table with seven leaves, a perfect size for the occasions when the house wasn't quite half filled with guests. You will also observe four rich Flemish tapestries ornamenting the walls of Italian marble; it is said that the room was decorated around the tapestries.

In a similar manner, this Gilded Age mansion was built around an 1832 Greek Revival home located on the same spot. The Greek Revival home was built by Morgan Lewis, a Revolutionary War colonel and the state's third governor, and his wife, Gertrude, sister of Chancellor Robert R. Livingston, to replace another house destroyed by fire in 1832.

The home passed through generations of the family, and in 1888 it was inherited by Lewis's great-granddaughter, Ruth Livingston Mills, wife of financier and philanthropist Ogden Mills. They felt the property needed to be enlarged and re-odeled, so they chose the New York architectural firm McKim, Mead and White, who designed many of the millionaires' mansions during the Gilded Age, to do the work.

They added two large wings on opposite ends of the house and embellished a new exterior with floral swags, pilasters, and balustrades. Inside, they brought in the styles of Louis XIV, Louis XV, and Louis XVI with gilded ceilings, ancient objets d'art, the tapestries, and marble fireplaces. The finished product was a sixty-five-room mansion Ogden Mills was proud to call his country retreat.

The Millses also kept a seaside retreat in Newport, Rhode Island, a California retreat in San Mateo, a European retreat in Paris, and a town house in Manhattan. This Hudson River mansion was their home when a chill invaded the air and the leaves began to lose their green; the family came here in September after closing its Newport home for the season and left about four months later. When the urge to go skating or ice boating struck them in the dead of January, they would use this place as a midwinter getaway, and on rare occasions they would come here for a spring fling. Most of the time, however, this was their autumn home.

Considering aesthetics alone, the Millses were luckier than their neighbors. The railroad tracks that crawl up the Hudson River Valley pass by the front of this house, close to US 9, rather than through its backyard on the fringes of the river, making it one of the few estates in this vicinity in which the river view is not marred by the railroad. The best river scene may be from the round room, part of the original 1832 house. This vantage point boasts a stunning view of the late afternoon sun setting over the glistening Hudson with the faint outline of the Catskill Mountains in the distance.

Companion to the round room is the drawing room, also part of the original Greek Revival mansion. A Ming-dynasty teak-and-jade incense burner joins five Greek vessels dating from 500 to 400 B.C. as a few of the plentiful fine furnishings in the drawing room. Women would withdraw to this room after dinner – the name "drawing room" was a shortened form of "withdrawing room."

The drawing room was used by most American commercial royalty as a showcase for their most valuable ornaments and objets d'art. Modern home owners apparently take a dim view of such ostentation; site manager Melodye Moore reports that the most often heard comment from visitors on the tour is that the drawing room is "too busy."

As the women were leaving the dining room table for the drawing room, the men were likely heading downstairs to the billiards room, which unfortunately is not open to the public. But in a house boasting sixty-five rooms and fourteen bathrooms, no tour could exhibit all of them.

The library, architectural companion to the dining room, is on the tour, and its 1,800 volumes will impress even seasoned veterans of mansion-hopping. The collection represents five generations of the Lewis-Livingston-Mills families, and many volumes are personalized. If the books don't make an impression on you, perhaps the nineteenth-century Steinway piano and the silk damask draperies will.

Even when the Millses weren't entertaining, they had a full house on their hands. They traveled with nineteen servants from home to home; five additional servants lived at the mansion year-round, so when the family was in residence, there were twenty-four servants keeping them company. But that two dozen pales in comparison to the ten dozen people employed to care for the grounds. There were greenhouses, outbuildings, and a full complement of livestock, including cattle and horses, to care for.

The mansion and grounds have become part of Mills-Norrie State Park, actually two connecting state parks composed of land donated by the daughter of Ruth and Ogden Mills and the sister of Margaret Lewis Norrie. The park has eighteen holes of golf, a campground, cabins, the Norrie Marina, the Dutchess Community College Environmental Site, a fitness trail, a clubhouse restaurant, hiking trails overlooking the river, and picnic tables, all operational in warm months. In winter the park is open for cross-country skiing on groomed trails and sledding on the mansion's lawns.

Location: Staatsburg is three miles north of Hyde Park. Take US 9 to Old Post Road (a side street to the left as you head north) to the mansion. Mills-Norrie State Park can be reached from either US 9 or the mansion.

Admission is free for the mansion, the park, the environmental site, and for cross-country skiing. Admission is charged for golf and camping.

Hours: From mid-April to Labor Day the mansion is open all day Wednesday through Saturday and on Sunday afternoons; Labor Day through late October, afternoons only Wednesday through Sunday. The park is open daily, year-round. Call to check on specific activities. Camping season is mid-May through late October.

Allow fifty minutes for the mansion tour, considerably longer to walk the grounds or use any park facilities.

Information: Mills Mansion State Historic Site, Staatsburg, NY 12580, 914-889-8851. To contact Mills-Norrie State Park call 914-889-4646.

Events: Summer musical concerts; September, floral show, Celtic Day in the Park; October, antique auto show; December, A Gilded Age Christmas.

Note: Restoration on the mansion is ongoing. However, public access is not blocked and the mansion is open for tours as usual. Tours, even in the heart of vacation season, are given every half hour. The good news for golfers is that, according to the park staff, there is usually no lengthy wait during the week; reservations are needed on weekends.

If you are staying overnight: Dutch Patroon Motel, US 9 (half a mile north of the FDR home), Hyde Park, 914-229-7141; The Roosevelt Inn, US 9 (a mile north of the FDR home), Hyde Park, 914-229-2443; Super 8 Motel, US 9, Hyde Park, 914-229-0088; Beekman Arms, US 9 (at junction with State 308), Rhinebeck, 914-876-7077. Camping and cabins at Mills-Norrie State Park: in peak season, fourth Saturday in June to Labor Day, minimum reservation for one week, maximum reservation for two weeks; in off-season, opening day to fourth Saturday in June, and Labor Day to closing day, minimum reservation for two nights (three nights when holiday falls on Friday or Monday), maximum reservation for two weeks.

When in the area: Franklin and Eleanor Roosevelt's homes and the Gilded Age mansion of Frederick Vanderbilt (pages 1–8) are a five-minute drive south in Hyde Park. And biplanes, triplanes, and other classic aircraft take off on weekends at the air shows at Old Rhinebeck Aerodrome (pages 141–144).

14 Old Westbury Gardens
Old Westbury

Just after the turn of the century, John and Margarita Phipps, heirs to steel and shipping fortunes, decided to spare no expense in building Westbury House, their Long Island country estate. The oak-paneled dining room was moved in its entirety from the Phippses' Fifth Avenue Manhattan town house. The master bathroom is no less plush than the master bedroom, with silver-plated plumbing fixtures and wicker covering the toilet.

Paintings by such masters as John Singer Sargent, Joshua Reynolds, and Richard Wilson dot the mansion walls. And when the west porch was expanded in 1924, the Phippses added hydraulic windows, the same ones you see today, which can be lowered into the basement so a flow of fresh air will rush into the room.

Yet to those who come in spring or early summer, the glorious mansion is secondary to the gardens. Through much of the year, but especially in late May and early June, the floral fiesta is in its full glory. "The gardens were Margarita Phipps's pride and joy," said our guide, Marcie. And it's easy to see why. There are about a dozen separate gardens encompassing eighty-eight acres, and the scent of roses and a rainbow of rhododendrons surround visitors in late spring, the favorite time of year for most visitors.

Several months later, the welcoming of autumn is announced by asters, dahlias, and chrysanthemums, lighting up the gardens in fireworks of yellow, red, purple, and orange. Lily pads on East Lake, now and then topped with an obligatory frog, bespeak summer, while foxgloves and other herbs offer color throughout the months the house and gardens are open to the public.

Classic statuary is ubiquitous. A twin set of eighteenth-century female sphinxes stare from the mansion, admiring the garden view, while Milo of Crotona stands in anguish against the hemlock hedge outside the Walled Garden. There's a terra-cotta statue of Diana the Huntress, sitting inside a rose-covered Corinthian colonnade in the Boxwood Garden. In fact, as you stroll through the gardens and purposely get lost wandering the grounds, you can never tell when you may come face-to-face with a sprightly faun – part man, part goat – or the solemn visage of a Roman emperor.

Several gardens – the Lilac Walk, the Ghost Walk, the Cottage Garden, the Woodland Walk – have their own stories to tell. A step outside the Lilac Walk brings visitors to the pet cemetery, where Doreen and her canine companions are buried; the Phipps family were unapologetic dog lovers. The lead eagles down the stairs from the pet cemetery along the Lilac Walk were gifts from an English family, given as a thank-you to the Phippses. When the Battle of Britain was raging during World War II, the Phipps family made it possible for thirty English children to come to America and stay in their mansion to escape the bombs. It was in exchange for the safe haven for their offspring that the family donated the eagles.

Margarita Phipps, née Margarita Grace, had roots in England. An heir to the Grace shipping family, Margarita lived before her marriage with her sisters and parents at a mansion called Battle Abbey in Sussex, England. In the Ghost Walk at Old Westbury Gardens is a hemlock replica of the yew walk that exists at Battle Abbey. The pair of bronze peacocks, with topiary tails and blossomy bodies, are symbolic of the real peacocks who once roamed in the gardens.

For a long time, the bridge spanning the narrow end of East Lake on the Woodland Walk was an actual gangplank used on a Grace Line ship; it was recently replaced by a more traditional bridge. In the Cottage Garden is a miniature English cottage, with timbers and thatched roof. Inside you will find the hallmarks of childhood, a play tea set and teddy bears and dolls, once the property of the Phippses' only daughter, Peggy. The three Phipps boys, Ben, Hubert, and Michael, played in three little log cabins, also in the Cottage Garden. The white cedar replica cabins you see today replace the originals, long since destroyed by the elements.

Portraits are seen throughout the Charles II–style mansion. A pensive Michael with pet pit bull, Spike, hangs in John Phipps's green-paneled study, which at one time was the family dining room. (Spike and the other family dogs were treated royally, just as one might expect. A china food bowl in the master bedroom has a French phrase inscribed on it which in English means "Love me, love my dog.")

Sketches of all four Phipps children hang in the master bedroom, but it is likely that Margarita saw more of the paintings that did her husband. Marcie said, "It was fashionable for the ladies of the day to sleep in until one or two in the afternoon," adding coyly, "I still think it's fashionable." So while Margarita slept in, John would wake early and head to his personal dressing room, complete with its own mahogany tester bed with clawed feet and carved posts, to dress for the morning hunt or some other typical men's activity of the day.

While Margarita was without her own dressing room, she did have her own study downstairs. Filled with books, it is a more mannish room – square in shape with sharp angles – than some might expect for a woman's study of that time. But there are armchairs and a couch with floral upholstery, and you will likely find a bouquet of flowers on a center table.

Both Margarita and John were avid readers, and titles on the shelves range from volumes of Shakespeare's works to the *Memoirs of the Duke of Urbino*. Try to spot the bookcase section that is fake; the book spines facing you are as phony as Michael Jackson's nose – they conceal a secret closet where John Phipps kept his Stradivarius and Guarnerius violins.

Much softer is the White Drawing Room. It also contains chairs and a sofa with floral upholstery. But unlike Margarita's study, it is bathed in white with gold brocade draperies framing the view of the gardens. As a native of England, Margarita observed afternoon tea regularly, often in this room. A tea table is set with the family's silver set, including pieces dating to the eighteenth century.

But on all but the rainiest and coolest days – and keep in mind that the mansion was used mainly as a spring and summer retreat – teatime took place in the open and airy West Porch. The hulking windows, when not hydraulically lowered into the basement, offered a stellar view of the gardens and let in oceans of light. On a clear day one could admire the terrace, hedges, pond, and lawns from the comfort of a cushy upholstered couch. Marcie noted that this is probably the favorite room of those who come to tour the mansion today. It was also the Phippses' most used room, not only for teatime, but also when they were alone.

When the mansion was built, the West Porch was quite a bit smaller, but it was expanded to its present size in 1924 when the hydraulic windows were added. Keep a sharp eye out for the shape of a rectangle on the southeast corner of the porch floor. It hides a dumbwaiter, also added in 1924 to make serving at teatime easier.

But of all the rooms in the mansion, the one that served the most purposes is known today as the Children's Dining Room. It was at various times part of the kitchen and butler's pantry, a smoking room, a billiards room, and a housekeeping room. During World War II, however, it was the place where the English children escaping the war had their meals. Today it is used for changing exhibits.

Location: From the Long Island Expressway (I-495), exit 39S

(Glen Cove Road), continue east on the service road that parallels the expressway for 1.2 miles, then onto Old Westbury Road (first right) and continue one-quarter mile to the gardens. An alternate route is to take the Northern State Parkway east to exit 30, turn right onto I.U. Willets Road; at the dead end, turn left onto Old Westbury Road and continue a tenth of a mile. From the south shore, take the Meadowbrook Parkway north to the Northern State Parkway, exit 31; turn left onto Glen Cove Road to I.U. Willets Road and continue as above. From eastern Long Island, take the Long Island Expressway (I-495), exit 39S, cross over the expressway, and follow the service road as above. *Admission* is charged.

Hours: Late April through mid-December, Wednesday through Monday.

Allow an hour to see the gardens and about forty minutes to take the guided mansion tour.

Information: Old Westbury Gardens, P.O. Box 430, Old Westbury, NY 11568, 516-333-0048.

Events: A few of the many include: early May, Arbor Day Celebration; May and June, antique auto shows; late June-early August, Picnic Pops Concerts, six-week-long series of name orchestra and band concerts; fall, Scottish Games, bagpipe playing, dancing, tossing the caber, Scottish food and marketplace; Halloween Program for Children, pumpkin painting, hayrides, magic show, spooky ghost walk; Christmas at Westbury House, holiday decorations, gifts and music, Santa Claus, hayrides; year-round, dried flower workshops.

Note: You can buy separate admissions for the house or the garden only, or a combination ticket for both. The sprawling grounds are perfect for relaxing walks, and there are plenty of picnic tables for a leisurely lunch.

If you are staying overnight: Island Inn, Old Country Road (Meadow Brook Parkway, exit M1), Old Westbury, 516-228-9500 or 800-FOR-ROOM; Holiday Inn, 369 Old Country Road (Long Island Expressway [I-495], exit 39S), Carle Place, 516-997-5000; Comfort Inn, 101 Jericho Turnpike (Long Island Expressway [I-495], exit 40W), Jericho, 516-334-8811; Howard Johnson Motor Lodge, 120 Jericho Turnpike (Long Island Expressway [I-495], exit 40W), Jericho, 516-333-9700. Note that lodging on Long Island is very expensive.

When in the area: The homes of illustrious Americans Theodore Roosevelt (pages 263–269) and Walt Whitman (pages 231–237) are to the north. Hungry for more wealth and splendor? The Vanderbilt Museum and planetarium are in Centerport (pages 9–13). Old Bethpage Village Restoration, the re-created village representing nineteenth-century Long Island, is to the east (pages 52–57).

The lighthouse at Fire Island National Seashore

15 Waterfalls and Gorges of the Finger Lakes

Find legends fascinating? Then you will love hearing how according to Iroquois Indian lore the Finger Lakes were created. The great Spirit, it was said, made the Finger Lakes region for the use of the Iroquois people, who then asked how they would recognize their homeland. In response, the Great Spirit extended his hand to them and said, "You must have faith and press onward. You should know your lands, for I have pressed my hand upon them and in my fingerprints rest the blue waters."

There is another version of the same story, this one told by biologists and other scientists. A million or so years ago, rivers flowed in the Finger Lakes region valleys. During the Ice Age glaciers carved out deeper valleys, and when the glaciers melted, the depressions filled with water.

Those who come to this part of west-central New York, whether purposely or serendipitously, can't help but admire the beauty of the entire region. The glens, valleys, and lakes combine to form vistas that remind many observers of the Scottish highlands or the Irish countryside. Come here looking for sights for sore eyes and you will not leave disappointed. The same goes for the recreation-minded. Boating, camping, swimming, hiking, and, in winter, cross-country skiing are found in abundance.

The area can claim a total of eleven deep lakes—Seneca is

the deepest at 632 feet – and eighteen parks. Watkins Glen State Park, at the south end of Seneca Lake, is perhaps the most famous of all the Finger Lakes parks. It is also the oldest regional state park and the most spectacular. Its gorge is so inspiring it makes one giddy.

There are nineteen waterfalls and 300-foot-high cliffs in Watkins Glen, as well as a mile-and-a half-long trail that takes visitors up and down stairs and over and under waterfalls, all the while skirting the gorge's edge. Look down and you see a multilevel wonderland of cliffs and crags, mosses and pools, and powerful, plunging rockets of water. At the bottom is Glen Creek, which started forming the gorge 10,000 years ago. The process continues.

Before you walk the trail be sure to get a copy of the park leaflet. Ten posted numbers along the trail denote landmarks, all explained in the brochure. The trail walk is fairly easy, but there are 832 stone steps in all. To avoid the mass of steps near the trail's start, you can take a shuttle bus to a farther entrance. In any case, you should wear good hiking shoes, for the footing can be slick.

While all the stops are worthy of a good look, Cavern Cascade at number 3 and the Cathedral at number 6 are two of our favorites. You can actually walk behind the high falls at Cavern Cascade, thanks to the force of the water that has worn away a thin layer of shale in the cliff wall. Step on the stone slab with the rippled surface at the Cathedral and you are standing on the floor of an ancient sea. These ripples were once in sand at the bottom of an inland ocean hundreds of millions of years ago.

After you have walked the gorge, try a second or third hiking trail, or relax at poolside by reading that paperback you brought along. The park is graced with a fifty-meter pool as well as a children's pool.

Come back to Watkins Glen at nighttime and you go back

Climb the gorge at Watkins Glen State Park

eons in history. An outdoor sound-and-light spectacular called "Timespell" utilizes lasers and music to take you to the beginnings of the earth and specifically to the formation of Watkins Glen gorge. Says the stirring voice of the narrator, "We are about to leave human time altogether and go far, far back into the geologic past—almost a million times five thousand years. We are going back to a time when the earth was young—over four and one half billion years ago."

The bare features of the gorge blackened in the night serve as the stage on which the show takes place. The vivid laser lights are cast on cliff walls while the resounding narrator's voice bridges the time from the dawn of the gorge's creation to the Ice Age to the thriving Seneca Indian communities that were here a few hundred years ago to the glen's first tourists in the mid-nineteenth century. Lights, all the while, dance off waterfalls and canyon walls; sounds imitate erupting volcanos, crackling ice, and the rhythmic, steady beating of the Senecas' drums.

Indian legends also played a role in the naming of the major feature in another park, Taughannock Falls State Park, by Cayuga Lake. One says that Chief Taughannock, a Delaware Indian, was slain in battle against the Cayugas and the Senecas and his body thrown over the falls. Another says simply that "taughannock" is an Iroquois or Algonquian word translated as "the great falls in the woods."

Taughannock Falls, 215 feet high, is the highest vertical waterfall in the eastern United States. A three-quarter-mile-long trail extends from the park office by the lake shore through a gorge to the base of the falls. As at Watkins Glen State Park, a leaflet has descriptions corresponding to posted numbers at nature trail stopping points.

Stop at the little waterfall at marker number 2 and you see evidence of a waterfall's power. The constant pouring of water has gradually eaten away at rock supporting it. The same principle applies to supersize Taughannock Falls, which in 10,000 years has sculpted the three-quarter-mile-long gorge you must walk through to reach its base. Some 10,000 years ago, the falls were right at Cayuga Lake's shore.

In addition to hiking trails, there are a swimming beach, a bathhouse, playgrounds, and playing fields in the park. Fishing is permitted in nearby Taughannock Falls Creek and Cayuga Lake.

Buttermilk Falls State Park, just south of Ithaca, has falls that refresh rather than overwhelm. A natural pool forms at the base, and park spokespersons don't exaggerate when they compare the atmosphere to that of an old-fashioned swimming hole. Stretching out by pool's edge and taking a dip can invigorate even the most jaded and worn-out vacationer.

Cool and shaded trails take hikers uphill and alongside Buttermilk Creek, which drops more than 500 feet in a series of cascades and rapids. All together there are ten waterfalls and two glens. The potential danger to those acting carelessly caught the attention of filmmakers back when the movie industry was young. *The Perils of Pauline*, filmdom's first successful serial, was shot in Buttermilk Glen.

A few words about some other Finger Lakes region parks:

Keuka Lake State Park, another hilly and wooded refuge, is in the heart of wine country. Stunning views combining vineyards and the lake are commonplace. Swimming is available, and trails take hikers among the surrounding trees and hills.

Favored activities at Cayuga Lake State Park near Seneca Falls include swimming and fishing, while swimming and boating enthusiasts should consider making Seneca Lake State Park near Geneva their base of operations.

There are two more gorges worth noting. On the southwest fringes of the Finger Lakes region is Stony Brook State Park near Dansville. The trail bordering Stony Brook Glen extends three-quarters of a mile, climbs about 250 steps, and passes three waterfalls. Stony Brook does Buttermilk Falls one better by providing swimming in two stream-fed ponds.

Finally, while it is technically out of the Finger Lakes region, Letchworth State Park near Portageville, about twenty-five miles west of Dansville, deserves a mention since this is the single other area park whose sheer wonder rivals Watkins Glen. The walls of the park's seventeen-mile-long Genesee River Gorge reach over 600 feet high. Three waterfalls, all plunging over 100 feet, highlight this creation, crafted on one of Mother Nature's best days. Swimming, hiking, fishing, white-water rafting, and white-water canoeing are recreation options, after your eyes have been sufficiently amazed.

Location: Watkins Glen State Park's main entrance is on State 14 (Franklin Street) in the village of Watkins Glen. Taughannock Falls State Park's entrance is on State 89, eight miles north of Ithaca, near Trumansburg. The main entrance to Buttermilk Falls State Park is along State 13, two miles south of Ithaca.

Admission is charged to enter all three parks and there is an additional fee for "Timespell." Parking fees at Taughannock Falls and Buttermilk Falls state parks are waived in winter.

Hours: Watkins Glen, Taughannock Falls, and Buttermilk Falls state parks are open year-round, although gorge trails are closed at all three in winter. Watkins Glen State Park is open in winter for hiking, cross-country skiing, and snowmobiling. Taughannock Falls State Park is open in winter for beginners' downhill skiing, skating, some hiking, and cross-country skiing. Buttermilk Falls State Park is open in winter for hiking and cross-country skiing. "Timespell" is presented early May through

October, twice nightly late June-late August and once nightly rest of the season.

Allow one to two hours to walk the gorge trail at Watkins Glen State Park and an hour to ninety minutes to walk the gorge trails at Taughannock Falls and Buttermilk Falls state parks. Allow forty-five minutes for the "Timespell" presentation.

Information: Watkins Glen State Park, P.O. Box 304, Watkins Glen, NY 14891, 607-535-4511. Taughannock Falls State Park, Box 1055, 2221 Taughannock Park Road, Trumansburg, NY 14886, 607-387-6739. Buttermilk Falls State Park, RD 10, Ithaca, NY 14850, 607-273-5761. "Timespell," SMRL Corporation, Box 6, Franklin Street, Watkins Glen, NY 14891, 607-535-4960. For information on the other mentioned parks, contact Taughannock Falls State Park.

If you are staying overnight: Best Western University Inn, 1020 Ellis Hollow Road, Ithaca, 607-272-6100; Econo Lodge, 2303 North Triphamer Road, Ithaca, 607-257-1400; Taughannock Farms Inn (seven-room country inn in former Victorian summer home), 2030 Gorge Road (State 89), Trumansburg, 607-387-7711; Chieftain Motel, 3815 State Route 14 (at junction with State 14A), Watkins Glen, 607-535-4759; Falls Motel, 239 North Genesee Street (just off State 14), Montour Falls, 607-535-7262.

Camping: Watkins Glen State Park (303 sites), Taughannock Falls State Park (72 sites), Buttermilk Falls State Park (61 sites)— see addresses and phone numbers above; Watkins Glen–Corning KOA (112 sites), State 414 (four and a half miles south of junction with State 14), 607-535-7404; Spruce Row Campsite (185 sites), 164 Kraft Road (State 89), Ithaca, 607-387-9225.

When in the area: The wineries of Hammondsport (pages 156–161) are to the west, on the south shore of Keuka Lake. To the southwest is the famous museum and factory of glass, the Corning Glass Center (pages 283–287) in Corning.

16 Adirondack Sampler

New York State's Adirondack Mountains are made in part from the oldest rocks on the face of the earth, so it is appropriate that this rugged chunk of northeastern New York state is one of the oldest resorts in the country and contains what is claimed to be the country's oldest tourist attraction as well.

The Ausable River, flowing for about fifty miles from the slopes of Mount Marcy to Lake Champlain, is responsible for much of this region's beauty. At High Falls Gorge in Wilmington, the river's cold waters drop 700 feet over the course of several waterfalls. Near the river's mouth is Ausable Chasm, with its massive sandstone cliffs sheltering the rushing river and the nature lovers who stroll on walkways high above it and ride on boats inside it.

Ausable Chasm has been open to the public since 1870, and its management claims it to be "probably America's oldest organized tourist attraction." Ever since Maj. John Howe, the chasm's discoverer, first journeyed inside it while suspended on ropes, people have been awestruck by the sights inside this ponderous river-carved gash in solid sandstone.

The walk inside Ausable Chasm takes you up and down 178 stairs over a three-quarter-mile-long course. You walk along a stone floor and wooden stairs and now and then cross the chasm on steel bridges. Markers along the path explain a little about the huge gorge and help you identify natural landmarks.

At one you learn that the rocky cliffs encasing the gorge are made from Potsdam sandstone (named for the northern New York state town, not the German one), which ranges in texture from a soft, brittle sandstone in some spots to a hard, dense quartzite. Geologists estimate that it took at least 15,000 years for the Ausable River to cut through the rock and carve the chasm. The cliffs, it is estimated, were created by glacial action 500,000 million years ago.

Elephant's Head, across the chasm, looks as much like its name as any rock formation we've ever seen. It was formed when deep cracks occurred in the sandstone cliffs. The Cathedral, another appropriately named feature, offers a sheltered refuge in a large, open, grotto-like sanctuary behind you. Jacob's Well, by a ledge high above the cleft, is a natural pothole — smooth, sleek, deep, and dry, the result of the action of stones repeatedly whirling in an eddy, boring gradually into the stream bottom. To look at the depth of the pothole and think that it was made by many, many small stones makes one's mind reel.

You will feel dampness as you walk in the chasm, but you won't feel the spray of water until you reach Table Rock. At this point you hop in a red wooden dory and take off on a ten-to-fifteen-minute ride down a part of the river called the Grand Flume. It is quiet at first, but a guide will break the silence with a few tales of the long natural and human history that has taken place inside these sandstone walls. As you ride through the chasm's narrowest point, you will hear that the cliffs are less than twenty feet apart and the water there can be as deep as ninety feet.

There is no boat ride at High Falls Gorge but there are thrills nonetheless. You cross the Ausable River on foot three times and so are given a wide spectrum of views of the natural curiosities that it has spawned.

While the most memorable feature of Ausable Chasm is the deep and craggy chasm itself, the highlights of High Falls Gorge are the Ausable River's four gushing waterfalls, each of which you see, from varied vantage points, close up, directly above, and far away.

Your view gets bigger and broader as you gradually wind your way along the wooden path, up and down stairs, across bridges, and precipitously perched on the cliff's edge, following the trail outlined in the descriptive brochure and map you are given when you buy tickets. Between stops 4 and 5 you cross the Ausable River and are afforded a glance at both Main and Mini Falls; at stop 5 you peer directly into torrential Rainbow Falls.

Between stops 7 and 8 you once again cross the Ausable River at a point called "best view." You will understand why when you get there. Climax Falls has joined the scene, making a quartet of power-packed, gushing cataracts. Take time to stand on the bridge and savor the setting. This is one sight you will remember long after you have left the area.

The brochure explains some of the Ausable River's more subtle alterations of the land, such as the lichens at stop 8 that are really a marriage of algae and fungi cohabiting together as a means of survival. Then there is the metallic brown tint of the river's waters. At Rainbow Falls you read that the drab color is the result of dissolved iron ore mineral from the surrounding mountains. As at Ausable Chasm there are potholes of all sizes here and explanations as to how they came to be.

You don't need to be in top shape to walk through Ausable Chasm and High Falls Gorge, but you do need to be able and willing to climb more than 100 steps. To experience a mountain-top view, however, you need to be in even better shape, which is why we recommend that less energetic view seekers drive to the top of Whiteface Mountain, the only one of the forty-six Adirondack peak summits that can be reached by car.

Here it is your automobile that puts forth the effort to reach the top . . . well, most of the way to the top. You drive a distance of about five miles from the ticket booth at the base of Whiteface Mountain Veterans Memorial Highway to just a few hundred feet short of the 4,867-foot-high peak, the state's fifth-highest mountain. From there you have a choice of walking up the Whiteface Mountain Nature Trail, a fifth of a mile long, or taking an elevator to the summit. The nature trail consists mostly of stones rather than steps, so wear good sturdy shoes or don't risk the climb. The trail is closed during and just after rainstorms, for good reason.

Even though the star attraction of Whiteface Mountain is the view from the summit, don't ignore the sights on the drive up. Notice how the soil grows thinner and rockier as you rise in elevation. The trees slowly but certainly become smaller and thinner and are akin to stunted dwarfs as the auto drive ends. Stop at some of the numerous parking areas on the way up and feel the air gradually cooling.

If you do walk the short trail from the highway end to the summit, pause a few moments to read the markers along the way. You can tell the direction of the prevailing wind by checking the balsam firs, known as flag trees, along the left side as you climb. At these high altitudes, the trees grow few branches on their windward sides.

As you continue climbing, you ultimately reach the timberline, the point where the climate is so harsh and cold that trees can no longer grow. Although you won't see trees in the alpine zone above the timberline, you will spot herbs and stubby small shrubs like the bearberry willow (bearing fuzzy fruits similar to the pussy willow), the alpine goldenrod, and the alpine bilberry (a cousin of the blueberry).

The view from the summit is a lot like pizza. When it's good, it's great. When it isn't so good, it's still pretty good. You can see the Montreal skyline, Lake Champlain, and Vermont's faraway Green Mountains on a sparkling day. If it is hazy or cloudy, you will still have an unobstructed view of the village of Lake Placid, the entire Ausable River Valley, cars working their ways up the same snaking path you just drove, and untold mountaintops in every direction.

A complex housing a gift shop, a cafeteria, and rest rooms offers shelter from the chills and winds. The silo standing next to it is home to New York state's equipment for the Atmospheric Science Research Center.

Location: Ausable Chasm is reached by taking I-87 (the Northway), exit 34, onto US 9 north to the chasm. It is twelve miles south of Plattsburgh. High Falls Gorge is reached by taking I-87, exit 30, onto State 73 north to Lake Placid, then State 86 northeast to the gorge. (From Ausable Chasm and I-87 heading south, take State 9N to Jay, then State 86 south to the gorge.) Whiteface Mountain Veterans Memorial Highway is reached by taking State 86 (north from Lake Placid or south from Jay) to State 431 to the highway toll house.

Admission is charged to all three attractions.

Hours: Ausable Chasm is open daily mid-May to early October. High Falls Gorge and Whiteface Mountain Veterans Memorial Highway are open daily late May to mid-October.

Allow an hour and a half to two hours for Ausable Chasm, forty-five minutes to an hour for High Falls Gorge, and an hour for the drive up and down Whiteface Mountain with some time to enjoy the view.

Information: Ausable Chasm, P.O. Box 490, Ausable Chasm, NY 12911, 518-834-7454. High Falls Gorge, Wilmington, NY 12997, 518-946-2278 in season, 518-946-2211 off-season. For Whiteface Mountain drive: Olympic Regional Development Authority, Olympic Center, Lake Placid, NY 12946, 518-523-1655, or 800-462-6236 toll-free in the U.S., 800-858-7782 in eastern Canada.

Note: Ausable Chasm: the boat ride will not take place during times of high water. At those times, a reduced admission fee is charged and visitors are given a free pass for a return trip. Still, even with the boat ride, the admission isn't cheap for an attraction where the average visitor spends no more than two hours—in 1993 it was $11.95 for adults and $7.95 for children. A cross-country ski center operates here in winter.

High Falls Gorge: picnic tables are on the grounds.

Whiteface Mountain Veterans Memorial Highway: the highway climbs at an average grade of 8 percent. Check your radiator, brakes, oil, and water before taking the drive. The auto road is part of a larger tour of the 1980 Winter Olympics facilities, which includes the Olympic Jumping Complex, Olympic Sports Complex (Mount Van Hoevenberg), and Whiteface Mountain Chairlift (to the top of smaller Little Whiteface Mountain). Contact Olympic Regional Development Authority for more information (see above).

If you are staying overnight: The following are in Plattsburgh off I-87, exit 37: Holiday Inn, 518-561-5000; Howard Johnson Inn, 518-561-7750; Econo-Lodge, 518-561-1500. The following are in Lake Placid on State 86: Lake Placid Hilton, 518-523-4411; Holiday Inn, 518-523-2556; Art Devlin's Olympic Motor Inn, 518-523-3700. The following are in Wilmington on State 86: Landmark Motor Lodge, at junction with Whiteface Mountain Highway, 518-946-2247; Grand View Motel, 518-946-2209; Holiday Lodge, 518-946-2251.

The following campgrounds are all at Ausable Chasm: Ausable Chasm KOA (135 sites), State 373 (east of US 9), 518-834-9990; Holiday Travel Park (48 sites), State 373 (east of US 9), 518-834-9216; Ausable River Campsite (100 sites), State 9N, 518-834-9379. Also consider: Adirondak Loj Campground (34 sites, three miles south of town on State 73, then five miles west on Adirondack Loj Road), Lake Placid, 518-523-3441; Lake Placid–Whiteface Mountain KOA (200 sites), Fox Farm Road (State 86), Wilmington, 518-946-2171; North Pole Campground (70 sites), State 86, Wilmington, 518-946-7733.

17 Seafaring Museums of Long Island
Sag Harbor and Amagansett

It's hard to believe as you drive through the environs of Sag Harbor and East Hampton on eastern Long Island, through the woods, past the manicured lawns and hidden estates, and along the country roads, that you are on the same island on which the urban jungles of Brooklyn and Queens sit. The eastern third of Long Island is the wilderness part of the island, where you can escape for a day in the country without having to head north or west, and where maritime history is the main draw for inquisitive visitors. Two of the better repositories for seafarer's artifacts and memoirs are the Sag Harbor Whaling Museum and the East Hampton Town Marine Museum in Amagansett.

Sag Harbor's boosters call their village the "un-Hampton Hampton," a reference to the towns of Southampton, East Hampton, and others containing the suffix "hampton" in their names, where well-to-do Manhattanites retreat during the summer, whether for a weekend or a whole month. Depending on one's point of view, the Hamptons are snobbish or sophisticated, but no matter what you think of them, you won't be lacking for human company at any of the Hamptons on a summer weekend.

What makes Sag Harbor the "un-Hampton Hampton"? For one thing, it sits on State 114, north of traffic-bloated State 27, the main drag from Manhattan to the south fork of Long Island, and is not prone to the congestion of the actual Hamptons (although you won't have a cloistered vacation here either).

But there is also Sag Harbor's atmosphere. It is reminiscent more of coastal New England than New York. There are weathered gray clapboard saltbox homes in town, along with elaborate mid-Victorian houses once owned by wealthy sea captains and merchants. There are also the requisite restaurants and shops, and you'll see everything from fashionable clothing to miniature people crafted from lobster claws and seashells in storefront windows, luring visitors inside to relieve their wallets of those cumbersome dollar bills.

Mostly, though, there is the whaling heritage. Like New Bedford, the whaling capital of New England, Sag Harbor was one of the country's major whaling towns in the nineteenth century, and dozens of ships sailed out of the port annually on trips as far away as the Bering Sea and the Pacific Ocean.

The best place in town to take a peek into Sag Harbor's nautical past is the Sag Harbor Whaling Museum, a Greek Revival mansion fronted by a quartet of sturdy Corinthian columns and built by a whaling-ship owner in 1845 at an astounding cost of $7,000. Some of the high cost of construction could be blamed on the hand-sculptured fireplace of imported Italian Carrara marble. Then there was also the sparkling stained glass skylight in the domed ceiling, which still reflects the sun's rays on a bright day.

The collection of authentic scrimshaw, elaborate carvings—many in minute detail—on whale bones and teeth, is certainly eye-pleasing, but the logbooks and displays tell the stories of intrepid whalers who went out to sea to catch whales in order to provide the oil that lit the country's homes in the early nineteenth century.

Whaling had been taking place here long before European settlers arrived. According to museum curator George Finckenor, Native Americans taught early settlers the patterns of the tides and currents and the locations of the sandbars. They also showed the new arrivals how they circled whales and drove them into shallow water or onto land, where the whales would die natural deaths. Whales farther out to sea, says Finckenor, were killed with a harping iron, a crude sort of harpoon connected by a twisted rope of vines and reeds to a float that was usually little more than a red cedar log.

Native Americans used whales for food, typically mixing whale oil with corn and peas and drying whale blubber for long-term use. But what became gold to non-Native American whaling men was spermacetti, a singular kind of oil found in the sperm whale's head. When boiled, cooled, and added to another liquid, the mixture was easily molded into candles that provided bright light. Says George Finckenor, a cavity in the head of one sperm whale could supply spermacetti for as many as thirty barrels of oil. For the first fifty years of the nineteenth century, whale oil was as valuable as fossil fuels are today.

Ironically, and contrary to common belief, it wasn't the discovery of oil in 1855 in Titusville, Pennsylvania, that killed the whaling industry, although it did hammer the last nail into its coffin. By the late 1840s, whales had migrated to points farther out to sea and the costs of voyages to hunt them was becoming exorbitant. The California gold rush of 1849 lured many whaling men west. By that time San Francisco and Honolulu were the only surviving whaling ports, the only ones still close to what remained of once sizable whaling pods.

Artifacts of the eastern whaling trade that survived hundreds of journeys out to sea are today at home inside and outside the Sag Harbor Whaling Museum. Three kettles used to boil blubber down to oil and a whale boat with mastodon-size oars guard the front of the museum. Arched over the entrance doorway are the jawbones of a right whale, so called because it was the right one to harpoon; this one was brought back to land by Sag Harbor whalers well over a hundred years ago.

Inside are tools, harpoons, and ship models in addition to a bevy of mounted sea predators. Also here are displays reflecting other aspects of the lives of Sag Harbor residents through the years. The portraits of children were done by itinerant painters in the 1800s. The bodies were already painted when the artist arrived in town; he painted in the face when he met the child.

Toys that these children might have played with, as well as the china and glass their parents would have displayed, are exhibited, and there is also a rare Giraffe piano with eighty-four keys rather than the standard eighty-eight, more of a percussion instrument than a keyboard. You will also find a complete kitchen reflecting the life-styles of the earliest settlers who lived here around the year 1700.

Across the street is the Custom House, home of a late-eighteenth-century customs officer named Henry Packer Dering, who for thirty years conducted official government business with whaling ships and trading vessels here. The Dering family's household inventories and account books still exist and were the basis for stocking the house with furnishings like those the Derings owned: a Newport tallcase clock from the 1740s, a Queen Anne side chair from the same period, and a Windsor chair, circa 1794, for example.

What the Sag Harbor repository does to preserve eastern Long Island's whaling history, the East Hampton Town Marine Museum in Amagansett, about a twenty-minute drive away, depending on traffic, does for fishing. From the museum's setting atop Bluff Road, visitors can see the fleets at work out in the Atlantic Ocean.

The galleries on the top floor are devoted almost exclusively to the world of the present-day commercial fisherman. Dioramas and models illustrate half a dozen or more fishing methods, some used commonly, like dragging, and others rarely practiced nowadays, such as harpooning. Then there is aquaculture, or fish farming, a fairly new practice, which is illustrated and described as "a technique in which fertilized fish eggs are grown to pan-size fish within a controlled environment."

A wall-size calendar shows a bay fisherman's typical year, which species of fish are caught at what times, and how reliant the profession is on the season, while a stocked aquarium and a gallery of watercolors feature fish indigenous to the area. The most popular areas for children are the discovery rooms, filled with "do-touch" displays, where they can see just how sharp the shell of a horseshoe crab or some other crustacean really is.

Further exhibits include salvage from shipwrecks, a diorama of the village of East Hampton on a busy summer day in 1916, a look at the evolution of yachts, and an original Gil Smith catboat. Behind the museum is the Fulweiler Garden, a relaxing place for parents to walk and take in the oceanside setting while kids with the energy of a speedboat can tackle the trawler jungle gym.

Location: Sag Harbor Whaling Museum is on Main Street opposite the library in the center of Sag Harbor. The Custom House is next door to the museum at the corner of Main and Garden streets in Sag Harbor. The East Hampton Town Marine Museum is on Bluff Road, a half mile south of the junction of State 27 and Atlantic Avenue in Amagansett.

Admission is charged to all three sites.

Hours: Sag Harbor Whaling Museum is open daily, mid-May through September. The Custom House is open daily, Memorial Day through Labor Day, and weekends in September. The East Hampton Town Marine Museum is open daily, July to Labor Day, and selected weekends or by appointment the rest of the year; call for specific weekend dates.

Allow an hour to see Sag Harbor Whaling Museum, a half hour to see the Custom House, and an hour to an hour and a half to tour the East Hampton Town Marine Museum.

Information: Sag Harbor Whaling Museum, Main Street, Sag Harbor, NY 11963, 516-725-0770; Society for the Preservation of Long Island Antiquities, 93 North Country Road, Setauket, NY 11733, 516-941-9444 (for information on the Custom House);

East Hampton Historical Society, 101 Main Street, East Hampton, NY 11937, 516-324-6850 or 516-267-6544 (for information on the East Hampton Town Marine Museum).

If you are staying overnight: Baron's Cove Motel, West Water Street, Sag Harbor, 516-725-2100; Seacrest Motel, State 27, Amagansett, 516-267-3159; East Hampton House (motel), 226 Pantigo Road, East Hampton, 516-324-4300; Maidstone Arms (country inn), 207 Main Street, East Hampton, 516-324-5006; Huntting Inn (country inn), 94 Main Street, East Hampton, 516-324-0410.

When in the area: Should a look at life on the sea make you thirsty for more waterside heritage, head about an hour west to the Long Island Marine Museum in Sayville (pages 37–41) or to Fire Island National Seashore (pages 126–132).

18 The Thousand Islands

Actually there are more than 1,800 islands in the Thousand Islands region, that fifty-mile stretch of the St. Lawrence River along the border separating New York State, U.S.A., from Ontario, Canada. The largest is Wellesley Island, over twenty miles long, while the smallest could fit inside your living room.

From high above, the view of these freckles of greenery on the body of the St. Lawrence is nature's masterpiece of water intermixed with land. This area is as friendly to boaters as it is to sightseers; computer wizards might be tempted to call it "cruiser friendly." There are two ways to get a good overall look at the islands: from high above, or if you fall into the category of pleasure boater or fisherman, from water level. Let's travel by water first.

Alexandria Bay, the hub and commercial center of the region, pats itself on the back, calling itself the "world capital of bass fishing." That's no idle boast, and you will find both small and largemouth bass in the waters. The town has been the setting for fishing tournaments many times, and it once hosted the Bass Anglers Sportsman Society's Bass Masters Classic, a meaningless title to most of us but to a bass fisherman the equivalent of the World Series and the Super Bowl rolled into one.

But Alexandria Bay is not the only place in the Thousand Islands to cast off your boat for a few hours of fishing. Cape Vincent, south of Clayton, is a choice spot for both black bass and muskie. Clayton is good for pike and perch. Chippewa Bay, north of Alexandria Bay, and Wellesley Island are likely places to haul in pike and largemouth bass. New York State fishing licenses may be obtained at many places, including Department of Energy Conservation offices, tackle-and-bait shops, chambers of commerce, and town clerk offices. You need a Canadian fishing license to fish in Canadian waters, and if you are caught without one you will probably be fined, have your fish confiscated, and be given so many hours to obtain the Canadian license.

If you don't know your bass from a hole in the ground and just want to take in the view of the islands, you can set out in your own boat – if you are one of the lucky few that owns one – or hop aboard one of several tour boats offering sights and river trivia. One line, Uncle Sam Boat Tours, operates out of Alexandria Bay, while several other outfits also give tours. The best known is Gananoque Boat lines, operating from the town of Gananoque, Ontario.

The various lines serve up a potpourri of choices. There are dinner cruises, sunset cruises, charter cruises, and express ferry shuttles to Boldt Castle. All depart several times daily on general

Romantic Boldt Castle, the Thousand Islands

tours of the Thousand Islands region, weaving amid and among the archipelago and stopping at the most famous island of all, Heart Island, home of Boldt Castle, where you have the option of seeing the castle and taking a later boat back. In addition, each boat line gives a bit of a tour. Uncle Sam has a live tour guide on board, Gananoque a taped guide. You will learn island tidbits and trivia regardless of which line you take.

What is an island? According to our guide it is any piece of land sticking at least two feet above water and supporting at least two trees. "That one to the right barely makes it," our guide called out, and our fellow passengers on the top deck rushed to the right side of the boat. "That's the smallest one in the river. Its name is Tom Thumb," he added.

Most of the islands are big enough to support a summer camp or a second or third (or fourth) home. The boat took us past those with mansions once owned by families with names like Astor and Strauss, although as in Newport, Rhode Island, these forty-room laps of luxury were humbly called cottages in their day.

As for trivia, how about the following food fact? Both Philadelphia Cream Cheese and Thousand Islands salad dressing have links to this area, while one also has a connection to Philadelphia, Pennsylvania. Which is which?

It's the dressing that connects Philadelphia, Pa., to the Thousand Islands. Hotelier George Boldt, owner of Boldt Castle, was sailing on the St. Lawrence in his yacht when his steward surprised him with a new dressing. Boldt enjoyed the taste so much he named it for the region where he first tasted it and served it in his hotels: the Waldorf-Astoria in New York City and the Bellevue-Stratford in Philadelphia. His steward later gained fame as Oscar of the Waldorf. Philadelphia Cream Cheese? It was developed in the mid-nineteenth century in nearby Philadelphia, New York.

The story of Boldt Castle, George Boldt's mansion away from home, is a parable of life at its most kind and most cruel, a towering testament to the ancient adage that money can't buy happiness. The turreted Rhenish-style stone castle and its surrounding outbuildings, as magnificent as the castle itself, occupy all of Heart Island in the St. Lawrence River. The castle and the entire island were to be part of the millionaire's gift to his wife, Louise. In fact, Boldt arranged to have the island, originally called Hart Island, reshaped to resemble a heart, hence the spelling change.

Work on Boldt's fantasy castle began in 1900. An arch of triumph planned to be the formal entryway for launches was raised. The main castle building, six stories of granite walls, steel and concrete roofs and floors, and terra-cotta decorations began taking shape. The bottom two floors included the ballroom, dining room, library, billiard room, and reception rooms. Bedrooms, each with a private bath and fireplace, were to occupy the upper floors. In total, the Boldts' dream home would contain 120 rooms.

By the end of 1903, the castle structure was complete and the interior was filling up with luxurious furnishings. All was proceeding on schedule with more than $2.5 million of George Boldt's money invested in it.

Then, just after ringing in the new year, 1904, George Boldt sent a telegram to the superintendent of construction. Louise Boldt was dead. A grieving and disheartened George ordered the crew to stop construction immediately. They did. The castle was about a year and a half from completion.

Today over 160,000 tourists annually visit the castle and explore its interior. But there are no rich tapestries from the looms of Flanders, no smooth marble mantelpieces from Italy, no sculptures from the artisans from France, as Boldt had planned. There is a bit of furniture, donated by local organizations, and there are photographs and commentaries on the castle's decorative idiosyncrasies, like its carved hearts (for Heart Island) and clovers (for Philadelphia's Clover Club, where Boldt once worked – he named his daughter Clover).

There are broken dreams here too. It nearly hurts to follow markers labeled "Miss Clover's Room" and "Mr. and Mrs. Boldt's Suite," only to find rooms as bare as the winter woods and walls scribbled with graffiti, remnants of seventy years of neglect when the elements and vandals had their way with Mr. Boldt's dream.

As if the castle were crying enough is enough, the Thousand Islands Bridge Authority took control of it in 1977 and has been operating it since. A restoration project is in effect. In recent years, the roofs and windows have been replaced, new brick walkways have been placed on the island, an Italian garden has been planted, and outbuildings, including the playhouse, powerhouse, and hennery, have been refurbished.

Back on the boat, keep your eyes open and you will see some further strange sights, including two-boat garages; Smugglers' Cove, where rumrunners hid during Prohibition; and the world's smallest international bridge, connecting two islands privately owned by one family: one island is in the United States, the other in Canada.

You will also be able to see the 1000 Islands Skydeck from your boat tour, but the more thrilling view is from atop the 400-foot-high observation tower. The Skydeck is on Hill Island, just a few hundred feet over the border in Canada, so be sure you have your driver's license, birth certificate, or other form of identification to present at customs. The perspective from the bridge to Canada is itself commanding, but you can enjoy just so much scenery from the window of a moving car.

If you want to look down your nose at all those island mansions, take the forty-second elevator ride to the observation deck. It is enclosed by glass, so even those suffering from mild acrophobia should feel secure. If you want a higher view and have the legs and the nerve, you can climb to two upper levels.

Stretch out your legs even more at one of New York's several area state parks. Wellesley Island State Park, surrounded by the river northwest of Alexandria Bay, offers the most facilities: nature trails, fishing, summer hiking, and a swimming beach. Keewaydin State Park, on the mainland a mile west of Alexandria Bay, boasts fishing, summer hiking, and a swimming pool. Formerly a private estate belonging to, among others, New York publishing magnate William T. Dewart, Keewaydin accommodates recreation-minded persons looking for both a romantic and an aquatic view, with two gazebos overlooking the river.

Other state parks with bathing beaches include, from north to south, Jacques Cartier (about twenty miles northeast of Alexandria Bay), Kring Point, Grass Point, and Cedar Point (about fourteen miles southwest of Clayton). Each of these state parks has picnic facilities and, as would be expected in any park along the waters of the St. Lawrence, each affords superb fishing opportunities.

If hunting for fish makes you hungry for knowledge about the area's long maritime heritage, plan a stop at the Antique Boat Museum in Clayton. The museum's collection contains more than 150 boats, thousands of nautical artifacts, and displays on related topics ranging from the evolution of the outboard motor to the life of a Prohibition rumrunner.

Location: To reach the Thousand Islands region, from I-81, take exit 50 (last exit before Canada) onto State 12 south to Clayton or north to Alexandria Bay. Boldt Castle is reached by tour boats or private boat.

Admission is charged for the boat rides, Boldt Castle, the Skydeck, the state parks, and the Antique Boat Museum.

Hours: Uncle Sam Boat Tours run generally from early May through October. Gananoque Boat Line tours run from mid-May through mid-October. Each company runs up to ten tours daily in July and August and as few as two daily in May and October. Boldt Castle is open daily, mid-May through early October. Skydeck is open daily, May through October. Wellesley Island State Park is open year-round; other state parks vary by season. The boat museum is open daily, mid-May through mid-October.

Allow two and a half hours for the Uncle Sam tour and three hours for the Gananoque tour. Allow one to two hours for Boldt Castle, depending on how much time you wish to spend walking the grounds. Allow forty-five minutes for Skydeck and about an hour for the boat museum.

Information: 1000 Islands International Council, Box 400, Alexandria Bay, NY 13607, 800-8-ISLAND or 315-482-2520. Uncle Sam Boat Tours, Alexandria Bay, NY, 315-482-2611 or 800-253-9229 in New York state. Gananoque Boat Lines, 613-382-2144. 1000 Islands Skydeck, 613-659-2335. Thousand Islands State Park, Recreation and Historic Preservation Region, Box 247, Alexandria Bay, NY 13607, 315-482-2593. Antique Boat Museum, 750 Mary Street, Clayton, NY 13624, 315-686-4104.

Note: Picnic tables are on the grounds at Boldt Castle. You can buy food at the castle or bring your own picnic.

If you are staying overnight: Pine Tree Point Resort, Anthony Street, Alexandria Bay, 315-482-9911 or 800-ALEX-BAY; Bertrand's Motel, 229 James Street, Clayton, 315-686-3641; Fairwind Lodge Motel and Cottages, State 12E (two and a half miles west of town), Clayton, 315-686-5251. Just about every state park here offers camping and reservations are recommended. Write to Thousand Islands State Park (address above) for a reservation form. A private campground is Merryknoll Campground (85 sites), State 12E, Clayton, 315-686-3055.

19 Sonnenberg Gardens
Canandaigua

With my garden fair and sweet,
My thoughts full often stray
To greet again the lovely flowers
Along the accustomed way.

—Mary Clark Thompson

We walked along, ten of us and tour leader Florence Richardson, from a greenhouse by the parking lot up the sloping walkway to benefactress Mary Clark Thompson's formal gardens, better known as Sonnenberg Gardens, in Canandaigua. As we walked uphill we could see fragments of the estate's Richardsonian-style mansion. Turrets, chimneys, windows, and bits and pieces of geometric patterns came into view. But like the famous plantation gardens of Charleston and other parts of the South, the gardens are the primary attraction here, the mansion secondary. And so Florence Richardson identified all the trees on the grounds as we strolled past them.

"There's a weeping beech, similar to a banyan, but it doesn't take root like one."

"Here's a Kentucky coffee tree. It grows a pod with big brown beans that were brewed for a beverage. And over there is a purple beech. In wet weather, the leaves take on a dark reddish tint."

As we reached the mansion, Florence asked us to turn around and look into the distance. Here we discovered the inspiration for the name of the grand estate. Sonnenberg means "sunny hill" in German. In between the trees on this bright, blue western New York day were the waters of Canandaigua Lake and the blue-gray domed hills in the distance.

Then we embarked on the formal garden tour, made up of jaunts to several small gardens on the grounds: the Italian garden, the sub-rosa garden, the pansy garden, the Japanese garden, the rose garden, the moonlit garden, the old-fashioned garden, and the rock garden. Ironically, casual neglect was responsible for saving much of the floral kaleidoscope at Sonnenberg today. The story begins shortly after the turn of the century when Mary Clark Thompson started the gardens as a memorial to her husband, banker and philanthropist Frederick Ferris Thompson, who died in 1899.

Mary continued to practice his charitable ways, donating large sums of money to colleges, museums, and other worthy causes, and regularly opened up the blossomy wonders of Sonnenberg to the general public. She often saw up to 7,000 visitors a day ambling along the footpaths, admiring the fragrant roses, studying classic Greek statuary, and gazing at the placid, clear waters of the reflecting pool.

When she died in 1923, Sonnenberg was inherited by a nephew, who later sold the estate to the United States government. A Veterans Administration hospital was constructed on the grounds with the mansion serving as a nurses' dormitory.

The gardens and grounds were neglected and fell into disuse but were never destroyed. So when restorers came here in the early 1970s they already had a living skeleton sketch of the estate. Old photographs from the early 1900s and a 1916 description of the grounds from the director of the New York Zoological Gardens further enhanced the restoration project, letting planners and workers know exactly what went where.

The restored Sonnenberg Gardens opened to the public in 1973 and have gradually been brought back to full bloom since then. Although there is still work to be done—a Roman bath along with its marble pillars and flooring sits as a silent victim of many upstate New York winters—the gardens are 95 percent completed; in fact, the Smithsonian Institution has recognized them as "one of the most magnificent late Victorian gardens ever created in America."

Each individual garden was designed so it could be viewed apart from the rest. We took notice of that during our tour, when the blue sky darkened and a drizzle began to fall. Richardson led us to the belvedere separating the Italian garden from the rose garden.

In one direction we looked down upon a classic European garden, which reminded us of those we had seen at Old World palaces like Versailles and Nymphenberg, with its four sunken parterre forming a modified fleur-de-lis design. Despite its name, the Italian garden borrows greatly from French influence. In the other direction we saw rows of roses: pink, red, and white. The rose garden was the first to be restored when more than 4,000 rosebushes were planted by volunteers, reestablishing the original beds.

We turned a corner and there was the sub-rosa garden, the term meaning "under the roses," referring to its chapel-like location. The hedges bordering this garden, Florence Richardson reported, were supposedly so thick that the family cat couldn't sneak through them.

The tour continued, the rain let up, and we reached *Diana Robing,* a nineteenth-century sculpture modeled after a fourth-century Greco-Roman statue now in the Louvre in Paris. That's not all the statuary here. The Italian garden is garnished with *Hercules Slaying the Hydra,* while the Japanese garden is dominated by the soft visage of a bronze meditating Buddha.

The Japanese garden, complete with a teahouse based on one in Kyoto, Japan, was designed and built by a man named K. Wadamori with seven workers whom Mary Thompson brought over from Japan. The rest of the landscaping was the work of Ernest K. Bowditch, a well-respected Boston landscape architect, and an area landscaper named John Handrahan. Bowditch was a firm believer in variety, as evidenced by Sonnenberg Gardens' multiformity, which doesn't let up even as you approach the tour's end. That's when you come across the old-fashioned garden, the rock garden, and the moonlit garden.

The old-fashioned garden is like a colonial garden and is similar to those you may have visited at places like Colonial Williamsburg and Mount Vernon; its design, however, can be traced as far back as Pompeii. The moonlit garden, predominantly white, is arranged so its blossoms are illuminated by the moon. Of course you can't see this on the guided tour in full daylight, but it's not difficult to imagine.

Circular in shape, the rock garden is composed of pudding stone and Onondaga limestone, two conglomerate rocks selected for their natural indentations and pockets, which make perfect homes for rock plants. Geysers and simulated springs shoot up, and a climbing hydrangea wraps around the walkway up to the Lookout Tower, a favorite spot for children. A statue of the mythological Pan, with his human body and goat's legs, horns, and ears, can't help but fascinate kids.

As Richardson left us and the garden tour came to an end, we were invited to enter the mansion. Staffpersons are on duty inside, but there is no guided tour. You move at your own pace and read about the house on posted descriptions.

An elk head, a bear skin, and a minstrel gallery all draw your attention in the medieval Great Hall. Next to the hall is the Tudor-style front room with its arch and half-timbers, while down the hall is the drawing room used to entertain guests on formal occasions. Like many of the wealthy in her time, Mary Clark Thompson collected treasures from the Orient, and you can see the melange of jades, porcelains, and ivories in the tiny trophy room. But her favorite room was the library because the axis of the Italian garden lined up directly with its French doors and the view of the garden was commanding.

Location: From the New York State Thruway (I-90) heading west, take exit 43 onto State 21 into Canandaigua, where it becomes Gibson Street, then follow the signs. From I-90 heading east, take exit 44 onto State 332 into Canandaigua, where it becomes Main Street; take a left onto Gibson Street (State 21) and follow the signs. From the south, take I-390 to exit 2 at Cohocton onto State 21; follow State 21 north for thirty-seven miles into Canandaigua and follow the signs.

Admission is charged.

Hours: Mid-May through mid-October, daily.

Allow two to three hours to take the guided garden tour, walk the grounds, and explore the mansion.

Information: Sonnenberg Gardens, 151 Charlotte Street, Canandaigua, NY 14424, 716-394-4922.

Events: Late June, Rose Sundays; Christmas in July.

Note: Admission fee admits you to the property. You can either take the ninety-minute-long guided garden tour or walk around on your own. There is no extra charge for the tour, but tours are offered only two times daily. The tour may be lengthy for children or adults with little interest in gardens, but you may leave the tour at any time. Buy admission tickets near the greenhouse closest to the parking lot. Picnic tables are available for your use by the duck pond next to the greenhouse.

If you are staying overnight: Canandaigua Inn, 770 South Main Street (one block south of junction of State 332, State 5, and US 20), Canandaigua, 716-394-7800; Econo-Lodge, 170 Eastern Boulevard (on State 5 and US 20, a half mile east of junction with State 332), Canandaigua, 716-394-9000; Georgian Motel, State 332 just north of center of town), Canandaigua,

716-394-2321; Finger Lakes Bed & Breakfast Association, P.O. Box 862, Canandaigua, NY 14424; Canandaigua Lake Area Bed & Breakfast Association, P.O. Box 334, Canandaigua, NY 14424, 716-229-2834.

When in the area: About half an hour east along US 20 and State 5 is historic Seneca Falls, birthplace of women's rights and home of Women's Rights National Historical Park and the National Women's Hall of Fame (pages 133–140). About half an hour to the north is the city of Rochester, home of the International Museum of Photography at the George Eastman House (pages 288–294).

20 Fort Stanwix National Monument
Rome

Benedict Arnold is a great guy, you hear when you visit the American troops stationed at Fort Stanwix National Monument in Rome. Arnold is a hero, a highly praised general who helped defeat the British at the Battle of Saratoga the year before.

It is summer 1778 at Fort Stanwix. The enlisted men and officers and their wives you meet cannot answer a question relating to a later time. If you ask where the nearest McDonald's is, you will be sent to the quarters of Corp. Donald McDonald, who actually served here in 1778.

You see, the staff members at Fort Stanwix National Monument, an accurate reconstruction of the real Fort Stanwix that existed here more than 200 years ago, don't simply interpret life during the Revolutionary War. They play the roles of actual men and women who lived here. Corporal McDonald, Sgt. Stephen Adams, Capt. and Mrs. Joseph Savage, drummer Cornelius Buttson, and all the others are stuck in a time warp.

If you ask a question about a time later than summer 1778, or about an unheard-of country called the United States of America, you will get a blank stare as a response. If you ask a question beyond the scope of the residents of Fort Stanwix in 1778, you will be directed to the visitors center, the only place inside the fort where staff members are living in the present, where personnel on duty will be pleased to answer your questions.

As with most National Park Service sites, the visitors center is the first place you should stop. It is located in the west barracks inside a door marked GREGG. A sentry will show you the way if you need help. An audiovisual presentation describes the true-to-life setting and acquaints you with this site's special method of living-history interpretation. In the visitors center you will absorb the background you need to converse with the 1778 fort residents.

Ask Sergeant Adams, for example, how the war is going and he might say that there is no end in sight, that the war should be raging for some time, but that it doesn't look hopeless. After all, just last fall General Burgoyne surrendered his army at the Battle of Saratoga, a major victory for the colonists.

And two months before that, the very men to whom you are talking successfully staved off a twenty-day siege by the British army, composed mainly of Indians and Canadian Loyalists. Much of the credit went to Col. Peter Gansevoort, commanding officer of the fort, but reliable and trustworthy Maj. Gen. Benedict Arnold also played a vital role. Arnold was sent from Albany to assist the men at besieged Fort Stanwix, and soon rumors reached the British camp that Arnold was coming with a tremendous force of Americans. The British commander, Gen. Barry St. Leger, seeing low morale and desertion by Indians who had joined his cause, ultimately lifted the siege and retreated to Canada.

The residents are incredibly cordial to visitors from the twentieth century. They will let you enter their living quarters and put your hands on just about anything in sight. Feel a straw mattress on which they slept, lumpy as a sack of dirty laundry, and keep in mind that none had the luxury of a pillow. We wanted a closer look at the portable writing table in the staff dining room, the place where Colonel Gansevoort and his high-ranking officers would have eaten. The table comes with a quill pen and some cloth covering its surface; an officer explained that the cloth was necessary because quill breaks when used directly on wood. Inside the table are maps and currency. The maps, too, had cloth attached to make them last longer. It is easy to forget that things weren't disposable and replaceable at the time–1778 on the edge of the wilderness was hardly a throw-away society.

Survival here means making do. Ask an officer's wife what's cooking in the hearth of her coarse quarters and she will likely respond chicken pie or stew. Bread was mostly cornbread. There wasn't much wheat grown around here. Ask an officer what his garb is made of and you will probably be told it's linen. You could count on the fingers of one hand the number of bales of cotton that arrived in Boston annually.

Ask to pick up some draughts (in our time they are called checkers) on the checkerboard in the enlisted men's bunkhouse and you will see they are made of melted-down bullets. You may find up to ten soldiers here on the busiest days, but in 1778 there would have been twenty-eight, with four sharing each of the seven bunk beds. The twenty-eight cooked over one fireplace and ate at one table, all in a space the size of your living room. Sanitary conditions were primitive; no visitor from the 1990s would have been able to stand the stench of an eighteenth-century bunkhouse.

That is one of the few cases where lines are drawn short of complete realism. You see the past as it was, but up to a point. Says Fort Stanwix staff member Bill Curtis, "We're not going to get typhoid or eat bad meat or go without showering for months."

But they do accurately enact everyday events that would have occurred in such an outpost. Some weapon is commonly fired each day as part of a drill or ceremony. At times a mis-behaving soldier is led to the whipping post in the middle of the parade ground where everyone can see. It was up to the company drummer to apply the lashes to the miscreant, but before the whip is cracked today, an officer will rush out to stop the punishment, calling out something like, "There are enough injured people here already." Darn!

Drummer Cornelius Buttson, played adeptly by staff member Bill Sawyer, is seen throughout the day on the parade grounds, where he dispels the false image of young drummer boys. Drummers ranged in age from their teens to their thirties and forties and were found all over the battlefield. They acted as orderlies for officers and gofers for doctors, helping collect the wounded or doing light hospital work, tasks that could not have been handled competently by a boy.

Most important, they gave signals with their drums. Everyday at noon, drummer Buttson marches to the parade ground and calls the militiamen to rations. Then at 4:30 he plays retreat, signaling to the soldiers that it is time to come back inside the fort. The drummer's responsibilities were never cancelled on account of the weather; he is out there in any condition, summer sunshine to upstate New York drizzle.

In one sector of the fort, the time warp is suspended. Inside the west casemate is a museum serving as a repository for relics from the original fort found during excavation. Articles like cloth and woodwork have long disintegrated, but buttons from French or British uniforms have survived the centuries. So have digging tools, pottery and pieces thereof, scissors, and toothbrushes. A short slide show on the process of reconstructing the fort is also shown there.

Location: Fort Stanwix National Monument is in the center of downtown Rome. To reach the fort from the east, take the New York State Thruway (I-90), exit 31, onto State 49, which becomes East Dominick Street in Rome. When you reach the fort, circle around it until you get to the parking garage on North James Street on the west side of the fort. There is free parking for fort visitors for three hours in the garage. From the west, take the Thruway, exit 33, onto State 365, which becomes Erie

Boulevard East in Rome. Just before you pass the fort take a right onto North James Street to the parking garage.

Admission is charged.

Hours: April through December, daily. The full living-history program is in effect Memorial Day through Labor Day. A modified living-history program is in effect at other times.

Allow an hour and a half to two hours in peak season, up to an hour and a half in the off-season.

Information: Fort Stanwix National Monument, 112 East Park Street, Rome, NY 13440, 315-336-2090.

Note: Separate tours of the fort's exterior and interior, black powder demonstrations, and a topical talk called "Ranger's Choice" are usually offered once daily in peak season.

If you are staying overnight: Quality Inn, 200 South James Street (in the center of Rome on State 46, 49 and 69), 315-336-4300; Paul Revere Lodge, 7900 Turin Road (three miles north of Rome on State 26), 315-336-1776; Esquire Motor Lodge, 1801 Black River Road, Rome, 315-336-5320.

When in the area: Also in Rome is Erie Canal Village (pages 118–125), another example of living history in the form of a re-created canalside village of the 1840s.

21 On the Erie Canal
Rome and Syracuse

You talk of making a canal 350 miles long through the wilderness. It is little short of madness to think of it at this day.

> — Thomas Jefferson in a speech to New York
> State representatives just prior to the start
> of construction of the Erie Canal

> *I've got an old mule and her name is Sal*
> *Fifteen miles on the Erie Canal.*
> *She's a good ol' worker and a good ol' pal,*
> *Fifteen miles on the Erie Canal.*

> — A Tin Pan Alley song written by Thomas S. Allen

Even Thomas Jefferson was fooled. But he was in good company. Few people thought the building of a canal across upstate New York was even remotely possible. For one thing, the canal would have been the longest in the world. For another, there was no machine power in 1816, just muscles in arms and legs. Trees had to be cut, stumps pulled, brush burned, and the canal bed dug with only shovels, scoops, and human strength.

But DeWitt Clinton campaigned for governor in 1816 on one issue: the building of the canal he hoped would connect the Hudson River to Lake Erie. He knew of the potential commerce made up of freight and passengers itching to move west. The voters agreed with him. It was just six months into his term, on July 4, 1817, that the first shovel of dirt was turned. That spot is now occupied by a re-created village composed mainly of authentic buildings transported from within a fifty-mile radius of its location.

When we visited we took a ride on the *Chief Engineer of Rome,* a canal-style packet boat, near that same spot. As in the early 1800s, a team of mules trudged along a towpath pulling us as we sang songs like "Low Bridge, Everybody Down," "Buffalo Gals," and "Jimmy Crack Corn." It was a slow ride as we crept rather than cruised, but we were intrigued as we heard the tale of the canal they said couldn't be built.

The packet boat ride is one of many ways to pass your time while visiting Rome's Erie Canal Village. This model community is similar to many that grew up around the dawdling canal during its early years of shuffling people and freight to Buffalo.

On any given day in peak season you will see a couple dozen staffpersons in period dress on the grounds and inside the Wood Creek School, Bennett's Tavern, H. M. Farmer's general store, the blacksmith shop, and aboard the *Chief Engineer of Rome.* But before you enter the living-history portion of the village you are ushered into a building where an introductory slide show is presented. The sequence of slides begins with a melange of cars and sounds of honking horns followed by the words "What if all this hadn't been invented yet?"

You learn that the Native Americans of the area carried their canoes from the Mohawk River to Wood Creek, actually little more than a trickle, and by following natural though barely passable waterways could navigate themselves to the Great Lakes. They called this stretch the Great Carry.

Four artificial waterways would eventually be constructed on this site. The first, built in 1794, simply connected the Mohawk River and Wood Creek, a total of three miles, removing forever the inconvenience of the Great Carry. The Erie Canal was next, built in shifts over the course of eight years. But the acrid Erie's waters were only four feet deep, and except for one site near its terminus, the canal was equipped only with single locks. In many locations along its 363-mile route, the canal was obsolete soon after it was completed.

So it was widened and deepened in the 1840s and served

the people of New York until the 1910s, when it was gradually replaced by the bigger New York State Barge Canal System. The barge system is still in use today. In fact, many travelers on the New York State Thruway, especially those from other states, mistakenly assume the barge system paralleling the interstate is a remnant of the original Erie Canal.

The barge system actually bypasses the historic waterway. But visitors to Erie Canal Village can see remains of the original Erie Canal, referred to as Clinton's Ditch, which runs through the village, although it is not used for boat rides. When you ride on the *Chief Engineer of Rome,* you are on the bed of the enlarged canal that came through Rome in the 1840s.

Off the water, nineteenth-century village life goes on as usual. The teacher in Wood Creek School takes a pointer in hand to show us, as she would her students, the Erie's location on an 1845 map. A *McGuffey's Reader* sits on each stern, gray desk, and the chalkboard is covered with platitudes extolling the virtues of humility and generosity: "People who think big of themselves make small packages" and "Man is sometimes more generous when he has little money than when he has plenty."

In addition to the classroom, respectable women would have been found in the home and the marketplace. So you shouldn't be surprised to find the lady of the house in any of the three village residences, each presenting a look at life in different periods when canal commerce was booming.

She will likely be baking cookies or perhaps a loaf of bread in the circa 1840 Crosby House. If you have the knack of being in the right place at the right time, you will be able to sample such a treat hot from the woodstove.

There was no luxury like a woodstove for the residents in the little Cape next door, built forty years earlier in another part of Rome. They relied on a fireplace for heat and had to retrieve water from an outside well.

The third home, the Shull House, representing Victorian Rome, was built in 1869 by a farmer and cattle dealer in nearby Little Falls. It faced the canal in its original location, and the Shull family was one of many that prospered because of the waterway.

Another who made a living thanks to the canal was H. M. Farmer, whose typical canalside store can be visited. While Farmer's sold foodstuffs and cloth like any general store at the time, it also dealt with products serving a particular clientele. Ropes, whips, and harnesses were for sale to aid those Buffalo or Albany bound who might have broken a rope or harness en route. There was one other difference between Farmer's and most other general stores. Farmer ran a cash-only business. Unlike merchants dealing with a local farming community, Farmer couldn't afford to extend credit to transients he might see in his emporium just four or five times a year.

The blacksmith was similarly busy. All who lived here needed animals for work, and all animals needed shoes. Visit in peak season and you will hear the clanging of the hammer and iron from the blacksmith in residence.

Staying overnight? You'd probably grab a room in Bennett's Tavern. Proper ladies relaxed in the parlor since the taproom was off-limits. Then as now, salesmen took to the road to earn a living, and the second-floor guest room serves as a showcase for a peddler's wares as he might have displayed them for a potential buyer. Enter a smaller guest room and you see a suitcase, top hat, and frock coat, giving the appearance that someone just stepped out for a pint.

Downstairs in the tavern you can cool off too with a brisk drink of less potent potables than nineteenth-century guests would have sampled. The choice is usually root beer, iced tea, or lemonade.

If you have additional time, consider a trip less than an hour west to Syracuse, home of the Erie Canal Museum, the only museum of its kind dedicated solely to this legendary waterway. The site itself breathes history; it is in the only weighlock building still in existence, a place where 100-foot-long canal boats were weighed before being assessed tolls.

An old photograph shows the building alongside the canal, now Erie Boulevard, in the early twentieth century, hemmed in by the buildings of downtown Syracuse. Boats lined up here, one behind another, waiting to be weighed. A brochure available at the museum describes the scene in the 1850s: "Brightly colored boats with men and women busy about their decks moved up and down the canal – horns blowing, whips cracking at teams of weary mules, rugged and impatient canallers shouting and sometimes fighting. The air was thick with the smell of sweat, dampness, wood smoke, grain, potatoes, apples and other foodstuffs."

Today in the same spot where boats were weighed is a replica of a canal boat, the *Frank Thomson,* in eternal dry dock. A statue representing an 1850s immigrant, most likely from Ireland or Germany, stares out a window of the boat, while close by are three beds hanging by rope, one atop the other, which were the passengers' sleeping accommodations. Passenger fare was four cents a mile in the 1840s.

Busy in his office in the weighlock building is the weighmaster, also represented in the form of a statue. He leans at his rolltop desk with his head on his hand, likely poring over that day's toll collections – tolls were discontinued in 1883 – under the watchful eye of his clock, stove, trunks, and for some R&R, a checkerboard. A reproduced lock tender's garden sprouts period plants like Harrison's yellow rose and nicotiana outside his window.

Upstairs are reproduced shops and businesses that would have been frequented by Syracuse residents in an earlier time. A print of tall-masted sailing ships hangs by the bar in Bartolotta's Tavern, where the cash register looks like a prop from an episode of *Gunsmoke*. In the Farmer's and Trader's General Store are Brown's Mandrake Pills and Halsam's Balsam Myrrh for what ails you, and there is also the Onondaga Pottery, a canalside industry, located in Syracuse because of the ease of shipping clay and finished products.

Before leaving, spend a few moments admiring the trompe l'oeil mural on the building wall just outside the museum. It is a cross-section of a nineteenth-century canalside general store, and you will swear that it is three-dimensional. Be sure to notice the open doors and windows on the left end and the glimpse of the canal seen through them.

Location: Erie Canal Village is on State 49 and 46 west of Rome. From the New York State Thruway (I-90) heading west, take exit 32 (Westmoreland/Rome) onto State 233W to State 365 to State 69 to the village. From the New York State Thruway (I-90) heading east, take exit 33 (Verona) onto State 365 to State 69 to the village.

Admission is charged.

Hours: Mid-May through September, daily.

Allow three to five hours.

Information: Erie Canal Village, 5789 New London Road, Rome, NY 13440, 315-337-3999.

Events: Early summer, Canal Day, boat rides, traditional crafts, period children's games, canal-related folk music; late summer, Harvest Festival, cow milking, cheese making, agricultural demonstrations; December, Christmas Carol Sing, music, decorations, food, sleigh rides.

Note: Picnic tables are on the grounds. There is a snack bar, although you can also bring your own picnic.

If you are staying overnight: Quality Inn, 200 South James Street (in the center of Rome on State 46, 49 and 69), 315-336-4300; Paul Revere Lodge, 7900 Turin Road (three miles north of Rome on State 26), 315-336-1776; Esquire Motor Lodge, 1801 Black River Road, Rome, 315-336-5320.

When in the area: Spend a day in 1778 at Fort Stanwix National Monument (pages 113–117), a re-created fort in the center of Rome where first-person historical interpretation is the rule.

Location: The Erie Canal Museum is on the corner of Erie Boulevard East and Montgomery Street in Syracuse. From the New York State Thruway (I-90), take I-81 south to the Salina Street exit, then turn left onto Erie Boulevard.

Admission is free.

Hours: Year-round, Tuesday through Sunday.

Allow an hour.

Information: Erie Canal Museum, 318 Erie Boulevard East, Syracuse, NY 13202, 315-471-0593.

Note: Parking is a bit of a problem. There are a couple of spots in the lot next to the weighlock building. Otherwise, you will have to settle for on-street parking or pay lots. The weighlock building also serves as the home of the Syracuse Urban Cultural Park, and a brochure mapping out self-guided walking tours of historic Clinton and Hanover squares is available.

If you are staying overnight: Sheraton Inn Syracuse, 441 Electronics Parkway (at I-90, exit 37), Syracuse, 315-457-1122; Arborgate Inn, 430 Electronics Parkway (at I-90, exit 37), Liverpool, 315-453-6330; Motel 6, 6577 Court Street Road, East Syracuse, 315-433-1300; John Milton Inn, Carrier Circle, Syracuse, 315-463-8555; Howard Johnson Lodge, Carrier Circle, Syracuse, 315-437-2711.

When in the area: Sainte Marie Among the Iroquois (pages 14–20) in Onondaga Lake Park will take you back to an even earlier point in time, with its first-person historic reenactments of the seventeenth-century meeting of two cultures: Native Americans and French settlers. Also in the park is the Salt Museum.

22 Fire Island National Seashore
Long Island

Fire Island National Seashore is a string bean-thin patch of seaside recreation – some of it pure wilderness – within a suburbanite's commute of midtown Manhattan. To its majority of visitors, Fire Island National Seashore is a summertime beach destination.

To those who look a little further, the national seashore is a refuge for a bevy of wild birds, a place to touch a horseshoe crab to see just how sharp it really is, an opportunity to walk through an outdoor environment unaffected by human alterations, and a place to explore the life of a lighthouse keeper.

There are four separate areas that make up the thirty-two-mile-long barrier island. Access to the Lighthouse Area in the west and the Smith Point Area in the east is by car. The two areas in the heart of Fire Island, Watch Hill and Sailors Haven, can be reached only by private boat or by ferry from Long Island in season. In between the areas are expanses of protected land or clusters of small communities or a combination of both, but no roads.

For the quickest getaway from the city, take the Robert Moses Causeway from West Islip to the Lighthouse Area, which borders Robert Moses State Park. The state park and the national seashore both offer beaches and lighthouses, but only Fire Island National Seashore's visitors center has educational programming and exhibits to explain about this land of sun and recreation.

Fire Island has long been an area for shipwrecks, the first recorded one occurring on May 8, 1657. A rash of wrecks for well over a century and a half led to the building of a lighthouse, which began operation in 1826. The current brick, striped lighthouse was completed in 1858.

The walk from Field 5, the closest parking lot, is just 0.6 mile to the lighthouse. The visitors center, the stone building next to the light, was formerly the keeper's home, and displays inside tell the tale of a lonely existence. There are twelve rooms in the keeper's building, which when used regularly was divided in half by a staircase, splitting it into separate residences for the keeper's and his assistant's families.

Fire Island's out-of-the-way locale – it wasn't connected by bridge to Long Island until relatively recent times – made it a haven for rumrunners during Prohibition. A display about the island's past delves into this illegal era and says that a captain and former boat builder, Bill McCoy, was known for bringing batches of high-quality liquor to the island. Compared to the cut or impure alcohol of other bootleggers, his was referred to as "the real McCoy."

Though associated with an easy and carefree beach life, Fire Island has always faced a pretty harsh climate. To see evidence, take the half-mile-long boardwalk trail past mountainous sand dunes and cranberry bogs along the shore of the Great South Bay, and past patches of pitch pine and bearberry. You will pass some trees with bald south sides, appearing as if an army supplied with pruning clippers has gone on a rampage. These trees are the results of salt winds constantly blowing in from the ocean.

Want to learn more? Take one of the regularly scheduled interpretive walks or sit in on a Park Service program. Topics range from the history of the Fire Island Lighthouse to a sing-along of old sea chanteys.

At Great South Bay, as in all areas of the national seashore, it is important to remind visitors to stay on boardwalks and other designated walkways. Human feet trample fragile plants and dunes, and poison ivy grows in abundance on the island. Also, staying on the boardwalks will help diminish chances of bites from ticks carrying Lyme Disease (see note at the end of this section).

One other precaution: the national seashore beach at the Lighthouse Area is for all practical purposes a nude one. There is also a nude beach in the vicinity of the Smith Point West area. If you find nudity offensive, bear those facts in mind, or you might expose yourself to the naked truth of naturalist bathing.

To get to Sailors Haven, the next national seashore area heading east, most visitors take the ferry from Sayville, Long Island, although those lucky ones with access to private boats use the thirty-six-slip marina. Expect to find a party flavor in season when you step off the boat.

Aside from the swimming beach (a lifeguard is on duty in summer), the main draw is the Sunken Forest Trail, a stroll of a mile and a half along a boardwalk that takes casual ramblers through an unusual maritime forest. In addition to the ever-present poison ivy you will encounter more than a dozen other shrubs, trees, and plants, including sassafras, cattail, inkberry, black oak, and American holly.

Midway along the trail you reach an area called The Canopy, where treetops have grown laterally instead of vertically, blocked by high levels of salt concentration in the air above the height of nearby sand dunes. With the trees unable to grow above the level of the dunes, they have formed a thick canopy, keeping this stretch of forest shaded and cool. As you walk through the forest, don't be too surprised if a deer, fox, or rabbit should appear within eyeshot.

The Sailors Haven area is also home to a visitors center with a "do-touch" table, showers, changing rooms, picnic tables, concession stands, and even a dog-walk area. It doesn't, however, have a campground. The only family campground on Fire Island is at the Watch Hill facility, the next area heading east, also accessible only by ferry or private boat.

The twenty-six-site campground is about one-quarter mile from the ferry terminal, reached by a boardwalk trail. Park service personnel recommend that campers with heavy or large amounts of equipment bring a cart or wagon to help haul their gear to their campsite. But don't start packing yet. As you might guess, with a campground this small on such a popular island destination, reservations are necessary and are for the most part selected by lottery. There is also a limit of five days and four nights per stay, and there are no sites for RVs. Watch Hill also has a small visitors center, a nature trail, concessions, picnic tables, showers, and a swimming beach with a lifeguard in summer. The marina has 150 slips.

A seven-mile-long wilderness area, the only federal wilderness area in New York State, connects Watch Hill to Smith Point, the easternmost point on Fire Island. You can explore this wilderness area on foot or with a four-wheel drive vehicle, but you can drive a vehicle there only if your intent is to hunt or fish. To do so, you must fill out an application for a permit at the Smith Point visitors center. Driving season for off-road vehicles is most of spring and fall. The area is closed to off-road vehicles at all other times.

Camping is allowed in the wilderness area, but it is true wilderness camping. Campers must hike in and out, check in at the Smith Point visitors center, and be completely self-sufficient. There is no available parking, so campers must be dropped off and picked up. (The Smith Point County Park parking lot near the visitors center has a $3.00 fee for day parking in season.)

Park rangers say that fall and spring are the best seasons for camping here, spring a little less popular because of frequent rains. Summer camping is discouraged thanks to masses of mosquitos. Fall and spring are also the best seasons for bird watching since Fire Island is on the Atlantic Flyway, a major migratory route. While the entire island is a feast for friends of feathered flyers, Smith Point may be the best place to see rare birds, being less settled than areas west.

Like the Sailors Haven area, the Smith Point visitors center maintains a "do-touch" table full of surprises for children as well as parents. The razor clam is only a little sharp, but you still wouldn't want to step on one. The waved whelk egg case is soft, almost spongy. The baleen, which forms the plates of whales' upper jaws, feels almost like a soft wood and its ends are like feathers. Baleen plates have been used throughout the years to make everything from corset stays to buggy springs, and as a result whales, like the North Atlantic right whale, are now endangered.

All specimens in the visitors center are labeled, but if you can't tell the shells without a scorecard, plan to take part in one of the ranger-led walks. In addition to shells you can find out about shipwrecks and other human history or just learn about all the edible plants growing wild on the island.

Then consider taking time to walk the three-quarter-mile-long trail here that will take you past beach plums, one of Fire Island's most edible plants. Other edibles? How about sarsa-parilla, rose hips, glassworts, Juneberries, and blueberries – it's a veritable beachcomber's banquet.

Location: Fire Island National Seashore consists of unsettled portions of Fire Island located between several communities. To reach the Lighthouse area from the Sunrise Highway (State 27), take exit 41, then take the Robert Moses Parkway south; cross the Robert Moses Causeway and continue straight to the island. To reach Sailors Haven from Sunrise Highway, take Lakeland Avenue south onto Main Street and follow the green-and-white signs for Fire Island ferries. The ferry terminal is off River Road. To reach Watch Hill from Sunrise Highway, take Waverly Avenue south to the ferry terminal. To reach Smith Point West from the Sunrise Highway, take exit 58, then take the William Floyd Highway south and cross Smith Point Bridge to the island.

Admission is free to all parts of the national seashore. Parking fees are charged in season for the beaches at Robert Moses State Park and Smith Point County Park. Admission is charged for the ferries from Long Island to Sailors Haven and Watch Hill.

Hours: Fire Island National Seashore is open year-round. Peak season is late June through Labor Day weekend – some visitors centers open earlier and close later depending on staffing. Sailors Haven Marina is open late April to mid-October. Watch Hill Marina is open mid-May to mid-October. Ferries generally run from early May through October.

Allow half an hour to walk the Lighthouse Area Trail, an hour to walk the Sunken Forest Trail, and forty-five minutes to walk the Smith Point West Trail. Allow thirty minutes for the ferry ride to Sailors Haven and twenty-five minutes for the ferry ride to Watch Hill.

Information: Superintendent, Fire Island National Seashore, 120 Laurel Street, Patchogue, NY 11772, 516-289-4810.

Note: Trail guides are available for free and are located at Smith Point and Watch Hill.

The William Floyd Estate, home of a signer of the Declaration of Independence, is also part of Fire Island National Seashore even though it is located on Long Island (20 Washington Avenue, Mastic Beach). It is open July to early September, weekends and holidays. Admission is free. Call 516-399-2030 for more information.

Park service personnel emphasize that visitors should take precautions to avoid being bitten by ticks carrying Lyme Disease. First recognized in Old Lyme, Connecticut, in 1975, Lyme

Disease is carried by ticks the size of pinheads and initial symptoms include a rash followed by flu-like symptoms, which can become more severe if the disease is left untreated. Some ways to help avoid contact with the ticks are to stay on trail boardwalks, avoid walking through wooded and brushy areas, wear long pants with cuffs tucked into socks, and wear light clothing to help spot ticks.

If you are staying overnight: Holiday Inn, 3845 Veterans Memorial Highway (just over four miles southeast of I-495, exit 57), Ronkonkoma, 516-585-9500; Econo-Lodge, 3055 Veterans Memorial Highway (off I-495, exit 57), 516-588-6800; Best Western Strathmore, 1730 North Ocean Avenue (off I-495, exit 63), 516-758-2900; Summit Motor Inn, 501 East Main Street (State 27A), Bay Shore, 516-666-6000; Watch Hill Campground, Fire Island National Seashore, 516-597-6633. (Summer camping applications are accepted in February and March with a drawing taking place in April to assign campsites. For an application for the lottery, write to Fire Island National Seashore at the Laurel Street address above and be sure to enclose a self-addressed stamped envelope; you won't receive an application without one. Fire Island staff members say that no-shows are common even in summer and especially on weekdays. Feel free to call and check on last-minute availabilities if you get the sudden urge to set up your tent.) If no space is available on Fire Island, consider Heckscher State Park, one mile south of East Islip off Heckscher Parkway, 516-581-2100.

When in the area: To explore further into Long Island's oceanside lore, stop at the Long Island Maritime Museum (pages 37–41) in West Sayville.

23 The Birthplace of Women's Rights
Seneca Falls

It was called "the other Declaration of Independence." But this one contained demands the majority of Americans found ludicrous. The most laughable stated that women be allowed to vote. The Declaration of Sentiments, as it was officially titled, was signed by 100 men and women in the Wesleyan Methodist Chapel in Seneca Falls on July 20, 1848, and soon it was the cornerstone of the crusade for human rights. And today this small upstate town is regarded as the birthplace of the women's rights movement. You can explore its history by visiting several sites here, including Women's Rights National Historical Park and the National Women's Hall of Fame.

Although Women's Rights National Historical Park was established in 1980, it was in 1993 that the park reached full maturity. The temporary visitors center was closed and a new permanent one opened next to remnants of the historic Wesleyan Chapel. The space between the two buildings was landscaped and designated as Declaration Park, with a waterfall covering a 140-foot-long bluestone wall on which the Declaration of Sentiments is inscribed.

There are two other parts of the park, both a short drive away. The home of Elizabeth Cady Stanton, engineer of the convention that resulted in the Declaration of Sentiments, is in Seneca Falls, while in the neighboring Waterloo is the home of Mary Ann M'Clintock, another pioneering feminist.

As with any National Park Service site, the first place to investigate is the visitors center. But unlike most other such parks, it is likely you will spend most of your time inside it. For this visitors center is a virtual museum, filled with laser disc technology and interactive exhibits, devoted to both the history made here in 1848 and the women's rights movement in general.

Step up to a bevy of video screens where you'll hear two

sides of various gender-related issues and be given a chance to register your own opinion with the push of a button. Those who expect to be brainwashed with a barrage of one-sided rantings are in for a surprise. Balanced points of view are expressed on issues like single-sex schools, gender superiority at specialized jobs, and sexual harassment. (However, it is assumed that you agree there is such a thing as sexual harassment and that things have gotten better, not worse, for women since the 1950s.)

On one video terminal a female proponent of single-sex colleges states that women take control of their education at women's colleges and boasts that many graduates of women's colleges have gone on to careers in politics. A female opponent opines that single-sex colleges don't offer cultural diversity and that the impetus behind the political careers stems more from the wealthy background of the women who attend single-sex colleges than from the campus environment. "Do women from women's colleges become more successful?" appears on a screen, and you are implored to register your opinion. When we visited, 88 said yes, 111 no.

On another pair of monitors, a man states that he would love to work in elementary school education but women have a monopoly on jobs in that field. A woman counters that young children need motherly nurturing care, something men can't provide. "Are women better at teaching younger children?" you are asked. The answers, when we visited, were overwhelmingly in the "no" column.

There are more questions. A man wants to ask a woman he works with for a date, but the specter of a sexual harassment accusation hangs over him. "Is it sexual harassment to ask a co-worker for a date?" A total of 51 said yes, while 443 said no. However, at the time we were there visitors felt by a margin of 491 to 317 that pinups are a form of sexual harassment.

Some exhibits ask questions without giving answers. A toy

shelf is painted with pink on one side and blue on the other. Among the toys stacked on the pink side are a cheerleader doll, a kitchen stove, and a washing machine. Among those on the blue side are two boxing "Knockout Champs," a soldier, and a model fire station. A question posted in front of the exhibit reads, "Would you want to play with some of these toys but not want anyone to see you?"

The centerpiece of the visitors center is the grouping of twenty full-size statues depicting persons who attended the initial women's rights convention. Eleven are anonymous figures, representing the rank and file who attended; among the nine identified statues are Stanton, M'Clintock, and Frederick Douglass.

All the emphasis on this moment in history gives rise to a natural question: "Why Seneca Falls?" The visitors center tells the answer. The town in 1848 was going through severe changes, turning away from agriculture in favor of milling and manufacturing. Women were getting off the farms and going to work in factories for the first time. But existing laws mandated that any money they earned was the property of their husbands.

The list of "could nots" for women stretched as long as the Erie Canal itself, which passed through this town. Women could not vote. They could not own property. They could not become guardians of their children in case of separation. And women heard this list repeated over and over again by resident and transient reformers, many of whom stopped in Seneca Falls to speak as they traveled the famous canal en route to the vast and open West. This, along with the rising numbers of working women, spurred on the start of the movement.

The woman who started the chain reaction was Elizabeth Cady Stanton, a transplant from Boston weary with life in this out-of-the-way milling town. Her Seneca Falls home was restored and opened to the public as part of the national historical park in 1985. However, one should not enter it expecting to see heirlooms or rare antiques. The house's furnishings are sparse, its main feature being the story of the woman who lived here, a radical whose then far-fetched ideas are routine today.

Stanton believed in equal education for boys and girls, including physical education for girls and sewing and knitting for boys. She believed that wages earned by a woman should be hers to keep. She believed that women should be given the right to vote.

You meet Stanton as both a firebrand who fought for equal rights and a family woman who gave crowd-pleasing parties and cared for seven children in this six-room Greek Revival house. One wonders how she managed to find the time and space to write, speak, organize rallies, and raise seven youngsters in this modest home. It is said she kept a flagpole in the front yard that her neighbors recognized as a kind of combination semaphore and birth announcement. She would raise a red flag after giving birth to a boy and a white flag for a girl. A Stanton son is on record as saying, "There was never an empty seat in the house."

As we stood in the formal parlor, our guide described Henry and Elizabeth Stanton as community activists and listed a who's who of progressives, abolitionists, and feminists who gathered in this room: William Seward, William Lloyd Garrison, Lucretia Mott, and Susan B. Anthony, for starters. (Surprisingly, Anthony, the most famous feminist, had little to do with the Seneca Falls convention, since she was busy working in the abolitionist movement in Rochester.) The Stantons entertained in many ways, throwing open the piazza doors during a formal dance one day and conversing casually with a few friends the next.

With seven kids who garnered reputations as neighborhood hellions, the Stanton household was filled with mischief and adventures that today's sitcom writers would be hard put to imagine in their most creative moods. In the upstairs nursery, our guide told us about the time when the three oldest boys decided to strap baby brother Theodore to the chimney. Watchful neighbors informed the Stantons that their youngest son was on the roof. Then the boys, curious to see if Theodore would float, took him to the Seneca River and tied him with ropes and corks. Theodore did float, and since he was used to baths in big tubs, he had a marvelous time splashing around until rescued by his mother, who described him "as blue as indigo and cold as a frog."

Admittedly, the name of Stanton might be new to you. But how about these other names: Florence Sabin, Mary McLeod Bethune, Dorothea Dix?

If your response is a blank stare, you are in the majority, which is exactly why the National Women's Hall of Fame was founded. Located down the street from the national historical park visitors center, the hall is a vital stop for people with a passion for social history.

Said a hall of fame staffperson, "Women have traditionally been left out of history books. We hope there will be a day when we won't need a special house for women." Until then, this is where you can learn about such women as Sabin (a scientist and researcher), Bethune (a civil rights leader and college president), and Dix (an educator and reformer concerned with the struggles of the handicapped). Of course, some of the enshrined women are household names: Eleanor Roosevelt, Pearl Buck, Helen Keller, Sally Ride, and Clara Barton.

During a visit here you can pore over exhibits such as blues singer Bessie Smith's sheet music and Amelia Earhart's scarf that Sally Ride took into space. Or read the life stories of the more than forty-five enshrined women. You can also hear their actual or re-created voices in a series of audiotapes. Eleanor Roosevelt says understatedly, "My husband knew I would not be satisfied just to be an official hostess," a fitting statement for a woman who would serve as a delegate to the United Nations and help draft the Universal Declaration of Human Rights and who once cooked up for guests a dinner of macaroni, potatoes, creamed chicken, and for dessert, pancakes with syrup. And you hear nineteenth-century civil rights crusader Sojourner Truth answer a man who said God favored men because Jesus was a man: "Where did your Christ come from? From God and a woman. Man didn't have nothing to do with it."

A question that inevitably arises at these sites is how many men visit. The answer is quite a few, and on any given day you can find as many men as women poring through any of these sites. Says Terry Roth, Chief of Interpretation and Visitors Services at Women's Rights National Historical Park (and a man), "This park is not a feminist park. You don't have to be female. It's about people having rights. What your rights are today may not be what your rights are tomorrow or next year or the next century."

Location: Seneca Falls is midway between Syracuse and Rochester and about an hour from each city. Take the New York State Thruway (I-90), exit 41, onto State 414 south to State 5 and US 20 (Fall Street) in Seneca Falls. Women's Rights National Historical Park visitors center is at 136 Fall Street. The National Women's Hall of Fame is at 76 Fall Street. From the Thruway well-marked signs direct you to both sites.

Admission to both sites is free; donation requested at the hall of fame.

Hours: The national historical park sites are open year-round, daily, with extended hours in summer. The hall of fame is open daily May through October, and Wednesday through Saturday and Sunday afternoon the rest of the year.

Allow two to three hours to see the main attractions at the national historical park and half an hour to an hour at the hall of fame.

Information: Women's Rights National Historical Park, P.O. Box 70, Seneca Falls, NY 13148, 315-568-2991. National Women's Hall of Fame, 76 Fall Street, Seneca Falls, NY 13148, 315-568-8060.

Events: Weekend nearest July 19-20, Convention Days, boat tours of canals, bicycle tours, speakers, historic reenactments; Saturday nearest August 26, Women's Equality Day, speakers and events.

Note: Ranger-led walking tours of historic Seneca Falls are offered several times a week. There are two additional related sites in Seneca Falls: (1) Seneca Falls Historical Society Museum, located in a wholly Victorian Queen Anne mansion at 55 Cayuga Street, houses artifacts, letters, and photographs relating to the 1848 convention as well as collections of fine and decorative arts, 315-568-8412; (2) Seneca Falls Urban Cultural Park, 115 Fall Street, with fiber-optic maps and other high-tech exhibits on the industrial and social conditions that precipitated the convention, 315-568-2703.

If you are staying overnight: Holiday Inn Waterloo-Seneca Falls, State 414 (a mile and a half east of the junction with US 20 and State 5, Waterloo, 315-539-5011; Starlite Motel, 101 Auburn Road (State 5 and US 20), Seneca Falls, 315-568-6149; Sleepy Hollow Motel, US 20 (east of town), Auburn, 315-253-3281; Grant Motel, 255 Grant Street (State 5 east of town), Auburn, 315-253-8447; Guion House (three-room B & B in 1876 Second Empire-style house), 32 Cayuga Street, Seneca Falls, 315-568-8129; Hubbell House (two-room B&B in circa 1855 Gothic Revival cottage), 42 Cayuga Street, Seneca Falls, 315-568-9690.

When in the area: A twenty-minute drive east along State 5 and

US 20 in Auburn is the home of President Lincoln's secretary of state and fervent abolitionist, William Seward (pages 213–217). Head south down State 89 along the shore of Cayuga Lake for the cascades of Taughannock Falls and Buttermilk Falls state parks, while a bit to the west is the majesty of Watkins Glen State Park (pages 80–87).

24 Old Rhinebeck Aerodrome
Rhinebeck

It is World War I all over again in the skies over Rhinebeck on summer and fall Sundays. On Saturdays a time machine takes you back to a period a bit earlier. And later.

Weekend air shows are high points at the Old Rhinebeck Aerodrome. Using only original aircraft and accurate reproductions with original engines, Aerodrome founder Cole Palen's staff stages a World War I dogfight on Sundays and a show featuring pre- and post-World War I aircraft on Saturdays. On weekdays there is no air show but the aerodrome museum collection is open for viewing.

A Sunday visit introduces you to Sir Percy Goodfellow, a pilot on the side of the Allies, and his foe, German flying ace Der Black Baron, as they compete in the air for the heart of heroine Trudy Truelove. Tara Sherman, who plays Truelove, calls the ninety-minute show "a classic confrontation between good and evil" and describes Percy as a bumbling pilot with only the best intentions. Der Black Baron, played by John Barker in a Fokker Triplane, manages to outwit Percy several times, but good conquers evil in the end when Trudy promises the Black Baron a kiss only to blow him up with a TNT detonator and cry out, "That was a dynamite kiss."

The Saturday show doesn't tell a story but offers a full range of aerial dramatics performed by pilots in numerous airplanes from the years before and after World War I, which Palen has categorized as the "pioneer" and the "Lindbergh" eras. The airplanes include the famous Curtis Jenney; the cumbersome Curtis Fledgling, called an "aeronautical dinosaur" by the show's announcer; the Nieuport 11, a French plane dating to 1915, used after the war for flight school training; and the Hariot, another 1910 French creation tagged by Palen as "a racing skiff with wings"—it flies only under certain wind conditions.

In both shows pilots spin and roll in the air, executing stunts guaranteed to inflict the rest of us with vertigo. They do quick spins called snap rolls; wider, barrel-shaped spins called barrel rolls; spins in which the plane's nose falls downward and the plane appears to crash; and classic barnstormer's loops. At the end of their performances they are right side up and on the ground and ready to answer your questions.

Founder Cole Palen is most proud of the aerodrome's accuracy. The duplicate airplanes are exact copies. The stunts performed are those one would have seen in an aerial barnstorming show seventy years ago. The hangars are copied from early photos, and even the benches on which the audience sits are historically accurate reproductions.

Cole Palen's own history with aircraft goes way back, though not as far back as his earliest aircraft. A Hudson Valley native, Palen grew up next to the old Poughkeepsie airport. His father ultimately bought the farm property next to the airport and young Cole became acquainted with several pilots. "They were my heroes," he says. After serving in World War II (he stayed on the ground), Palen, bit with what he calls "aeromania," purchased six aircraft from Roosevelt Field in Long Island just before it closed. In time, he bought property to use as an airport for his antique planes and did his first air show in 1960.

The museum consists of three hangars, each devoted to different periods in aviation. (A fourth museum building, constructed in 1993, houses the aerodrome foundation.) Airplane enthusiasts will be euphoric when walking through the museum, admiring aircraft that kept people and their dreams aloft. The 1918 Sopwith Snipe, made in Britain, was utilized near the end of World War I by successful fighter pilots like Canadian ace Billy Barker. The plane is in the World War I era hangar and is one of Palen's originals. The completely original French 1911 Bleriot, powered by a 71-horsepower rotary engine, had a long-range gas tank and was commonly used in the great circuit races of Europe.

What some might call the Model T of American airplanes is the original Waco 10, an open-cockpit biplane with a Curtiss OX-5 engine, dating from 1927 and typical of many American aircraft during the Lindbergh era. Lindbergh's Atlantic crossing inspired many to learn to fly, and with the Waco and a World War I surplus engine, it was affordable.

But the museum is not for airplane buffs only. Even those who wonder whether thumbtacks hold the plane up will enjoy looking at some of the earliest flying machines. A reproduction of the Wright brothers' famous glider, the first heavier-than-air machine .with a mechanical control system, will vie for your attention with a reproduced Chanute glider with two wings and no engine, both in the pioneer era hangar.

The wreckage of a reproduced World War I era Fokker triplane has a jarring effect. The plane crashed on May 2, 1987, and the twisted shell is there to examine. The red Monocoupe 90, a 1930 American propeller-driven plane in the Lindbergh era hangar, was flown in several cross-country and pylon races. One flying racer, Phoebe Omlie, had winnings of $3,250 in 1930, when the national hourly wage was 50 cents.

If you have the urge to be more than a bystander, note that flights lasting fifteen minutes are offered before and after the weekend shows. You'll be a passenger in a rebuilt 1929 open-cockpit biplane called a New Standard D-25. Those even more brave can model clothes that were hot off the racks from 1903 to 1920 in a fashion show before the air show; so far it is only women's apparel that is on parade.

Location: From the junction of US 9 and State 199 in Red Hook, take US 9 south one and a half miles to Stone Church Road, turn left, and follow road to the aerodrome; the old stone church is on the right. From the New York State Thruway (I-87), take exit 19 (State 199) and follow directions above. From the Taconic Parkway, take the exit for State 199.

Admission is charged.

Hours: The museum is open mid-May through mid-October, daily. Air shows take place between mid-June and mid-October on Saturday and Sunday afternoons.

Allow forty-five minutes to an hour and a half to tour the museum. On weekends allow four hours to see the fashion show, the air show, and the museum.

Information: Old Rhinebeck Aerodrome, 42 Stone Church Road, Rhinebeck, NY 12572, 914-758-8610.

Events: Air and early 1900s fashion shows Saturday and Sunday through season.

Note: Passenger flights are first come, first serve. No advance reservations are taken, although you can sign up as early as 10 A.M. on Saturday or Sunday. The museum is closed when air shows are taking place. Picnic tables are on the grounds.

If you are staying overnight: Village Inn of Rhinebeck, US 9 (half a mile south of junction with State 308), Rhinebeck, 914-876-7000; Rhinebeck Motel, US 9, Rhinebeck, 914-876-5900; Ramada Inn, State 28 (just west of I-87, exit 19), Kingston, 914-339-3900; Beekman Arms Hotel (historic inn dating to 1766), 4 Mill Street (junction US 9 and State 308), Rhinebeck, 914-876-7077.

When in the area: To the south in historic Hyde Park are the homes of Franklin and Eleanor Roosevelt and the Gilded Age palatial home of Frederick Vanderbilt (pages 1–8). A monument to the same era is the Mills Mansion (pages 69–73) in Staatsburg, just north of Hyde Park. Within a half-our drive to the north along the Hudson are the singular Persian-style mansion home of artist Frederic Church, Olana (pages 195–200), and the American Museum of Fire Fighting in Hudson (pages 33–36).

25 Huguenot Street Houses
New Paltz

Houses made of stone are not commonly seen in the United States, so when you first set eyes on the group of stone houses near the banks of the Wallkill River in New Paltz, your first feeling may be one of curiosity. The houses were built as early as 1692 by Huguenots, French Protestants, who despite the abundance of natural hardwoods in the Hudson Valley chose to build their new homes in stone as they had back in France.

Who were the Huguenots? They emerged during the Protestant Reformation in sixteenth-century Europe and were ultimately forced to flee their homes because of relentless persecution. In 1685, King Louis XIV revoked an official edict that granted Huguenots religious and political freedom. Over the next several years more than a quarter million Huguenots fled France, settling in England, Holland, Prussia, and the colonies of America.

These were hardly stereotyped dirt-poor refugees. Most were successful upper-middle-class merchants, artisans, and craftsmen. While these immigrants had the financial capabilities to build large homes, they were lacking in manpower. So they started with two basic rooms that included a loft for sleeping and a kitchen in the cellar. Most of the houses were expanded within a decade and were further altered by later generations. Some you see still look European in style, others have been remodeled to reflect styles of later periods. One example is the Hugo Freer House, which is believed to date from 1694. Within twenty years it had doubled in size, and late in the eighteenth century a wooden extension was added.

While the Huguenots emigrated to escape religious persecution, they did not resist assimilation. Their children were not discouraged from marrying the offspring of Dutch settlers and adopting their ways of living. And they were willing to borrow and learn from their neighbors. In the Abraham Hasbrouck House you will see examples of Dutch influence. Wooden shoes rest silently in the cellar kitchen, and a wall bed, reached by ladder and with a big door to shut out drafts, is seen in an upstairs bedroom. A big wooden kas (cabinet) is also in that bedroom; a smaller one is in a bedroom next to it.

The Huguenots adopted the Dutch kas not simply for practicality or aesthetics. There was a closet tax at the time, so the kas and other storage alternatives like a three-section wardrobe in a bedroom were common. A similar tax was levied on glass; little wonder that several houses, including the Hasbrouck House, have tiny windows with no more than six panes, making the rooms depressingly dark. There is also the Dutch door, a handy development seen in the Bevier-Elting House, circa 1698.

In addition to serving as showcases for antiques and oddities, each of the six Huguenot Street houses (and one church) is warmed by its own distinct personality. The Hugo Freer House is basic stone adapted to afford comfortable latter-day living. The Abraham Hasbrouck House is known for its big hearth in the expansive cellar kitchen with a bumpy stone floor. The Bevier-Elting House also served as a general store; note its thirty-paned window, pure decadence in the time of heavy glass taxes.

Another store was across the street in the Jean Hasbrouck House. This store also served as a tavern, and in spite of hardened Calvinistic attitudes toward drinking, the residents of Huguenot Street were known to bend an elbow there now and then. Old bottles resting on the tavern counter attest to that.

The Jean Hasbrouck House has a rare central hallway dividing the residential portion of the house from the store. It also has an unusually handsome kitchen. But even though the pots, roaster, toaster, wafer irons, and pewter ware all surround the bountiful hearth, the Hasbroucks leaned toward frugality. The room still has its original six-paned window, which makes the interior as dark as twilight in the nearby Hudson River woods.

Getting tired of Dutch colonial New York? Then step inside the LeFevre House and the Deyo House. The Federal-style LeFevre House first took shape in 1799 and was built by a member of the Elting family. (Many Elting women married into the LeFevre family, giving the home its name.)

The LeFevre House also served as a store, but it appears that business was not good enough. Since brick construction was a status symbol, Ezekiel Elting cleverly put brick on the front and side so people arriving by ferry on the Wallkill River would think it was a wealthy family's home.

Should you need a reason to be thankful you live in the twentieth century, climb upstairs in the LeFevre House and enter the re-created early-nineteenth-century doctor's office. The good country doctor served as a dentist too, and this one was thoughtful enough to place rings on his patients' chair so they could hold onto something while having teeth yanked out in those days long before anesthetics.

Victoriana rules the Deyo House, which, though hard to believe, was once a little stone structure. Remodeled in 1890, this rambling home features a wedding cake ceiling with plaster of paris frills and Tiffany glass globes on the lights.

Only one building in this group is not original. A French Reformed church was built in this neighborhood in 1717 and destroyed in 1795. After seven years of painstaking research, a reproduction was raised in 1972 near the spot where the first one stood. The cupola might be the most eye-catching of the church's physical facets, but in its day it was important to the building's spiritual role. In the 1700s, a man or boy would climb to the church's cupola and blow a conch shell to alert area residents that services were about to begin. (Placing the cupola was the most cumbersome part of reconstructing the church. A helicopter was needed to do the job.)

Services were austere, lasting from morning to sunset with a single break only for lunch. Cold, hard-backed, wooden pews made sleeping during services uncomfortable, and even so, a man was hired specifically to watch the congregators to make sure they didn't nod off while they should be praying.

Before leaving the area make one last stop in Deyo Hall (as opposed to the Deyo House, a completely different building). The museum on the second floor, called the Howard H. Grimm Memorial Gallery, contains a variety of Huguenot possessions and a smattering of paintings. You can see everything from silver teapots to swords and pistols and a circa 1714 chocolate pot, evidence that chocoholics have been around for centuries.

Location: From the New York State Thruway (I-87), take exit 18 to State 299 into New Paltz, where the road becomes Main Street. After the junction with State 32, take a right onto Huguenot Street, then a right onto Brodhead Street to Deyo Hall, where the tours start.

Admission is charged to all buildings with the exception of the Howard H. Grimm Gallery in Deyo Hall.

Hours: Memorial Day through September, Wednesday through Sunday; weekends only in October.

Allow two and a half to three hours for the full seven-building tour; one and a quarter to one and a half hours for the shorter three-building tour (two houses and the church); a half hour to forty-five minutes for the tour of the Jean Hasbrouck House, the only house one can see without taking a longer tour; and fifteen minutes to see the Grimm Gallery in Deyo Hall.

Information: The Huguenot Historical Society, P.O. Box 339,

New Paltz, NY 12561, 914-255-1889 (tours), 914-255-1660 (office).

Note: We recommend casual visitors take the three-building tour. The complete tour is best for persons with specific interests in this period of history or architecture. Those with little time or passing interest will be happy with a visit to just the Jean Hasbrouck House. All tickets are purchased in Deyo Hall on Brodhead Street (not to be confused with the Deyo House, which is seen only on guided tours).

If you are staying overnight: DayStop of New Paltz, 601 Main Street (State 299), New Paltz, 914-883-7373; Mohonk Mountain House (a national historic landmark and noted resort), 1000 Mountain Rest Road (off State 299), New Paltz, 914-255-1000; Ramada Inn, 679 South Road (US 9), Poughkeepsie, 914-462-4600; Edison Motor Inn, 313 Manchester Road (State 55, four miles east of the center of Poughkeepsie), 914-454-3080.

When in the area: The area explodes with history. Hyde Park, home of the Roosevelts and the Vanderbilts (pages 1–8), is about a twenty-minute ride away, on the east bank of the Hudson. The Mills Mansion (pages 69–73), a Gilded Age palace, is in Staatsburg, a bit north of Hyde Park. The nation's aviation heritage is preserved at Old Rhinebeck Aerodrome (pages 141–144), about ten minutes north of Staatsburg and home of regularly scheduled weekend air shows.

26 Niagara Falls

To live in the United States and never visit Niagara Falls is a shame. To live within a day's drive and never visit Niagara Falls is a crime. Like the Grand Canyon and Old Faithful, Niagara Falls is a work of nature that has become an American icon. It's a must-see for tourists of all nations, and you'll find area brochures printed in French, Spanish, German, and Japanese. And you will hear plenty of foreign tongues spoken here.

According to Stan Rydelek, director of tourism for the Niagara Falls Convention & Visitors Bureau, approximately eight million people visit the falls each year. Suffice it to say that nobody will ever be lonely here, especially in peak season. Most observers say the Canadian side, known as the Horseshoe Falls, is the prettier of the falls—and they are right. The Canadian cascades are over twice as wide as the American falls and curve dramatically, whereas the American falls tumble over a straight brink.

Niagara Falls, Canada, also has what some have called the tackiest street in the country, with wax museums and other tourist magnets exposing the sordid and the sensational. Although neither city is shy about telling visitors how to spend their money, Niagara Falls, New York, is the more sincere.

If all you want to do is see the falls, you can do so from several vantage points. Whirlpool State Park, on the Robert Moses Parkway, is one of the best, permitting a view overlooking the whirlpool that forms as a result of the Niagara River's 90-degree bend.

Other superb vistas are yours from Goat Island, reached by pedestrian and vehicular bridges, and from 242-foot-high Prospect Point Observation Tower in Niagara Reservation State Park. The state park visitors center, opened in 1987, may be the best place to begin your visit. Displays on water power and a

70-millimeter film on the majesty and potency of the falls set the mood.

It is the sheer power of Niagara Falls that impresses the most. There are higher waterfalls; Taughannock Falls near Ithaca is 215 feet high. Although Niagara Falls is only 184 feet high on the American side and 176 feet high on the Canadian, the falls are dramatically wide. The curved brink of the Canadian falls is about 2,200 feet long; the American brink covers about half that width, still a formidable span. The water flow over the falls is about 700,000 gallons per second, and when you feel the mist at Prospect Point, the falls at Niagara will earn your respect.

To see the falls from a distance is one thing. To meet the falls head-on is another. From the American side there are two ways to experience Niagara Falls at their own level, confront the spray face-to-face, and expose your ears to its perpetual roar. To many, the *Maid of the Mist* and the Cave of the Winds are the only means of fully encountering the beauty and raw force of Niagara Falls. Short of going over the falls in a barrel, you can't get any closer.

The first *Maid of the Mist* set sail in 1846 when James K. Polk was president, and it was a president who some sixty years later gave the boat ride its mightiest endorsement. Theodore Roosevelt called it "the only way to fully realize the Grandeur of the Great Falls of Niagara." Since then, world leaders and other VIPs have donned black rubber raincoats and faced the falls from the deck. Actress Marilyn Monroe, Indian statesman Jawaharlal Nehru, and Soviet Premier Alexei Kosygin were a few. Kosygin, it is said, refused to protect his head with his rain hood until the *Maid* was virtually on top of the Horseshoe Falls, telling an aide he enjoyed the feel of the mist on his face.

You may not want to be as brave as Kosygin. The *Maid* trip climaxes by taking passengers to the base of the American falls and into the basin of the Horseshoe Falls. The thirty-minute ride starts at the dock at the Prospect Point Observation Tower's base, and for the first ten minutes or so, feels no different than any other river cruise. As you approach the falls, mist starts to dance off your face, the boat bounces to the rhythm of the river, and the fortissimo of the falling water becomes a thunderous drone. If you bring your camera aboard–and we recommend you do–your prize shot will probably be the one of the inevitable rainbow. However, we wish to caution you not to expect too much from photos taken in the basin. Water will spray your lens, likely fogging up photographs. Rely on your memories, which will truly be made of the mist.

Your memories also will be made of tales and legends about the falls that the captain imparts on his way up and back. The

You can feel the spray on your face at Niagara Falls

most memorable is about Roger Woodward, a seven-year-old boy who was swept over the falls in a boating mishap on July 9, 1960. Roger unbelievably survived the fall and was rescued by the *Maid of the Mist* crew, becoming the fourth person to survive the fall and the only one to go over the falls and live while wearing just a bathing suit and a life preserver. In 1980, at age twenty-seven, Roger Woodward returned with his wife, Susan, to take a more conventional look at the falls.

We don't know whether Roger embarked on the forty-minute Cave of the Winds trip, but it, too, is an institution and is highly recommended to complement the *Maid*. Here, your perspective is from land – Goat Island.

After buying tickets, visitors change into felt booties and yellow raincoats, then take an elevator down 180 feet and prepare to be hit by another misting. You walk through a small tunnel and are at the base of Bridal Veil Falls, the rushing cataract of the American falls sandwiched between Luna and Goat islands. A web of wooden catwalks and staircases takes visitors to numerous points on the cliffside from which views of the American and Bridal Veil falls are astounding. The ever-present rainbow is best seen at the tour point called Rock of Ages, while the climax is at the last stop, Hurricane Deck, just twenty-five feet from Bridal Veil Falls. Prepare, once again, to get wet.

Cave of the Winds guides also relate stories of Niagara past, and you shouldn't be surprised to hear some of those you also heard on *Maid of the Mist*. Other tantalizing bits of falls trivia relate solely to Cave of the Winds. The two elevators taking raincoat wearers up and down were open to the public in 1925. Prior to that a 279-step staircase was used. Imagine the trip back up after being soaked from your look at the falls. And as at Howe Caverns, two young lovers felt this was a perfect place for their wedding. A Pennsylvania couple was married here in 1893, and they didn't have to travel far to reach everyone's favorite honey-moon destination.

The most romantic view of Niagara Falls can be seen for up to three hours after sunset – starting at 7:00 P.M. in the dead of winter and at 9:15 P.M. in the heat of summer – when the falls are spectacularly illuminated. One look and you will know why honeymooners still come to Niagara Falls for the most romantic vacation of their lives.

Location: From the New York State Thruway (I-90) take I-290 (Youngmann Expressway) in Buffalo to I-190 toward Niagara Falls. After crossing the North Grand Island Bridge take the first exit onto the Robert Moses Parkway and follow the parkway to Niagara Reservation State Park. *Maid of the Mist* departs from the base of the Observation Tower at Prospect Point in the park. The Cave of the Winds trip departs from Terrapin Point on Goat Island, connected to the state park by a pedestrian bridge and to the Robert Moses Parkway by a vehicular bridge.

Admission is charged for both *Maid of the Mist* and Cave of the Winds. A nominal admission is charged for the observation tower.

Hours: *Maid of the Mist* trips take place mid-May to late October, daily. Cave of the Winds trips are offered Memorial Day to mid-October, daily. The Prospect Point Observation Tower is open year-round, daily.

Allow half an hour for the *Maid of the Mist* ride; four boats are in operation and they depart every fifteen minutes in summer and every half hour in spring and fall; there is rarely more than a thirty-minute wait for a boat. Allow forty minutes for the Cave of the Winds trip.

Information: Maid of the Mist Corp., 151 Buffalo Avenue, Niagara Falls, NY 14303, 716-284-8897. Cave of the Winds, 716-282-8979. Niagara Falls Convention & Visitors Bureau, 345 Third Street, Suite 101, Niagara Falls, NY 14303, 716-278-8010.

Events: Thanksgiving through early January, A Festival of Lights: holiday lights illuminating the falls, parades, fireworks, entertainment.

If you are staying overnight: The following are among the best budget values among motels in Niagara Falls, New York: Beacon Motel, 9900 Niagara Falls Boulevard, 716-297-3647; Driftwood Motel, 2754 Niagara Falls Boulevard, 716-692-6650; Travelers Budget Inn, 9001 Niagara Falls Boulevard, 716-297-3228; Sharon Motel, 7560 Niagara Falls Boulevard, 716-283-5646; Bel Aire Motel, 9470 Niagara Falls Boulevard, 716-297-2250; Anchor Motel, 2332 River Road, 716-693 0850.

When in the area: The cultural and historic landmarks of Buffalo, including the legacies of the 1901 World's Fair—the Buffalo and Erie County Historical Society and Theodore Roosevelt Inaugural National Historic Site (pages 255–262)—and the Naval and Servicemen's Park (pages 58–63), with its aircraft and ships, are just to the south.

27 Wineries of the Finger Lakes
Hammondsport

In spite of publicity both in state and out, many people still don't realize New York state's stature as a major wine producer. The fact is that New York is ranked number two among states in total wine production in the nation. (California is number one.) There are more than eighty active wineries in New York, and regardless of where you live, you are no farther than a Sunday afternoon drive from fertile land where vines sport grapes like dandelions on a suburban front lawn.

The best-known area for winemaking is the Finger Lakes region, and for good reason. Nearly half of New York state's wineries are found along these shores. When it comes to Finger Lakes wine, the most famous name is Taylor. That's what drew us to Hammondsport and to Bully Hill Vineyards, founded by Walter S. Taylor, grandson of the man who started a family fortune more than a hundred years ago.

A funny thing, though, is that Walter S. Taylor's family name is mentioned nowhere on the property of his own winery. In places where it has appeared in print it is blotted out as if it were an obscene word. Whenever he is quoted, he is duly noted as Walter S. Blank or Walter S. XXXXXX or Saint Walter de Bully. You hear the story behind the man with no name as you start the winery tour at Bully Hill.

You don't have to take the tour to taste the wine. Sampling is yours for the asking. If you have the time though, follow your tour guide—or your nose—as you walk through the winemaking process, from the vineyard to the fermenting rooms, champagne cellar, aging cellar, and other points where the pungent scents of alcohol hang in the air like a low valley fog.

Our favorite stops were the vineyard's views and the aging cellar's elephantine wooden barrels, a wine connoisseur's paradise. In mid-May the grapes were in tiny clusters, but they would soon grow plump in the warm summer sun, even here in upstate New York. In fact, it's the presence of the lake water and the chilly spring air that makes the region such prime wine country. Because the lakes are so deep (Keuka Lake, within walking distance, is 187 feet deep), it takes a long time for the air to warm, keeping the grapes from coming out too soon. In fall, the lakes help the air stay warm longer. The longer the grapes stay on the vine, the sweeter they taste.

The barrels in the aging cellar, each seemingly big enough to contain a Toyota, are capable of holding 6,800 gallons of wine each. With good care, each barrel can last a century. The room smells like vinegar, but the scent numbs after a while. Our guide told us that aging is basically a form of oxidation and explained a basic difference between red and white wine; red is usually aged longer, up to two years, while white commonly ages in less than one.

Our guide also told us about Walter S. Taylor, who himself has been aging gracefully as company head since the early 1970s. He was once a part of Taylor Wines, like many members of the Taylor family, but he broke off a branch of the family tree and was booted out of the company after publicly criticizing New York state wines. He soon started his own company.

In 1976, Taylor Wines, now Walter's competitor, was purchased by Coca-Cola, who in turn sued him over the use of the Taylor name on his Bully Hill Wine products. The court ruled that Walter S. Taylor could no longer put his name on his wine labels unless it was accompanied by the words "Not connected with or a successor to the Taylor Wine Company" in sizable print. Walter took the decision to a visible extreme, referring to himself with no last name or with the phony ones mentioned earlier. He had his name crossed off every label of his wine and even put masks on drawings of ancestors on labels, making them look a bit like miniature Lone Rangers.

As if to confirm the adage "Nobody likes a wise guy," Coca-Cola took him to court again, suing him for contempt. And again, Walter lost. He was fined $11,000 and forced to turn over labels and other "offensive materials" to Coca-Cola for destruction. He did so, delivering them in a manure spreader.

Walter, meanwhile, began to wallow in all the publicity, becoming to many a folk hero, the proverbial little man clobbered by an impersonal corporation. A slogan for Bully Hill Wine grew out of it: "They have my name and heritage but they didn't get my goat." (Epilogue: several years later, Coca-Cola sold Taylor Wines.)

Taylor does own a pet goat, and the goat's face is depicted often on his wine labels. The labels that he designed and illustrated are unlike those you will see on conventional winery products. Most are scruffy illustrations of goats and spacecraft or even his self-portrait identifying wines with nonconventional names like "Love My Goat Red," "Space Shuttle Rose," and "Mother Ship Over Paris Rouge." (Actually, Walter did illustrate his labels until a tragic car accident in early 1990 left him paralyzed from the neck down.)

While Walter S. XXXXXX no longer has his grandfather's name, he does have much of his grandfather's old winemaking equipment, which is stored in three buildings known collectively as the Wine Museum of Greyton H. Taylor (Walter's father, not grandfather). It is grandfather's green and bulky 1883 wine press that you first see when stepping into the museum's champagne room. The archaic equipment from Grandfather Taylor's era gives visitors a peek at the day when the clarity of each bottle of champagne was checked by candlelight. A candle still sits at the end of an old riddling rack where champagne bottles were stacked so sediment could settle.

This was a time when wine corks were soaked in warm water for pliability and then placed on a corking machine on which a person could cork about 120 bottles an hour. One corking machine on view dates to the late 1700s. Bottles were reused after they were cleaned in a bottle washer, such as the one on display, circa 1897, which is little more than a keg fitted with pipes and faucets. Other machines used for clearing sediment from champagne, adding dosage (wine and sugar syrup used to sweeten champagne), and attaching wire hoods to bottle tops offer a complete look at wine and champagne making, turn-of-the-century style.

Another part of the museum is filled with tools a cooper would use, such as planes, adzes, and drawknives. There is also a 1917 Studebaker grape wagon once drawn by horses to carry boxes of grapes from vineyards to the winery. The view from Bully Hill, overlooking Keuka Lake and the distant hills, is as inspiring as any you will see. There couldn't be a better setting for sipping wine on an autumn day.

As any wine lover knows, there are literally dozens of wineries open for tastings and/or tours in the Finger Lakes region. A partial list includes:

Americana Vineyards Winery, Interlaken, 607-387-6801
Casa Larga Vineyards, Fairport, 716-223-4210
Castel Grisch Estate Winery, Restaurant & Manor, Watkins Glen, 607-535-9614
Cayuga Ridge Estate Winery, Ovid, 607-869-5158
Eagle Crest Vineyards, Conesus, 716-346-2321
Glenora Wine Cellars, Dundee, 607-243-5511
Hazlett 1852 Vineyards, Hector, 607-546-WINE
Hunt Country Vineyards, Branchport, 315-595-2812
Knapp Vineyards Winery & Restaurant, Romulus, 607-869-9271
Lucas Vineyards, Interlaken, 607-532-4825
Taylor Great Western Gold Seal Winery, Hammondsport, 607-569-6111

Wagner Vineyards, Lodi, 607-582-6450
Widmer's Wine Cellars, Naples, 716-374-6311

Location: Bully Hill Vineyards is one mile north of Hammondsport. From State 17, take State 54 in Bath to State 54A in Hammondsport; after about a mile, turn left onto Middle Road and follow signs (shaped like fish) to the winery.
Admission is free.
Hours: Winery, year-round, daily, closed Sunday morning. Museum, May through October, daily.
Allow an hour total for the tour (thirty to forty minutes) and tasting (fifteen to twenty minutes) and a half hour to see the museum.
Information: Bully Hill Wine Company, 8843 Greyton H. Taylor Memorial Drive, Hammondsport, NY 14840, 607-868-3210.
Events: Summer and fall, lectures on wine and winemaking.
Note: The winery maintains its own café. Also, you are welcome to bring your own picnic and use the picnic tables on the grounds. Harvest season, which depending on the weather can fall in any part of September or October, is the busiest season, but also the most fun. Come early during harvest season.

To receive lists and other information about New York state wineries, contact: The Keuka Winery Route, 9976 Rt 76, Hammondsport, NY 14840, or Cayuga Wine Trail, P.O. Box 123, Fayette, NY 13065.
If you are staying overnight: Hammondsport Motel, William Street (two blocks off State 54A on Keuka Lake), Hammondsport, 607-569-2600; Days Inn, 330 West Morris Street (a quarter mile east of State 17, exit 38), Bath, 607-776-7644; Holland-American Motel, State 415 (a mile and a half east of State 17, exit 39), Bath, 607-776-6057; Blushing Rose Bed & Breakfast (four-room Victorian home), 11 William Street (two blocks north of State 54A), downtown Hammondsport, 607-569-3402; Finger

Lakes Bed & Breakfast Association, P.O. Box 862, Canandaigua, NY 14424.

When in the area: The best of nature's beauty is found in the waterfalls and gorges of the Finger Lakes located to the east in Watkins Glen and the Ithaca area (pages 81–87). The Corning Glass Center (pages 283–287) is about half an hour south of Hammondsport along State 17.

Hanford Mills Museum, East Meredith

28 West Point

"At West Point, much of the history we teach was made by people we taught." These words are displayed in a poster above an artist's rendition of arguably the four most famous American generals since colonial times. There is Ulysses S. Grant, hard-faced and hirsute in his Union uniform; Robert E. Lee, with his flowing white beard blending into his Confederate grays; Dwight D. Eisenhower, determined and intent; and the jaunty profile of Douglas MacArthur, his ever-present corncob pipe protruding like a natural extension of his mouth.

The poster sums up the attraction of West Point to visitors. This is an institution of higher learning with a past as full of color and adventure as any storied college or university in the world. But the poster omits an additional lure: the stunning view looking down to the Hudson River. It is the spectacular setting that many casual visitors recall long after they have forgotten how many pipes the great Cadet Chapel organ has or the year that Ike graduated. Yet even the academy's beautiful cliff-side locale, a granite promontory jutting out into the Hudson, carries a macho, no-nonsense militaristic name: the American Gibraltar, coined by George Washington.

It was Washington who gave West Point its first role of service to the nation in January 1778. The British had hoped to

163

control navigation of the Hudson in order to split the colonies and isolate New England. Anticipating this, Washington stationed the first permanent garrison of troops here. The men placed a chain, more than 600 yards long and weighing 150 tons, across the river to Constitution Island, making enemy use of the river impossible. The states were bound together, linked literally and figuratively. The academy has taken this metaphor and run with it, boasting of its "long gray line" of living human links still providing service to their country. Several links of the famous chain can be seen at the west side of Trophy Point.

Most of what visitors wish to see can be toured on their own. The parts of the campus off-limits to visitors are clearly marked. Unfortunately, the famous Flirtation Walk is one place visitors can't go, since the riverside trail is saved for cadets and their guests only. Trophy Point is where most civilians will want to go. The view is commanding, and the setting is as romantic as Flirtation Walk. The crowds may be oppressive, but that's the penalty for being a civilian. From Trophy Point step up to the Battle Monument, cast your eyes downward, and you will understand why this is called "the million-dollar view."

The West Point Museum, which is worth a million dollars to military historians, means a stop even if you don't know the difference between a bayonet and the Bay of Pigs. Here is the nation's oldest (and one of the largest) public collection of military arms and equipment, arranged so that any visitor can appreciate and understand it, even those whose major interests lie elsewhere. Yes, there are weapons of all types, and some people may feel uncomfortable admiring cases filled with humankind's tools for killing one another. However, the museum doesn't glorify the displayed weapons. Instead, it chronicles their development.

You start your visit with a look at fourteenth-century English longbows and arrows and finish with an inspection of the ballistic case for the "fat man" atomic bomb, the type dropped over Nagasaki, Japan, at the end of World War II. You can decide for yourself whether this is progress or regression.

The museum also contains more lighthearted material, such as a somewhat whimsical life-size diorama of a French café scene during World War I and John Chapman's youthful portrayal of *George Washington as a Colonel in 1772* in the Craighead Gallery of Military Paintings.

The unforgettable agony of *Reveille on a Winter Morning* is immortalized on canvas by Henry Bacon, a field artist for *Leslie's Weekly,* a popular periodical during the Civil War. Each soldier is frozen in a moment of early morning routine, and the detail in each waking soldier's face is as amusing as it is fascinating. Don't neglect to notice the drummer boy blowing on his hands to warm frozen fingers.

The Civil War uniforms these soldiers would have worn are displayed among other military garb, including Dwight Eisenhower's winter service uniform, Joseph (Vinegar Joe) Stillwell's hats and boots, and Douglas MacArthur's cadet bathrobe.

In many cultures a soldier's uniform was extended beyond clothing to include his hair. You read that Napoleon's light horsemen wore braids and long, curling mustaches and that those physically unable to grow a mustache had to paint them on their faces.

One of the most popular exhibits at West Point would never fit inside the museum's walls. Fort Putnam, built in 1778 to protect the Hudson River, was refurbished for the bicentennial in 1976 using drawings of a Revolutionary War topographic engineer. It was threatened twice during the war – once by Benedict Arnold – but the men stationed here never saw combat. What you see today when taking the self-guided fort tour are the weapons, casemates, embrasures, and redoubts similar to those the Revolutionary soldier would have found here over 200 years ago. The colonial-era uniformed man probably uttered informal prayers for safety when in the old fort's vulnerable location, but today West Point is blessed with several handsome chapels, all open to visitors.

What is recognized as the largest church organ in the world sits inside the Gothic-style cadet chapel. With 18,700 pipes it is the building's most notable attraction, although the vaulted ceiling, buttresses, and stained glass are also worthy of attention. Windows are dedicated to each class from 1802 to 1976, and you should try to be here on a sunny day when the sun filters in through the stained glass.

The Chapel of the Most Holy Trinity, serving Catholic cadets, was dedicated in 1900 and widely expanded in the late 1940s. Although there have been Jewish cadets since the first class in 1802 – Simon Levy was one of the ten-man Corps of Cadets in the academy's first graduating class and one of two men commissioned a second lieutenant – and there have been separate Jewish services since 1939, there was never a house of worship for Jews until the Jewish chapel was completed in 1988. The gallery and museum inside highlight contributions Jews have made to the nation and the military.

Finally there is the Old Cadet Chapel built in 1836, the only existing chapel until the present Cadet Chapel was built in 1910. Robert Wier's mural *Peace and War* hangs above the altar. Black marble tablets pay tribute to general officers of the Continental Line and officers killed in the Mexican-American War. Each lists the officer's name, rank, and dates of birth and death, with one exception: Benedict Arnold. While he is honored for his service in the invasion of Canada and the Battle of Saratoga, he is noted by just his date of birth and rank. His name is omitted.

Location: From the northeast or northwest, take I-84 to US 9W south through Newburgh to the exit for Thayer Gate and follow the signs. From the south, take I-87 to US 9W north to State 218 through Highland Falls, which will take you to Thayer Gate. A visitors information center is located just outside Thayer Gate. A public parking lot is off Thayer Road between Clinton Field and "The Plain" parade ground.

Admission to all sites is free.

Hours: West Point Museum, year-round, daily; Fort Putnam, mid-May through mid-November, daily; Chapels, year round, daily (on weekends the Jewish chapel is open only in the afternoon).

Allow three to four hours to see all the major sites.

Information: West Point Visitors Information Center, USMA, West Point, NY 10996, 914-938-7079.

Events: Parades are held on "The Plain" parade ground from late August through early November and in April and May, usually on Saturday or late weekday afternoons. Athletic events take place throughout the school year. Contact the visitors information center (number listed above) or the West Point Public Affairs Office, 914-938-5650, for specific information.

Note: The visitors information center located outside Thayer Gate is open daily throughout the year and is helpful, although it is not essential to stop there. The academy offers no guided tours. You can pick up the brochure for a self-guided walking tour at the visitors information center. A private company, West Point Tours, gives hour-long guided tours of the campus in warm weather months. Contact them at 914-446-4724 or call the visitors information center. There are no public eating facilities on the academy grounds.

If you are staying overnight: Hotel Thayer (on USMA campus, inside Thayer Gate), 800-247-5047 or 914-446-4731; West Point Motel, 361 Main Street, (State 218), Highland Falls, 914-446-4180; Best Western Palisade Motel, junction State 218 and US 9W, Highland Falls, 914-446-9400.

When in the area: New York state's natural beauty can be explored at the adjacent Bear Mountain State Park and at Harriman State Park (pages 169–172). To the west along State 17 is the village of Goshen, home of the Hall of Fame of the Trotter (pages 279–282), while to the north are the humble and not so humble homes of President and First Lady Franklin and Eleanor Roosevelt, as well as the Vanderbilt Mansion, all in Hyde Park (pages 1–8). The commanding Mills Mansion is in Hyde Park's neighboring town of Staatsburg (pages 69–73).

29 Bear Mountain and Harriman State Parks

The stunning view from the summit of Perkins Memorial Drive, perhaps the best vista of all those in the Hudson River Valley, came very close to becoming hell on a hilltop. A few years past the turn of the century, the New York State Prison Commission decided that this isolated parcel of knolls and glens would be the perfect spot for a prison—specifically Sing Sing Prison.

The public was outraged and protested vociferously, full of the spirit of then-president Theodore Roosevelt, the most dedicated conservationist ever to sit in the Oval Office. To the rescue came Mary Harriman, who offered the state 10,000 acres of Orange and Rockland county lands and $1 million for the purchase of other nearby lands with two conditions: that the Palisades Interstate Park commissioners would become the new proposed park's managers and that the Bear Mountain prison site be scrapped. Both conditions were accepted, and in 1910 the adjoining Bear Mountain and Harriman state parks were created.

Almost every visitor who comes here nowadays drives to the summit of Bear Mountain along Perkins Memorial Drive. The summit measures 1,305 feet up from sea level, lilliputian by Rocky Mountains standards, but mighty high by those of the New York metropolitan area. On a clear day you may not see forever, but you can see Broadway, or at least the skyline of midtown Manhattan, forty-five miles south.

Most elevations in the two parks range from 1,000 to 1,200 feet above sea level. Many peaks have been named for animals: Catamount Mountain, Panther Mountain, Wildcat Mountain, and of course Bear Mountain. Other landmarks have names derived from Native American languages, such as Stahahe Lake ("stones in the water") and Lake Tiorati ("sky-like").

It is inevitable that hikers will want to tackle Bear Mountain, and the 3.3-mile-long Major Welch Trail on the north slope is fitting for all levels. The trail entrance is behind the Bear Mountain Inn, and the climb parallels the western shore of Hessian Lake before taking you up a gentle slope, then a steep slope of 800 feet to the summit. Splendid views abound throughout the trail.

The Popolopen Gorge Trail, another short hike, is 4.3 miles long and follows a brook and a gorge by that name; however, it's not really suited for children or the elderly. Able-bodied experts should consider the challenging Ramapo-Dunderberg Trail, 20.8 miles long, and the rugged Suffern–Bear Mountain Trail, which stretches 24.3 miles and is recommended for Grizzly Adams types. The Appalachian Trail also passes through the park, reaching 16.3 miles from Bear Mountain to State 17 and crossing nine summits along the way.

Outdoors people who would rather spend their precious leisure time on the water will be happy to learn that rowboats and canoes are allowed on ten park lakes and that rentals are available. A permit is needed to operate any craft on park waters and can be obtained in the park at Tiorati Circle and at Beaver Pond Campground. No gas-powered motorboats, sailboats, or inflatables are allowed.

Bear Mountain State Park, the more developed of the two parks, offers a potpourri of facilities: a 94-by-224-foot swimming pool, bathhouse, lockers, and a basketball court. Winter activities include ice-skating, sledding, and cross-country skiing with most trails falling within the easiest category. For those who would rather head out onto, as Robert Frost said, "the road not taken," there is ski touring on ungroomed hiking trails.

Regardless of the time of year in which you visit, you can come face-to-face with bullfrogs, catfish, garter snakes, and even copperheads. These are just a few of the creatures who make the parklands their natural homes and are also on view at the Bear Mountain Trailside Museum and Zoo.

There has been a museum building here since 1927, and throughout the years facilities have been added, enlarged, and expanded. Three buildings devoted to geology, botany, and history were added in the 1930s and have been given numerous face-lifts over the years, one as recent as the mid-1980s when the small animal museum was renovated. City residents whose experience with the animal world is usually limited to pigeons can learn how the other half of nature lives.

Location: Bear Mountain State Park is reached from US 9W or exit 19 off the Palisades Interstate Parkway. Harriman State Park is reached by taking the New York State Thruway (I-87), exit 16, onto US 6 (Long Mountain Parkway) to the Palisades Interstate Parkway south; from the parkway take exit 16 onto Lake Welch Drive into the park.

Admission is free to enter the grounds and the Bear Mountain Trailside Museum and Zoo, but there is a parking fee. Permits, obtained for a small fee, are required to take boats onto any park lakes, and fees are charged for most activities, such as swimming and skating. There is no charge to take your car up Perkins Memorial Drive to the summit of Bear Mountain.

Hours: Year-round, daily.

Allow an hour to drive to the summit of Bear Mountain. There are enough recreational opportunities in the two parks to last a full day or more.

Information: Palisades Interstate Park Commission, Administrative Building, Bear Mountain, NY 10911, 914-786-2701.

Events: There are many. A partial listing includes: spring—Earth Day, Teddy Bear Fair, Rockland County Family Fair, River Day/Shad Fest, "Hudson Valley Life" lecture series; summer—square dances, astronomy programs; fall—Arts and Crafts Show, Twin Forts Day (eighteenth-century encampment), Blue Crab Day, Fall Foliage Bike Rally, "Hudson Valley Life" lecture series;

December–Bear Mountain Festival (Christmas trees, gallery exhibits, outdoor lights display, Santa Claus in residence).

Note: Several other state parks, including Rockland Lake, High Tor, Nyack Beach, and Tallman Mountain, are in the immediate vicinity. Alcohol is not allowed in any of the state parks. For additional information, contact the Palisades Interstate Park Commission at the above address.

If you are staying overnight: Bear Mountain Inn (stone lodge with smaller buildings), Bear Mountain State Park, 914-786-2731; West Point Motel, 361 Main Street (State 218), Highland Falls, 914-446-4180; Best Western Palisade Motel, junction State 218 and US 9W, Highland Falls, 914-446-9400. Camping: Sebago Cabins (43 sites), Harriman, 914-351-2360; Beaver Pond Campground (220 sites), Harriman State Park, 914-947-2792 – call MISTIX (800-456-CAMP) for reservations; also camping at Tiorati Plateau Campsite in Harriman State Park, 914-351-2568 – no reservations taken.

When in the area: The museums and parades of West Point (pages 163–168) are just a musket shot away. Under half an hour west is the Hall of Fame of the Trotter (pages 279–282), while to the north are the homes of Franklin and Eleanor Roosevelt and the Vanderbilt Mansion in Hyde Park (pages 1–8) and the Mills Mansion in Staatsburg (pages 69–73).

30 Baseball Hall of Fame
Cooperstown

Nobody knows for sure how baseball got here. There is the creationist theory that the almighty Abner Doubleday invented the game on a slow day in a Cooperstown pasture in 1839. Then there is the evolutionist idea that the game slowly developed from similar British games such as rounders and one o'cat.

But this is not the time to think of such metaphysical mysteries as God and Baseball. Or with respect to diehards, Baseball and God. America's pastime has been here for well over a century, and despite strikes, contract disputes, and drug scandals, it endures. There is something about the game, something that draws thousands to watch men hitting and catching baseballs on any given summer day and to make year-round pilgrimages to the Baseball Hall of Fame and Museum in Cooperstown.

Opened in 1939, the centennial year of Doubleday's supposed invention, the hall of fame and museum (two separate entities housed under one roof) combine to form America's only major sports museum not located within sight of a major interstate highway.

That's the bad news for anyone who dislikes driving. The good news is that the maze of back roads on which you have to drive to get here takes you through some of the most beautiful countryside in the state. The view is no less lovely in Cooperstown itself, where verdant hills border shining Otsego Lake, immortalized in the novels of James Fenimore Cooper – whose father settled the town and lent his name to it – as Glimmerglass.

Appropriately, Main Street, with its geranium-bedecked street lamps, is home to the shrine to America's pastime. Its aged exterior belies the modern interior, which was extensively renovated in 1980. If you last visited the hall and museum prior to that, then you might find the old adage to be true – you won't even recognize the place. The bare floors and dime-store displays are gone, replaced by carpeting and state-of-the-art exhibits. There is much more here than just old baseballs and plaques.

Not that we want to minimize the significance of the Hall of Fame's plaques, which are to many the main draw. More than 200 players, managers, founders, and executives have their likenesses immortalized in bronze. The Hall of Fame Gallery is imposing: it's spacious, it has high ceilings and marble columns, and it commands respect as does a cathedral. To a serious baseball fan, that is not a far-fetched statement. This is where the greats are enshrined for eternity, from Cobb to Cronin to Clemente.

Throughout the remaining three floors, it is the game rather than individuals that is eulogized. A tattered glove with a pocket the size of a toddler's palm, once used by the legendary Ty Cobb, is on view. Keeping it company are the bat swung for career home run number 521 by Ted Williams, a jersey worn by Casey Stengel, and Babe Ruth's Yankee locker, as well as hundreds of other samples of baseball equipment and uniforms that belonged to the greats.

However, most items are not exhibited by themselves. They are on view in larger displays relating to specific themes. You may find some in the Great Moments Room, where through personal items, original art, and photographs, you recall just where you were when Roger Maris hit his sixty-first home run in 1961 or when Sandy Koufax pitched his fourth no-hitter. Other balls and bats and gloves are parts of sizable presentations devoted to diamond legends like Ruth and Stengel.

And still others could be in the History of Baseball section, which boasts nearly 1,000 such artifacts and which occupies most of the second floor. Arranged as a "time tunnel," it starts by discussing baseball's primeval ancestors and concludes with a look at the modern game.

It is here that you dive into the confusion about baseball's origins. A reproduced page in a British children's book includes notes about a game called "Base-ball"; the book was published in 1744, seventy-five years before Abner Doubleday was born.

Dynasties are glorified and rule changes are interpreted in the History of Baseball section, but some of the most appealing exhibits are in the area called Evolution of Equipment. Most visitors laugh in amazement and amusement when inspecting baseball gloves with no fingers and catcher's masks resembling wire chicken cages. Early bats and balls and heavy flannel uniforms from the days when players wore handlebar mustaches and the word "strike" meant only a good pitch are here for your pleasure too.

So are baseball cards. There's a colorful arrangement on 100 years of them, starting with tobacco cards (yes, baseball cards came with cigarettes long before they accompanied gum) of the late nineteenth and early twentieth centuries. But baby boomers will have their memories jogged by the classic Bowman baseball cards, sold from 1948 to 1955, and the Topps cards sold continually since 1951. As neither a current collector nor the father of one, I was surprised to see that, in the 1980s, Topps has major competition from the old Fleer and new Donruss companies, showing that this old childhood pastime is still as popular as when Mantle and Mays made headlines.

Other parts of the museum? There are sections devoted to every subcategory of baseball that you can imagine, including the World Series, the early Negro Leagues that barnstormed the country when major league baseball was segregated, the midsummer classic known as the All-Star game, the minor leagues and some of the grand old American ballparks—Yankee Stadium, Ebbets Field, and the horseshoe-shaped Polo Grounds, among them—guaranteed to bring out the sentimentalist in every fan. The Fetzer-Yawkey wing, which opened in 1989, is highlighted by a spectacular – and it truly is spectacular – thir-teen-minute multimedia presentation and the "Baseball Today" exhibit.

Then there's the Records Room, which brings you up to date on leaders in major league categories among active players; it's sort of like the old stock ticker, changing moment by moment, as you keep your eyes on the performances of your personal favorites. You will see who leads the majors in strikeouts, home runs, runs batted in, and more as you visit. You will leave here with only one question unanswered. Just how was baseball invented? Cooperstown doesn't say.

Location: From the west, take the New York State Thruway (I-90), exit 30 (Herkimer), and follow State 28 south to Coopers-town. From the east, take I-90, exit 25A, and follow US 20 west, then State 80 south. From the south, take I-88, exit 17 (Oneonta), and follow State 28 north. From New York City and the south-east, take I-87 to exit 21 (Catskill) and follow State 145 to I-88 west, exit 17 (see above). The hall of fame is on Main Street in the center of town.

Admission is charged.

Hours: Year-round, daily, open well into the evening in summer.

Allow an hour and a half if you are a casual fan, from two to four hours if you are a diehard.

Information: Baseball Hall of Fame and Museum, P.O. Box 590, Cooperstown, NY 13326, 607-547-9988.

Events: Induction ceremony and major league exhibition game, mid-summer.

Note: The Hall of Fame is incredibly crowded in summer on weekdays as well as weekends. Take advantage of the hall's evening hours in summer. A good idea is to have an early dinner and begin your visit around 5 or 5:30, when the crowds have thinned out. You won't feel as if you are part of a World Series crowd as you examine the exhibits.

If you are staying overnight: Deer Run Motel, State 80 (nine miles east of town), Cooperstown, 607-547-8600; Lake 'N Pines Motel, State 80 (seven miles north of town), Cooperstown, 607-547-2790; Bayside Motor Inn, State 80 (seven miles north of town), Cooperstown, 607-547-2371; The Inn at Cooperstown, 16 Chestnut Street, Cooperstown, 607-547-5756; Bed & Breakfast Leatherstocking (reservation service), P.O. Box 53, Herkimer, NY 13359, 315-733-0040 or 429-3416.

When in the area: The multifaceted Farmers' Museum (pages 178–183) is also in Cooperstown. Within half an hour are Howe Caverns (pages 190–194) and the Hanford Mills Museum (pages 225–230).

31 Farmers' Museum and Village Crossroads
Cooperstown

The Farmers' Museum and Village Crossroads in Cooperstown presents, in a nutshell, a slice of nineteenth century life in small-town upstate New York.

There was a country doctor, and you can visit his office, with its surgical instruments and skeleton. He often sent his patients next door to the pharmacy, where they would be introduced to all sorts of cures: dandelion root for menstrual irregularities or leeches for bloodletting.

Even though malpractice suits weren't the talk of the town then, the lawyer's office is conveniently close to the doctor's office. The simple structure served as the office of Judge Samuel Nelson, who practiced in Cooperstown and later served on the U.S. Supreme Court during the Lincoln administration.

After a hard day at work, citizens could be found unwinding at Ephraim Bump's tavern, a place for leisure for all but the tavernkeeper and his family, who were kept busy entertaining both the rowdy and the reserved. The tavern was an early American combination of Joe's Corner Bar and Grille and a modern Holiday Inn. Rougher patrons – drovers, teamsters, and some locals – sat in the taproom, indulging in lively spirits or spitting a chaw of tobacco onto the sawdust-covered floor as they played checkers or dominoes. Gentlemen and ladies – and they were indeed considered gentlemen and ladies – would retreat to one of several parlors while waiting for the next stagecoach.

A handful of other buildings where tradespeople earned their livelihood form a re-created village called the village crossroads part of the Farmers' Museum, but the village crossroads amounts to only a portion of the sights to see in the museum's massive complex.

Pass through the center of the village crossroads and step

Join a patriotic gathering at the Farmers' Museum, Cooperstown

onto a real working farm, the Lippitt Farmstead, thick with pungent odors of straw, hay, and livestock. The farmstead, with its farmhouse, barns, and adjacent fields, is where twentieth-century visitors meet nineteenth-century agrarian life.

In the farm kitchen you can watch as staff members prepare breads, puddings, and other dishes using traditional open-hearth cooking techniques. When we last savored the scents inside, catsup (in the days before "ketchup") was simmering in a cast-iron pot, and pork and beans were cooking in another. Staff member Andre Conklin was warming the baking oven with hot coals, preparing to make loaves of whole wheat bread; highly desired white bread was a luxury out of reach for all but the wealthiest citizens.

A typical farmwife would have likely spent six hours in the morning making dinner, the main meal, served at midday. She would commonly spend another six hours preparing supper, the smaller evening meal. While the condiments and main courses were cooking, Andre sat weaving rye straw into a work hat for a farmhand to wear while laboring in a hot field. Using one free hour every day to make the hat, she estimated it would be completed in two or two and a half months.

The Farmers' Museum staff encourages visitors to ask about any implements or curiosities that are within their view. That's how we discovered that the formal and fancy rooms in the Bump Tavern were for the convenience of gentlemen and ladies who preferred not to sit with the more earthy locals and transients who relaxed in the taproom, where liquor flowed like the nearby Susquehanna River.

The tavernkeeper told us that many visitors aren't familiar with the function of an early American tavern. The Bump Tavern, circa 1795, was constructed in the tiny hamlet of Ashland in Greene County. It served many purposes: an inn for weary travelers, a restaurant, a gathering place for social events, and a distribution point for news to residents within the community. Ardent spirits are no longer offered to visitors, but you can sit at a taproom table, sip freshly roasted coffee, play nine-men's Morris or checkers, or exercise your creativity with the innumerable formations of a clapping Jacob's ladder.

If you were looking for practical items or basic goods in the nineteenth century, you would try the general store or, surprisingly, the pharmacy. Offered village druggist Craig Haney, "Customers could come here to find paint, soap, bootblack, and other household items, which the pharmacist sold mainly out of economic necessity." This proud, pillared drugstore, built in 1832, has leeches in a jar, a variety of curatives for sale, and the thick scents of drying herbs.

Major competition would have come from the 1828 general store, filled with handmade crafts and other commonly stocked items for sale. They range from stick candy for ten cents (who says you can't buy anything for a dime anymore?) to woolen shawls and blankets for upwards of $75.

Here the wares made by the blacksmith, printer, cabinet-maker, and broom maker are for sale. Until you step inside the store you won't believe that brooms can come in so many varieties – hearth brooms, whisk brooms, house brooms, and pot scrubbers. One staff member says that they are the most popular gift that visitors purchase. It was common in the early 1800s to barter, and village residents would bring in cordwood, produce, or raw textiles to trade, but today only cash and credit cards are accepted.

You will meet the broom maker and other artisans, such as spinners and weavers, in the main barn, which could easily serve as a museum on its own. The barn's displays and collections interpret the lives of farmers and tradesmen in central New York state 150 years ago.

Examine tools and machinery, such as grain dolls, corn

shellers, plows, and carts, in an exhibit on the advancement of agriculture called "Beginnings." In another exhibit, "The Trades-man's Tool Chest," the tools and materials of twenty-one trades tell the tale of rural crafts, while "The Sheltered Nest" chronicles the development of domestic technology and includes displays on laundry, housekeeping, and food preparation and preservation.

Location: From the west, take the New York State Thruway (I-90), exit 30 (Herkimer), and follow State 28 south to Coopers-town. From the east, take I-90 exit 25A and follow US 20 west, then State 80 south. From the south, take I-88, exit 17 (Oneonta), and follow State 28 north. From New York City and the south-east, take I-87 to exit 21 (Catskill) and follow State 145 to I-88 west, exit 17 (see above). The museum is on State 80 (Lake Road), one mile north of the center of town.

Admission is charged.

Hours: May through October, daily; April, November and De-cember, Tuesday through Sunday.

Allow two to four hours.

Information: The Farmers' Museum, P.O. Box 800, Coopers-town, NY 13326, 607-547-2533.

Events: Independence Day celebration; summer, junior live-stock show; autumn, Harvest Festival, about two dozen crafts-people, performers, music, seasonal food.

Note: The legendary Cardiff Giant, the subject of a famous nineteenth-century hoax, is still part of the Farmers' Museum collection. But as this book went to press, some remodeling of the museum's exhibit space was planned and it was not clear exactly where the giant will be displayed.

If you are staying overnight: Deer Run Motel, State 80 (nine miles east of town), Cooperstown, 607-547-8600; Lake 'N Pines Motel, State 80 (seven miles north of town), Cooperstown,

607-547-2790; Bayside Motor Inn, State 80 (seven miles north of town), Cooperstown, 607-547-2371; The Inn at Cooperstown, 16 Chestnut Street, Cooperstown, 607-547-5756; Bed & Breakfast Leatherstocking (reservation service), P.O. Box 53, Herkimer, NY 13359, 315-733-0040 or 429-3416.

When in the area: The country's most famous hall of fame and the building that made Cooperstown famous, the National Baseball Hall of Fame and Museum (pages 173–177), is in the center of town. Half an hour away are Howe Caverns (pages 190–194) and the Hanford Mills Museum (pages 225–230).

32 Allegany State Park
Salamanca

Stand at the top of Stone Tower and look out over the ranges upon ranges of blue and gray hills in the distance. The view is humbling; human beings are insignificant in relation to the miles of untamed outdoors.

It is easy to be humbled at Allegany State Park, whose 65,000 acres in western New York State bump against the Pennsylvania border. This is the Empire State's largest state park and likely its wildest. The mountains are dominating, the lakes calming. Drive the curving park roads and you may be reminded of vacations in other places: the Blue Ridge Parkway in North Carolina and Virginia or the White Mountains in New Hampshire.

This is wildlife territory. Hardy hikers on any of the ninety miles of trails can have a chance encounter with deer and beaver, salamanders and snakes. (Don't expect to find the park's only poisonous snake, the timber rattler, as a dinner guest at a park campground. They are very uncommon.)

Nature is generous though. There is plenty of room for humans and much to do in all seasons. There are even activities for people who just want to relax and collect views. For one of the best, take the gravel road from Park Route 1 to Stone Tower, elevation 2,200 feet. Also try the junction of Ridge Run Road and Park Route 2 and the scenic point at the 4.0 mile marker on Park Route 1 south of Red House Lake for other all-encompassing looks at the world below.

For equally savorous scenes from the valley looking up, pull your car over at any of the roads that surround either Red House Lake or Quaker Lake. You won't need to walk more than a few steps in any direction to have varied views of green trees forming a buffer between the dark blue water and faint hills. There may be wildflowers of yellow and red at your feet and little white houses tucked in valleys sandwiched in by sturdy blue slopes and ridges.

Continue your nature show at Thunder Rocks, accessible by France Brook Road or Ridge Run Road, both gravel drives off Park Route 2. Thunder Rocks are house-size conglomerate boulders, heavy sandstone with quartzite pebbles embedded, that were not carried here by glaciers, as many believe, but remain where they were formed 180 million years ago. Recreation Specialist Grace P. Christy says that it is possible to climb the rocks without equipment and there have been relatively few accidents, but there is an element of danger.

Want less risky exercise? The network of hiking trails is vast, ranging from easy ones like the Sweetwater Ski Trail in the Red House Lake area and the Three Sisters Hiking Trail in the Quaker Lake area to the rugged Conservation Loop and Osgood trails in the Red House area. Experts will want to tackle the North Country Trail, by far the longest, covering eighteen miles and bisecting the park for much of its run before entering the Allegheny National Forest at the Pennsylvania State Line.

If you plan to hike, especially on the longer trails, bring along a canteen of water, food for energy, proper hiking shoes, and insect repellent. A small first aid kit isn't a bad idea, although serious injuries have been rare. The shortest jaunt is Bear Springs Trail, a leisurely half-mile walk off Park Route 1. Most park trails range from two and a half to five miles.

We recommend the Bear Caves–Mount Seneca Hiking Trail, which curves off Park Route 3 in the park's southern tier. Four miles long, it is somewhat difficult, taking you up some steep slopes and by rocky ledges, but it offers scenic rewards as you climb from point to point. Hikers can explore the three small caves along the trail on their own or venture into them as part of naturalist-led nature walks.

Looking to cool down? Lifeguards are on duty weekends from Memorial Day to the third Saturday in June and daily through Labor Day at beaches on Red House and Quaker lakes. Stretch out on the sand with a tube of sun screen and that paperback you've been planning on reading, and when you need a break from the printed page, awe yourself by taking in the pines, aspens, maples, and beeches surrounding the lakes.

Active recreation is in the form of boating, fishing, and hunting. Fishing is permitted year-round on Quaker and Red House lakes and on many streams during trout season (April through September). You must have a valid New York state fishing license and a permit from the Allegany Park police. Likewise, hunting for small game, turkey, and deer is allowed in season for those who have the proper permits and licenses.

The centers of summer family activity are three recreational areas, two of which are at Red House and Quaker lakes. The third, the Cain Hollow area, near Quaker Lake, is the newest, but not exactly new—it opened in 1971.

G-rated entertainment is provided at Quaker Lake all summer long in its open-air amphitheater. Films, including classic comedies like *The Great Chase* with Charlie Chaplin and recent features, are screened there. Also regularly scheduled are nature films such as *Yellowstone Cubs* and *The World of Jacques-Yves Cousteau* and such Disney magic as *Dumbo* and *The Black Hole*. You may also find a folk concert, puppet show, or sing-along on any given evening.

There are 230 cabins and a dozen-odd campsites at the Quaker Lake area, open early April through mid-December. At Cain Hollow Campground, 164 tent and trailer sites are available through Labor Day.

The Red House Lake area, named for a nearby Indian community that was itself named after a Native American who painted the door of his cabin red, has 144 cabins, of which 105 are winterized for year-round occupancy, and 134 campsites for tents and trailers.

Nature aside, the most eye-opening feature of Allegany State Park is the English Tudor-style administration building. It has a gift shop, a restaurant, and a museum devoted primarily to the park's natural history. Come here to learn about Allegany's birds, mammals, and geology.

Western New York winters may close historic homes or even businesses but not this state park. Ice-skating takes place on Red House Lake and ice-fishing on Quaker Lake. As in warm weather, a New York state fishing license and a park permit are required.

Three designated areas are set aside for tobogganing and sledding: one at the Summit area off Park Route 1 about 6.4 miles north of Red House Lake, another near the Beehunter Picnic Grounds off Park Route 2 near Camp Allegany, and the third on Park Route 2, two miles south of Red House Lake.

Utilizing Yankee ingenuity to the fullest, the park staff grooms twenty-four miles of cross-country ski trails on old logging roads and on the track bed of an 1890s narrow-gauge railroad. Skiers of all levels will find trails to match their skills. Those who want even more challenges are invited to try the more than fifty miles of ungroomed snow-covered hiking trails. Ski rentals are available, and there is a warming hut.

Snowmobiles are permitted on some park roadways and on fifty-five miles of off-road trails, but owners should check in with the park police before hitting the snow; certain areas are off-limits and park and state rules are in effect.

Rainy-day activities? The nearest sizable community is Salamanca on the adjoining Allegany Indian Reservation. Trivia fans will be interested to know that it's the only city in the world located on an Indian reservation. It's also home to the

Salamanca Rail Museum and the Seneca-Iroquois National Museum.

A passenger depot built in 1912 has been restored and converted into the railroad museum. Step inside an old caboose and examine its handsome red oak wainscoting, or take a summer or fall trail excursion along the route of the old New York and Lake Erie Railroad.

To learn about the people on whose land this city sits, open the door and enter the Seneca-Iroquois National Museum. Here you will have a look at authentic crafts (as opposed to the tomahawks with Day-Glo feathers sold at tourist traps). Wampum belts, beadwork, huskwork, paintings, and bone carvings are exhibited in displays telling the tale of the Seneca Nation's history and culture.

Or just walk and browse in the restored downtown area of the city called Salamanca Cityscape. There are more than forty shops and restaurants, and there is a self-guided walking tour focusing on Salamanca's background as a lumber and rail center.

Location: Allegany State Park is south of State 17, west of Olean and east of Jamestown. You can enter the park from State 17, exits 18 or 19, or from US 219 in Salamanca. A less-traveled entrance is in Limestone in the southeast corner of the park.

Admission is charged from Memorial Day weekend to Labor Day.

Hours: Year-round.

Allow two to four hours to have a good look at the main park sights.

Information: Allegany State Park, RD #1, Salamanca, NY 14779, 716-354-2545.

Location: The Salamanca Rail Museum is at 170 Main Street, between East and Wildwood streets, in Salamanca. The Seneca-

Iroquois National Museum is on the Allegany Indian Reservation, Broad Street Extension, west of Salamanca. From State 17, take exit 20.

Admission is free to both museums, donations accepted.

Hours: Rail museum: April through December, daily, afternoon only on Sunday; closed Mondays in off-season. Seneca-Iroquois Museum: February through December, daily in summer, closed weekends in off-season.

Allow one to two hours in each museum.

Information: Salamanca Rail Museum, 170 Main Street, Salamanca, NY 14779, 716-945-3133. Seneca-Iroquois National Museum, P.O. Box 442, Broad Street Extension, Salamanca, NY 14779, 716-945-1738.

If you are staying overnight: Park Inn, 2711 West State Street (just under two miles west of town on State 417), Olean, 716-373-1500; Castle Inn Motel, 3220 West State Street (just over two miles west of town on State 417), Olean, 716-372-1050; Motel 6, 1980 East Main Street (south of State 17, exit 13), Falconer, 716-665-3670; Old Library Bed & Breakfast (seven-room B&B in 1895 Victorian home), 120 South Union Street, downtown Olean, 716-373-9804.

Camping: Reservations are necessary for campsites and cabins in Allegany State Park and requests must be in writing. For March 15 through December 15, applications must be postmarked no earlier than January 1; for December 16 through March 14, applications must be postmarked no earlier than October 1. Applications are available from the park office, address above. Also, J.J.'s Pope Haven Campground (125 sites), Pope Road (State 17, exit 16, head east on State 394, then just over three miles go north on State 241), Randolph, 716-358-4900; Wood Ridge Camping Area (75 sites), Wood Ridge Lane (a mile and a half north on State 353, then a mile and a half west on New Albion Road to site), Little Valley, 716-938-6767.

33 Howe Caverns
Howes Cave

You can get married sixteen stories underground inside Howe Caverns. Why anyone would want to is beyond us. But you can do it. More than 350 couples have. You can also ride in a boat, have your picture taken, make a wish, and see a grown man hum into a rock.

Howe Caverns, in the village of Howes Cave, about forty miles west of Albany, is like most caves and caverns in the eastern United States privately owned. So unlike those operated as state or national parks, there are a lot of gimmicks on the tours and commercialization on the grounds.

Which isn't necessarily all bad. The Howe Caverns complex consists of, in addition to the tour underground and common tourist conveniences like a snack bar and gift shop, a twenty-four-room motel replete with swimming pool, especially convenient for the guests at your underground wedding.

On the other hand, it can get a little on the tawdry side when you enter the Bronze Room, named for the color of the ceiling and walls, and its guide takes a group photograph and offers you the opportunity to buy a five-by-seven-inch color reproduction.

During most of the tour you are looking at unusual rock formations, stalactites, and stalagmites or examining a remnant of human history. When we reached a landmark called the pipe organ, where stalactites and stalagmites have grown from floor to ceiling and melded together, our guide, Mike, smiled and said that when he hums into a nearby rock, known as the keyboard, the sound resonates and seems to come from the pipe organ.

"Now, it's a bit embarrassing to hum into a rock, but here goes," he said. "Hummmmmmm."

As Mike lifted his mouth from the keyboard, his captive

audience greeted him with a resounding round of applause.

There were encore performances, not of Mike's humming, but of stalactites and stalagmites growing in bizarre shapes and sizes. Continue on the tour and you see one resembling a pint-size version of the Leaning Tower of Pisa and another called the Great Beehive, You are given a geology lesson too. Stalactites and stalagmites are created by dripping water that picks up small amounts of limestone that are left behind when the water evaporates.

Stalactites (spelled with a *c,* as in ceiling), which grow from the ceiling downward, form as dripping water deposits limestone particles. This process occurs over millions of years. Stalagmites (spelled with a *g,* as in ground), which grow from the ground upward, are formed in a similar manner, except that the limestone particles in the water drip all the way to the floor before the water evaporates.

Flowstone, a first cousin to stalactites and stalagmites, is a limestone deposit that grows on cavern walls and looks like sheets of rippling ice. Touch these limestone landmarks growing 200 feet underground and you feel the sensation of stroking glass.

Time in a cavern is measured in aeons. Only about one cubic inch of a stalactite, or any other limestone formation, will form in a hundred years. The staff says that the caverns had their start about six million years ago, before the now-long-extinct woolly mammoth appeared on earth. At the time, this part of New York state was covered by seawater.

You can see where water has left its mark in the caverns, like the witch's profile in solid rock, carved bit by bit by dripping water. You cross under the balancing rock, a ponderous hunk of rock looking precariously lodged in place against the walls. In reality, it has been in this position for millions of years. Mike said that it is estimated that the last rock fell in the caverns 10,000 years ago; another isn't expected to fall for another 20,000 years.

Human history, on the other hand, is measured in years. About a third of the way into the tour, Mike told us the story of Lester Howe, the caverns' eponym, credited with being the first to discover and exploit the caverns. Farmer Howe followed the lead of his cows, who liked to stand in one particularly sunny spot on his property. On investigation, he discovered a dark hole in the earth through which streams of fresh air blew.

Before long, Lester Howe was operating a bona fide tourist attraction. For fifty cents he would supply visitors with a rain hat, a pair of rubber boots, and an oil lamp or torch and take them on eight-hour journeys into his caverns. He also threw in a box lunch. When you get to the Bronze Room, where your picture is taken, your guide will direct your eyes to soot marks on the walls. These were caused by oil lamps at rest while Howe's tourists ate lunch.

There are no oil lamps today. Your way is lit by multi-colored electric lights that lend a festive, if not natural, feel to the caverns. But if you want nature and prefer things completely natural, you will get that, too. During the second part of the tour, your guide will turn off all artificial lights. Chances are you have never been in such absolute darkness. The little red light on my camera's flash attachment glowed like a shooting star in the heavens.

No need to wait for a real shooting star to make a wish when you're inside Howe Caverns. Just toss a coin into the subterranean wishing well. The money is collected every two weeks and given to charity. Mike said, "Most people wish for a safe boat ride," since that's what happens next.

"Hop into one of our two luxury liners," Mike directed us with a sarcastic smile. Travel by boat is not a common way to explore a cave, but Howe Caverns has two twenty-two-passenger boats to carry you across the Lake of Venus. The lake is fed by the rushing water of the underground River Styx, named for the mythical river of Hades.

"One of our competitors," Mike continued, referring to nearby Secret Caverns, "has a hundred-foot waterfall. We have a waterfall, too. Ours is ninety-three and one half feet . . .," he said with a carefully placed pause, "shorter." Just before you reach the six-and-a-half-foot-high waterfall, the boats turn around and retrace their paths.

This is where you stop at the Bridal Altar, where all those weddings happen. Are you single and looking? Don't leave without setting foot on the six-inch-thick calcite heart embedded on the floor. Step on it, a legend says, and you will be married within a year.

Are you married and looking? Sit on the heart, advised Mike, and you will be divorced within a year.

We had no sitters, just a few optimistic, romantic standers.

Overindulging in romance may be fine, but not so wise for food, since everyone wraps up the tour with a journey through the Winding Way – the most fun part of the trip. It's a curving and twisting 560-foot-long path through the rock, carved over thousands of years by the natural power of water. At its broadest point, Winding Way is six feet wide; at its narrowest, it's three feet. It can make you wish you had started a diet or worn a tight belt before entering this limestone labyrinth.

Location: Howe Caverns is in Howes Cave, just east of Cobleskill. Take I-88, exit 22, onto State 7 and follow the yellow-and-black signs.
Admission is charged.
Hours: Year-round, daily.
Allow an hour and twenty minutes for the tour.

Information: Howe Caverns, Howes Cave, NY 12092, 518-296-8990.

Note: The temperature in the caverns is a constant fifty-two degrees, so wear a light jacket or other warm clothing. Also wear sturdy shoes; the ground can be slippery. There are picnic tables and fireplaces for cooking on the grounds. There is also a snack bar and restaurant. Secret Caverns, another privately owned enterprise, is nearby in Cobleskill.

If you are staying overnight: Howe Caverns Motel, at the caverns site, Howes Cave, 518-296-8950; Best Western Campus Drive (State 7, three miles south of Cobleskill), 518-234-4321; Hide-A-Way Campsites (72 sites), Woodman Road (two miles west of State 30A), Central Bridge, 518-868-9975; Locust Park (32 sites), State 7 and State 30A (a mile west of I-88, exit 23), 518-868-9927.

When in the area: Albany, the state capital and home of the New York State Museum (pages 246–250) and Schuyler Mansion State Historic Site (pages 251–254), is about thirty to forty minutes east. Cooperstown, home of the National Baseball Hall of Fame (pages 173–177) and the Farmers' Museum (pages 178–183), is a pretty drive of forty-five minutes to an hour west.

34 Olana State Historic Site
Hudson

We stood in the gallery in Olana, a masterpiece of a mansion built by artist Frederic Church, a master in his own right from the Hudson River School of painting. To the right and left of a door leading from the gallery to the studio are portraits of Church and his father.

"You can see who was the artist and who was the business-man," said our guide.

Church's father, a Hartford insurance executive, is depicted as clean-shaven, stern, and gray. The artist is bushy-haired but balding and has a walrus mustache; his eyes are tender and his expression is questioning.

We left the gallery and entered a long hallway, catching a glimpse of the Charter Oak chair, which will strike a chord in anybody who has lived in Connecticut. The Charter Oak was a tree that served as the hiding place for Connecticut's royal charter in colonial Hartford and is to this day Connecticut's most famous symbol. The tree was destroyed by a storm in the mid-1800s, and chairs made from its roots and branches were given to members of the seven families that originally settled Hartford.

Appropriately, the chair represents the severing of the artist's roots to Hartford. He shunned insurance and answered an-other calling, which made the world of art the beneficiary of his talents.

The tour of Olana (named after an ancient Persian fortress) begins with a ten-minute introduction of the man and his house. Frederic Church is regarded as the first American artist to receive international recognition. A worldwide traveler, Church intended to model his home after a French chateau until a trip to the Middle East in the late 1860s inspired him otherwise.

Impressed by the region's architecture, with its massive bearings, sense of eternal presence, and relationship of muted stone shades to highly decorated patterns, Church conceived a dream house with a distinctly Middle Eastern air.

The Persian carpets, the Arabic script on the walls and over the main portal, and the Syrian tiles make this a mansion unlike all others in the Hudson Valley. In fact the first sight of Olana from the crest of the access road that climbs 460 feet above the river is of a reckless Persian palace of Islamic arches and exotic stenciling set in a valley of mansard roofs and belvederes. Once inside you can study the spellbinding style in detail. Examine the Persian tile around the fireplace in Church's studio. Did you ever think there could be so many shades of blue?

Yet this architectural style, while an oddity in Columbia County, was not totally unheard of in Victorian times. There is an Ottoman smoking room in Victoria Mansion in Portland, Maine. Longwood, the unfinished home of cotton magnate Haller Nutt, brings a bit of Middle Eastern flavor to the magnolias and cotton boll of Natchez, Mississippi. Amid the palm trees and Spanish colonial homes of St. Augustine, Florida, is Villa Zurada with its Persian-style floor plan.

As a dutiful citizen of Victorian-era America, Church collected wherever he went. So it's not surprising to see South American and Mexican baskets and pottery in Church's studio and tables from Egypt and Morocco in the east parlor, which served as the formal guest reception room. The workmen employed by Church painted the doors in the east parlor silver and gold, and the busy and intricate rectangular designs simulate the markings he saw among the residences of the Middle Eastern upper middle class.

Church also admired Persian homes for their central courtyards. The Court Hall, seen early on the tour, was his attempt at duplicating this feature. But New York is not the hot, dry Persian

Gulf region, and Church ultimately abandoned the courtyard idea. At one time he considered skylights for this area, but the climate again dissuaded him. So he added an effect that couldn't be upset by the elements—Church painted the ceiling a light blue and varnished it to create the image of a clear, open sky.

A genuine nature scene is yours by looking through the ombra, a massive window with a shape falling somewhere between that of a Hershey's kiss and a Turkish turban, toward

Wander Frederic Church's Persian palace, Olana, in Hudson

a vista unparalleled by any oil on canvas. The ombra frames the woods, the rolling river, and the blue mountains beyond. Church was as proud of the natural setting around his home as he was of any man-made feature inside it, and he considered the combination of the ombra and the vast outdoors a three-dimensional painting. Come here in the fall and you will find the old adage true – you won't believe your eyes.

This, however, is not meant to detract from Church's best works, many of which hang proudly on the walls of Olana. *Solitary Lake in New Hampshire* is typical of the Hudson River School's subdued style; it was painted by Church's mentor, Thomas Cole. Church's *Autumn in North America,* on the other hand, is unusually vibrant. In the sitting room is the sketch for *The Great Fall, Niagara,* which was the painting that signaled the beginning of Church's career.

Church was intrigued with all types of art, and it is not surprising to hear that he viewed Olana itself as a distinguished work of art. He believed that art was never finished – that any effort could be altered and improved – and thus Olana was in a state of perpetual improvement. "As long as I live, this house will never be finished," Church is reported to have exclaimed. Our guide said, "Church had a very tolerant wife."

The biggest change Church made was the addition of the studio wing between 1888 and 1891. By that time he was suffering agonizing pain from arthritis in his right hand. His easel, palettes, brushes, and other tools of his trade are set up for a left-handed artist in this studio.

The deteriorating health of both Church and his wife curtailed any future expansion plans the artist might have had for Olana. The couple spent the winter months where temperatures were warmer, and not long after he built the studio Church hired his son to manage the estate. Church gradually devoted less and less time to Olana. His wife died in 1899, and he died one year later.

Location: From the Taconic State Parkway, take the Hudson-Ancram exit onto State 82 north, then to State 23 west, then to State 9G south. The entrance to Olana is on State 9G, five miles south of Hudson. From the New York State Thruway (I-87), exit 21, cross the Rip Van Winkle Bridge to State 9G south to the entrance to Olana.

Admission is charged.

Hours: Mansion open Wednesday through Sunday, Memorial Day weekend to Labor Day; variable hours in September and October; grounds open year-round.

Allow: forty-five minutes for the guided tour, up to two hours if you also explore the grounds.

Information: Olana State Historic Site, RD 2, Hudson, NY 12534, 518-828-0135.

Note: Because guided tours are limited to twelve persons, tickets can sell out early. According to James Ryan, site manager, the busiest months are July, August, and October. On weekends in those months, tickets for the last scheduled tour at 4 P.M. can sell out as early as 2:30 or 3 P.M. Wednesday is generally the busiest weekday. Tours on a summer weekday usually sell out by 3:30 or 3:45 P.M. Some reservations are taken, but most tours are first come, first serve.

A few picnic tables are on the grounds, and visitors are also welcome to bring a blanket to spread on the lawn or bring their own lawn chairs. There is also a visitors center with an orientation film and exhibits that should be viewed before seeing the house.

If you are staying overnight: HoJo Inn, 2764 State 32 (off I-87, exit 20), Saugerties, 914-246-9511; Super 8 Motel, 2790 State 32 (off I-87, exit 20), Saugerties, 914-246-1565; Red Ranch Motel, 4555 State 32 (nine miles north of I-87, exit 20), Catskill, 914-678-3380; Carl's Rip van Winkle Motor Lodge, State 23B (off I-87, exit 21), Catskill, 914-943-3303.

When in the area: The more modest yet eye-catching home of President Martin Van Buren, Lindenwald (pages 42–46), is about twenty miles north, while in Hudson is the noteworthy collection of fire-fighting vehicles and memorabilia at the American Museum of Fire Fighting (pages 33–36).

35 Grant Cottage State Historic Site
Wilton

In the 1880s most people went to the hills around Saratoga Springs to live life to the fullest. But in 1885, general and former president Ulysses S. Grant went there to die.

Grant was not a native of New York state or even the Northeast. He was a Midwestern product, born and raised in southern Ohio and as an adult lived in St. Louis and Galena, Illinois. But in 1880, following a two-year world tour, the former president left Galena for a brownstone on East 66th Street in Manhattan, where he lived and worked as a private businessman. (The house no longer stands.)

One trait that made Grant a great soldier—a lack of desire to be close to his fellow human beings—was responsible for his failure as a statesman and a businessman. He naively invested every cent of his savings, about $100,000 in all, in one banking firm, a company called Grant and Ward. His son Ulysses, Jr., was a partner, but the company head, a man named Ferdinand Ward, absconded with the firm's holdings. Grant and Ward declared bankruptcy in 1884 and the ex-president was penniless.

He said, "I have made it a rule of my life to trust a man long after other people gave him up, but I don't see how I can ever trust any human being again."

Soon he had an even bigger problem to face. In the summer of 1884, Grant bit into a peach at his summer retreat in Long Branch, New Jersey, and felt a menacing pain in his mouth. He was eventually diagnosed with throat cancer, the legacy of his many years as a passionate cigar smoker.

As caring about his own family as ever, the dying and broke former president chose to write his memoirs in order to have an inheritance to leave his survivors. And in February 1885, he signed a contract with his friend popular author Mark Twain to publish them.

The last five months of Grant's life have become a metaphor that has not gone unnoticed by military historians. It is viewed as a symbol of Grant's tenacity and courage, as he fought his last battle, this one against the Grim Reaper. It was essential for the security of his family's future that he be able to finish the massive project.

As his body increasingly weakened, Grant plugged on through the spring. But summer was approaching, and with it the repressive and stagnant New York City heat. It was thought that the cool mountain air upstate would be beneficial, and on June 26, Grant and his family arrived at a two-story cottage with a roomy front porch atop Mount McGregor in the hills above Saratoga in the village of Wilton. The cottage was owned by his friend and fellow New Yorker Joseph W. Drexel (founder of Drexel-Morgan, which evolved over the generations into the Drexel-Burnham-Lambert brokerage firm).

In early July, Twain made a visit to Mount McGregor, announcing that advance sales of the memoirs had already netted at least $300,000 in royalties. Grant finished the book on July 11, and eight days later he tied up the project's loose ends. Three days later, on July 20, Grant took a short walk to take an inspiring look at the valley below. On July 23 he surrendered to his battle with cancer.

The house atop Mount McGregor where Grant fought his final campaign looks almost exactly as it did on July 23, 1885, just as Joseph Drexel had arranged it for his friend. As soon as Grant exhaled his last breath, his son Fred stopped the French porcelain clock atop the mantel in the parlor. It was 8:08 A.M. The clock has not been altered since, and the time shown is still 8:08.

In another of the four downstairs rooms seen on the tour, this one known today as the sickroom, are two upholstered chairs facing each other. It is told that the pain caused by the cancer was so agonizing that Grant could no longer comfortably lie down. He spent his last days sleeping on these two chairs, sitting in one and extending his feet onto the other.

The mixture of water and cocaine applied to the former president's throat to ease the pain still sits in a jar atop a case with four shelves in the same room. Grant's pillow, brush and comb, toothbrush, and top hat all rest in the same case, just where they were left. His commode and washstand are here, as is the oil lamp he used when the power-producing dynamo was shut down.

The reception room, the room with the clock frozen at 8:08, bespeaks country Victorian splendor. Wicker rules here, with chairs and a small table made from malleable shoots resting atop busy carpeting. In a corner under a window is the bed in which Grant died. He had called for the bed two days before he died, and it was delivered from the 300-room Balmoral Hotel, on whose property the cottage sat.

Similar to a Murphy bed, which can be raised and folded into a closet, this bed folds handily to take the form of a desk. On the wall above the bed are sketches of Lincoln and Grant that Drexel had displayed just for Grant's visit.

By the time he died, Grant had earned the respect of southerners as well as northerners, and tributes came from throughout the country. Incredibly, several memorial floral arrangements were everlastings and survive to this day, although faded to a murky gray color, and are on view in the dining room. One assortment, in the form of the Gates of Heaven, was sent by financier Leland Stanford. Another, shaped like a pillow, was a gift of the Grand Army Post Grant belonged to; it rests, along with two others, on the dining room table on which the general was embalmed.

Grant's body lay in state for twelve days before his funeral on August 8 in Manhattan. It is estimated that a million people came to watch the funeral procession, which included 60,000 marchers and took five hours to pass.

Almost immediately after his death, the Victorian cottage where Grant died became a tourist attraction, opening to the public for the first time in 1890. A 1993 edition of *The Grant Cottage Chronicles,* the newsletter published by the Friends of the Ulysses S. Grant Cottage, featured the text of a letter written by a fifteen-year-old girl who visited the cottage in 1891. She wrote, "Every voice is hushed as we step inside the door. Though it was six years since the suffering hero passed away, we seem to stand in his very presence. Unconciously [*sic*] we bow our heads, step softly, and speak in whispers."

The only major change in the cottage's interior is the former secretary's office, a cozy little room converted into a gift shop and exhibit room. The exterior had been repainted several times since Grant was here, but in 1991 it was painted in what are believed to be its 1885 colors—yellow with maroon trim. The grounds have had several metamorphoses. The Balmoral Hotel burned in 1897, and the property served varied purposes before conversion to a medium security prison in 1976. Many Civil War purists are aghast that a historic site perceived as sacred by so many today sits on prison property.

They should be pleased that it even stands today. Because of its location and perceived obscurity, the building was to be closed and turned over to the Department of Corrections in 1985, but an active campaign of concerned Saratogans saved it.

Location: From the Northway (I-87), exit 16, head west on Ballard Road to the intersection with US 9; then follow the signs. From State 50 in Saratoga Springs, take US 9 north to the intersection with Ballard Road, turn left, and follow the signs. *Admission* is charged.

Hours: Memorial Day through Labor Day, Wednesday through Sunday; weekends in September and early October.

Allow half an hour for the tour.

Information: Friends of the Ulysses S. Grant Cottage, P.O. Box 990, Saratoga Springs, NY 12866, 518-587-8277 in season, 518-584-4768 in off-season.

Events: Around July 23, Grant Family Re-enactment, actors in roles as members of Grant family; summer, period concerts, singers performing period songs.

Note: The fact that the cottage sits today on the grounds of a prison might sound somewhat off-putting, but it is no real impediment to a visit, although you are required to stop at the entrance booth to check in. It is 2.8 miles from the junction of US 9 and Ballard Road to the check-in. A short path leads from the cottage to the spot where Grant admired the beauty of the surrounding countryside for the last time. It is spectacular in any season, even more so in fall.

President Grant is buried in – surprise! – Grant's Tomb, a mammoth monument officially known as the General Grant National Memorial, on Riverside Drive and 122nd Street on the outskirts of Harlem in Manhattan. The site has deteriorated over the years, and the neighborhood is not the best, but it should be fairly safe in the day. In addition to being the burial place of both President and Mrs. Grant, the monument houses a museum about the general's life.

If you are staying overnight: Saratoga Motel, 440 Church Street, Saratoga Springs, 518-584-0920; The Springs Motel, 165 Broadway, Saratoga Springs, 518-584-6336; The Turf and Spa Motel, 140 Broadway, Saratoga Springs, 518-584-2550, 800-972-1229; Landmark Motor Inn, US 9 (one mile north of I-87, exit 17N), Glens Falls, 518-793-3441, 800-688-8283.

There are dozens of bed and breakfasts in the Saratoga

Springs area. The following are in the city proper: Blue Moon Bed & Breakfast, 119 Nelson Avenue, Saratoga Springs, 518-583-4905; Six Sisters Bed & Breakfast, 149 Union Avenue, Saratoga Springs, 518-583-1173; Saratoga Bed & Breakfast, 434 Church Street, Saratoga Springs, 518-584-0920. For a more complete list of B&Bs contact the Saratoga County Chamber of Commerce, 494 Broadway, Suite #212, Saratoga Springs, NY 12866, 518-584-3255. Note that lodging rates during racing season are extremely high. It's not unusual for a room renting for $50 in winter to rent for over $100 in August. You will find more reasonable rates at that time in surrounding towns like Glens Falls to the north.

When in the area: A short drive away is historic Saratoga Springs, home of the Canfield Casino (pages 270–274) and the National Museum of Racing and Hall of Fame (pages 275–278). Saratoga National Historical Park (pages 47–51), which preserves the Revolutionary War battlefield, is to the southeast. If you are Adirondacks bound, keep in mind natural spectacles like Ausable Chasm, High Falls Gorge, and the Whiteface Mountain Highway (pages 88–93).

36 Genesee Country Museum
Mumford

Enter Genesee Country Museum, an expansive re-created village in Mumford, and you enter a world where white bread was like caviar to village residents and families advertised for hired help in this manner: "Wanted, by a respectable family, a smart girl 12 to 14 years of age whose parents or guardians would wish to bind out to do housework until she is of age."

Enter the village and you step into the nineteenth century in western New York State in an area once known as the Genesee Frontier. "Building a church then was like building a shopping mall today," said Cele Mills, a costumed staff member at the Brooks Grove Methodist Church. "It brought people to the area."

Today it's the village that brings visitors to this parcel of land about twenty miles southwest of Rochester. In the fifty-seven reconstructed buildings, most moved from within a ninety-mile radius and dating from the turn of the nineteenth century to 1870, you get a peek at the life-style of early New Yorkers.

As in most re-created villages, you get more out of your visit by talking with the craftspeople and others inside the buildings than by just breezing through them. It was Lorraine Dudley at the Jones Farm who shed light on the question of their daily bread. The warm, homey scents of baking drifted out of the windows of the farmhouse as we approached it. Dudley, in puffed sleeves and apron, stated that white flour was a rarity on the frontier, as was refined white sugar, even for a wealthy 1830s family of dairy farmers like the Joneses.

Dudley bent over and took a fresh-from-the-oven rhubarb pie from the fresh-from-the-factory cast-iron woodstove, which itself was an emblem of family wealth in these early days. Having a cast-iron stove in the 1830s was a rarity, sort of like being the first on the block to have a microwave oven in the 1970s. We asked Dudley what families like the Joneses would have used instead of the white sugar and flour so familiar today. "Molasses or brown sugar," she answered, "maybe honey," and added that she and other staff members cook whatever is in season, just as a cook in the 1800s would have been doing.

Step inside the Jones Farm kitchen on certain days and you are likely to see such nineteenth-century culinary arts as cheese making and butter churning in progress. On the other hand, proceed into the pioneer farmstead, representing the earliest period portrayed here, or the elegant Livingston-Backus House, built in portions from 1827 to 1840, and you will see cooking of different sorts. Three different working kitchens in the village allow for interpretation of the dramatic changes in food preparation, preservation, and technology during the nineteenth century.

Since the village interprets a span of seventy years, life is depicted as it was in various times. Cooking in the pioneer farmstead is done in a floor hearth, while in the Livingston-Backus House it's done either over an open hearth or inside a brick oven.

It's easy to see the changes in fashion and life-style over the years. Clothing is altered in ten-year increments, and the lavish Victorian homes in the far southeastern corner of the village offer a look at the plush living of which the wealthy Jones family could only dream.

There is the Hamilton House, an Italianate villa, with its rigid tower and mansard roof, relocated here from the town of Campbell, north of Corning. Next to it is the exotic Octagon House, whose porch extends around its perimeter and whose inside is filled with ostentatious Rococo Revival furniture and bric-a-brac. Eight-sided houses weren't uncommon in Victorian times, but they didn't spring up like weeds either. Their residents would have had slightly off-center tastes and may have leaned toward the eccentric. The owners of this one, the Hyde family, were members of a spiritualist group. When Corporal and Mrs. Hyde died within two days of each other, rumors arose that their spirits often came back to haunt their old house. We came across neither when we visited.

We did, however, meet several adept craftspeople from earlier periods throughout the village: a weaver, a spinner, a tinsmith, a blacksmith, a potter, a printer, a broom maker, and a basket maker. The blacksmith was banging out nails when we walked in. The basket maker, Betty Lennox, was plying her craft in Kieffer's Place, a two-story log home dating from 1814. She had already finished the tedious tasks of pounding out splints from a white ash log and shaving them to make them smooth and was in the process of making a cat-head basket. Why the name? Betty showed us the bottom of the basket, on which the splints took the shape of a cat's ears and face.

We toured more period buildings, including the school, the general store, the country inn, and the various churches. We also visited buildings that we have seen in few other re-created villages, such as the insurance office, the dressmaker's shop, the tackle shop, and the brewery and hop house. (The presence of the brewery is not surprising once you learn that the founder of the museum is John L. Wehle, chairman of the board of the Genesee Brewing Company.)

There is even a plot of hops growing in the back, one of many historically accurate gardens on the village grounds. In the brewery we discovered that beer, Archie Bunker's favorite beverage, was a staple on the *Mayflower* too. The ship's log says that Massachusetts rather than Virginia was chosen as the Pilgrims' destination because "we could not now take time for further research of consideration, our victuals having been much spent, especially our beer."

The collection of old buildings is embellished by two more specific collections: the carriage barn with forty horse-drawn vehicles, including coaches, cutters, sleighs, and fire-fighting equipment, and the Gallery of Sporting Art, which could stand by itself as a fine arts museum devoted to a single subject. The term "sporting art" here refers not to sports played with a ball and stick but to wildlife hunting and fishing. Inside are statuary, oils, and watercolors, including paintings by Batavia, New York, native Roy Mason; his oil *Duck Hunters at Sunset* is haunting.

A sculpture garden, featuring thirteen bronze works commissioned specifically for the museum by artists such as Kent Ullberg, Richard Greeves, Kenneth Bunn, and George Carlson, decorates the grounds near the museum.

Finally, after a visit here you should be able to answer the question "Where does the word 'Genesee' come from?" It's a word heard often in upstate New York, the name of everything from a river to streets to businesses. The word, like many here, comes from a Native American language. The Senecas called the northward-flowing river nearby the "Gen-nis-he-y," which means "pleasant valley." It was only a matter of time until the entire region would become known as Genesee Country.

Location: Westbound: from the New York State Thruway (I-90), exit 46, take I-390 south to exit 11 onto State 251 west to State 383 into Mumford and follow the signs. Eastbound: from I-90, exit 47 (Leroy), take State 19 south to State 5 east, then left onto Flint Lime Road and right onto Flint Hill Road into Mumford and follow the signs. Northbound on I-390: take exit 10 (Avon) onto US 20 west to State 5 west into Mumford and follow the signs.

Admission is charged.

Hours: Early May through mid-October, daily.

Allow four hours to a full day; if you can't spend at least three hours here, it is our opinion that you'd be best off saving your visit for another day.

Information: Genesee Country Museum, P.O. Box 310, Mumford, NY 14511, 716-538-6822.

Events: There are many, nearly one every weekend. A partial list includes: Memorial Day weekend, Homecoming, gardening clinics, sheep shearing demonstrations, traditional holiday ceremony; early June, Highland Gathering, bagpipe bands, genealogical displays; July 4, Independence Day celebration, old-fashioned observance with parades, patriotic music, cannon firings; August, Old-Time Fiddler's Fair, nineteenth-century music with fiddles, dulcimers, banjos, mandolins; Labor Day weekend, Salute to Autumn, farming and other chores needed to prepare for fall harvest; early October, Agricultural Society Fair, antique farm equipment, farmers' market, poultry show, draft horse exhibition.

Note: Two restaurants are on the grounds, one open all season, the other only in summer. Picnic tables are also on the grounds. The village is frequented by schoolchildren on field trips in spring, but most school groups are gone by about 1:30. When your feet get tired on hot summer days, consider taking the free trolley around the village; it runs daily in July and August and on weekends the rest of the season.

If you are staying overnight: Red Roof Inn, 4820 West Henrietta Road (State 15, at junction with I-90, exit 46), West Henrietta, 716-359-1100; Rochester Marriott Thruway Hotel, 5257 West Henrietta Road (State 15, just south of I-90, exit 46), West Henrietta, 716-359-1800; Genesee Country Inn (nine-room B&B), 948 George Street, Mumford, 716-538-2500; Adventures in Bed

& Breakfasts, P.O. Box 567, Geneseo, NY 14454, 800-724-1932 or 716-243-5540, for bed and breakfast listings in Genesee Country area.

When in the area: The father of modern photography is honored at the International Museum of Photography at the George East-man House (pages 288–294), a complex twenty miles away in Rochester where one can easily spend up to three hours.

37 The Man Who Could Have Been President
Auburn

The banks and schools are closed in Alaska every year on the last Monday in March in honor of William Seward, a New York native who negotiated the purchase of Alaska from Russia in 1867. Seward is as much a hero to the people of Alaska as George Washington is to the citizens of the United States as a whole, and it is not unusual to find Seward's home the target of many tourists from Alaska who travel 6,000 miles to see where the diminutive statesman slept, worked, and relaxed.

But Seward's accomplishments transcend the forty-ninth state. In fact, he came very close to being nominated in 1860 for the Republican candidacy for president of the United States, only to lose the nomination to Abraham Lincoln. "Seward thought he would win," offered our guide, curator Betty Lewis, "but the delegates at the Republican convention thought he was too radical and would get the Union into a war."

Prior to his bid for the presidency, Seward had won several elections, serving as state senator, governor, and U.S. senator from New York while espousing rigid antislavery views. So it wasn't surprising that Lincoln selected him to be his secretary of state, a position he held through the term of Lincoln's successor, Andrew Johnson. It was during Johnson's presidency that Seward negotiated the purchase of Alaska.

The event occurred early on an Alaskan morning when by gaslight Seward and Russian minister Edward Stoeckl signed the treaty turning "Russian America" over to the United States. The event was immortalized in oil by Emanuel Leutze, the artist best known for *Washington Crossing the Delaware*. Today, his *The Signing of the Alaska Treaty* dominates the second-floor stairwell of Seward's home, called the diplomatic gallery.

The gallery consists of Seward's collection of 132 prints and photographs of world leaders he met on diplomatic missions across the globe. A who's who of mid-nineteenth-century rulers, the collection is also an unusual mosaic of humanity.

The colors and creeds of the world are showcased, each handsomely presented. There is Gen. Giuseppe Garibaldi of Italy, bearded and in native costume. Nearby is Benito Juarez, president of Mexico, seeming forceful and determined. Side by side are Stephen A. Benson and J.J. Roberts, leaders of the African nation Liberia. Then there is the King of Siam, the same one immortalized in *The King and I,* appearing much unlike actor Yul Brynner.

Bearded Russian Edward Stoeckl, with whom Seward shook hands and traded Alaska for $7.2 million, is pictured, as is Seward's second presidential boss, Andrew Johnson. Seward himself appears on this wall of fame too, but likenesses of Seward also abound throughout the home. The most impressive may be the bust of Seward created by Daniel Chester French, the sculptor who's most famous for carving *Seated Lincoln* inside Washington's Lincoln Memorial.

It is said that while leading one of his guests past the gallery, Seward mentioned that many of the monarchs and elected officials pictured there had "passed from office or from earth in the brief period of eight years."

His guest answered, "It is a sermon on the instability of human greatness."

To which Seward replied, "Perhaps so. I can only hope that they all enjoyed the prospect of getting out of office as much as I do."

Seward's tenure as secretary of state was one of tragedy, caused indirectly by the war that nobody wanted but that couldn't be avoided. While John Wilkes Booth was shooting Abraham Lincoln at Ford's Theater as revenge for the defeat of the South, a hulking half-wit of a man and compatriot of Booth's named Lewis Paine made an attempt on Seward's life.

Seward was bedridden while recuperating from injuries suffered in a carriage accident when the attack took place. Paine came to the door of Seward's Washington residence and claimed to be a delivery boy bringing medicine to the secretary of state. Seward's son Frederick, who had answered the door, was promptly clubbed on the head by a gun Paine held in his hand. Paine then stabbed three people, including another son, Augustus, before reaching Seward and stabbing him repeatedly in the face and throat.

Paine was later captured and hanged along with three others found guilty in the conspiracy. Seward survived, thanks mainly to a steel-and-leather brace supporting his jaw, injured in the carriage accident. But the shock of the assassination attempt was too much for Seward's wife, who died two months later. One year later his daughter died. Seward's spirit was broken, but he continued in his capacity as Johnson's secretary of state and traveled the world after Johnson left office before dying in 1872.

Mementoes of his career stock the floors, halls, and walls of the handsome house. Since it was never sold out of the Seward family, most of the sixteen rooms open to the public are filled with original possessions just as Seward left them.

There is a somewhat grisly display of the sheet on which Seward lay after the attack by Paine. There is also a military uniform that he wore as governor of New York, looking as if it were custom-built for an adolescent but a perfect fit for the five-foot-four slightly-built Seward. Also displayed is Seward's commission as secretary of state with Abraham Lincoln's signature.

The most eye-opening displays are the treasures Seward brought back from his diplomatic journeys to far-off places or collected from foreign guests visiting Washington. In a dining room cabinet is a cobalt-tinted sixty-place setting of china, a gift of Prince Napoleon Joseph Charles Paul Bonaparte, the French emperor's nephew. On the buffet in the same room is a copper

Russian samovar. Also ornamenting the room are an alabaster Buddha from Siam and a pair of porcelain garden seats from China.

Most of the room is decorated as was fashionable in early Victorian times when Seward was in his prime. The North Library is typically dark and heavy, but the drawing room, added in 1870, is lighter and airier; favorite pieces there include the Oriental carpet from Turkey and the family portraits. The basement kitchen, however, is a throwback to the house's initial construction date of 1816. It is colonial in appearance, with a beehive oven, Sheraton bamboo chairs, and an oversize child's cradle that when turned over becomes a bench.

But no matter where you turn you'll encounter reminders of Alaska. You will see an Alaskan kayak not far from rare armor worn by Alaskan Indians. The biggest oddity is a product of more modern times: a forty-nine-star flag, produced after Alaska was admitted to the Union but before Hawaii achieved statehood. There were forty-nine states for such a short period (eight months) that few forty-nine-star flags were made. This one hangs upstairs and once flew over the United States Capitol.

Seward purchased Alaska with the country's national defense in mind, but the immediate reaction to his deal was ridicule and mockery. Americans laughed at the idea of purchasing the place they called "Seward's Folly" and "Seward's Icebox." Yet although Seward knew he was onto something big, even he couldn't have foreseen the riches in gold, oil, furs, and fish that we have reaped from the forty-ninth state.

Location: The William Seward House is at 33 South Street in the center of Auburn, near City Hall. From the New York State Thruway (I-90), take exit 40 onto State 34, which becomes South Street in Auburn.
Admission is charged.

Hours: April through December, Tuesday through Saturday afternoon. Allow at least an hour for the tour.

Information: William Seward House, 33 South Street, Auburn, NY 13021, 315-252-1283.

If you are staying overnight: Holiday Inn, 75 North Street (State 34), Auburn, 315-253-4531; Sleepy Hollow Motel, US 20 (east of town), Auburn, 315-253-3281; Grant Motel, 255 Grant Street (State 5 east of town), Auburn, 315-253-8447; Springside (eight-room B&B), West Lake Road (State 38, about five minutes out of town), Auburn, 315-252-7247.

When in the area: More history is to be explored in the birthplace of women's rights, Seneca Falls (pages 133–140). To the south are the gorges and waterfalls of the Finger Lakes region (pages 81–87).

38 The Accidental President
East Aurora and Moravia

Even Millard Fillmore seemed to know that his name was destined to be the target of mockery and ridicule. When he visited England in 1855, Fillmore declined an offer of an honorary degree from Oxford University. Said he, "They would probably ask, 'Who's Fillmore? What's he done? Where did he come from?' And then my name would, I fear, give them an excellent opportunity to make jokes at my expense."

Of all the forty-one chief executives, none—not Franklin Pierce, not Benjamin Harrison, not Chester A. Arthur—has suffered the pointed barbs and cruel ribbing tossed at Millard Fillmore.

Fact: the Students Committee for the Glorification of Millard Fillmore was founded in 1965. Its actual intent, however, is to vilify, not glorify, Millard Fillmore. At the committee's convincing, former Maryland governor Marvin Mandel issued a proclamation declaring Fillmore's birthday, January 7, Millard Fillmore Day in Maryland.

Fact: another group, the Millard Fillmore Society, brought its campaign to bring "respectability" to the name of Millard Fillmore to the general public by appearing on "The Tonight Show" with Johnny Carson.

Fact: one newspaper columnist said that Fillmore's most noteworthy accomplishment was being the only president to visit Elmira, New York. Others have said that the high point in the Fillmore administration was the installation of the White House's first bathtub. (Perhaps he should have visited Bath, New York.)

You can meet this much maligned man on a trip upstate and judge for yourself whether his impact on history deserves to be so derided.

Ruth Schmidt, curator of the Millard Fillmore House in East

Aurora, doesn't think so. She states, "He certainly was an upright person. There were never any scandals about him. He postponed the Civil War, giving the North a chance to get strong, they got very industrial and built up their factories and railroads. And he opened up Japan to trade. Commodore Perry's trip to Japan took place during Fillmore's administration."

Nobody who ever saw Millard Fillmore in his prime would have taken him for a loser. He was a tall, good-looking man, with blue eyes and a light complexion, and it was reported that Queen Victoria called him "the most handsome man in the world." His character was mellow. He was rarely known to lose his temper and seemed to have the perfect disposition for a statesman.

*President Millard Fillmore built this house
in East Aurora for his bride*

But Fillmore, like John Tyler before him, was an accidental president. He was elected vice president on the Whig ticket in 1848 and ascended to the top office after the death of President Zachary Taylor in 1850. Fillmore was later denied his party's nomination for the 1852 presidential election, and he stands as one of just five United States presidents who were not elected to the office.

Aside from a presidential visit to Elmira and the first White House bathtub, what is the Fillmore administration really known for?

Just months after taking office on July 10, 1850, Fillmore signed the Fugitive Slave Law as part of the Compromise of 1850. The law dictated that runaway slaves found in free states were still the property of their southern owners and that federal officials were responsible for recovering them. There were measures in the compromise that favored free states, and it may indeed have postponed the Civil War for a decade, but the Fugitive Slave Law caused many northerners to dislike Fillmore right from the start.

The Whig party weakened and crumbled during the mid-1850s, but instead of joining the ranks of the growing anti-slavery Republican party, Fillmore ran for president in 1856 on the ticket of the American party, also called the Know-Nothing party, which developed as an anti-immigrant, anti-Catholic party.

Most historians say that Fillmore didn't necessarily harbor nativist views but was more of an opportunist, using the third party as a vehicle for entering the 1856 campaign. But Fillmore finished a poor third in the general election, winning only one state, Maryland.

Fillmore lived twenty-one years in Buffalo after his term ended, speaking often on issues of the day, a favorite topic being the prevention of cruelty to animals. He even helped found a local chapter of the Society for Prevention of Cruelty to Animals. But according to several historians, his words were rarely noticed outside Buffalo. Millard Fillmore died on March 8, 1874.

Sadly, none of Fillmore's Buffalo homes survive. But the first house he ever owned, a little Greek Revival cottage in suburban East Aurora, still stands and has been restored to its nineteenth-century appearance. It is in this home that you hear another side to the story of Millard Fillmore.

Here you are told that the Compromise of 1850 was a positive action that delayed the Civil War and allowed the North a decade of industrial growth. Inside the home you enter the world of Fillmore as a newly married young lawyer. He built the cottage at age twenty-six as a dream house for his young bride, the former Abigail Powers. At the time Fillmore's life was new and full of promise.

The primitive desk and volumes of law books in the tiny cubbyhole he used as an office symbolize the struggling early days of his career. The meager financial situation of one just starting out in life is brought to mind as you climb the steep, narrow staircase to the second-floor bedroom. Some of the future president's white linen shirts are displayed on the bed, while adjacent to the bedroom in these tight quarters is a child's cozy playroom where it is believed Fillmore's son, Millard Powers Fillmore, was born.

You can judge for yourself if Queen Victoria was right when you enter the kitchen and see on the wall a sketch of the dark, wavy-haired Millard, drawn when he was in his twenties. Next to his is a sketch of Abigail, with brown ringlets dangling under a mop hat. The two young marrieds complement each other.

The wooden scrub-top table in the kitchen is one that Millard probably made. Should you be here at the right time you can sample goodies made in the Fillmore kitchen fireplace. Costumed guides are often baking delectables like cookies and bread, and a group of schoolchildren was once treated to a turkey feast, offered right from the authentically reproduced reflector oven.

You can examine an herb garden after leaving the house, but to study the roots of Millard Fillmore, you have to venture to the village of Moravia in the Finger Lakes region of the state.

About five miles from the actual birth site of the thirteenth president—marked by a commemorative plaque—is Fillmore Glen State Park. Just past the entrance is a log cabin built in 1965 to represent the one in which Fillmore was born.

Baby Millard was the son of a dirt-poor frontier farmer, and the cabin is emblematic of the luck and pluck that is the core of the American dream. Through determination and hard work, Fillmore rose from a log cabin to the White House. Step inside and you may shudder at the thought of raising a child in such sparse surroundings. The wooden boxlike bed is reproduced, but other items, such as the coarse chairs and tables, are authentic to the period.

Millard Fillmore is buried in Buffalo's Forest Lawn, a park-like cemetery that attracts its share of bird-watchers, joggers, and fall-foliage seekers. A granite obelisk marks the site of the graves of Fillmore and his family, although his actual grave is noted with nothing but a small stone bearing his initials.

Location: To reach the Millard Fillmore House in East Aurora from the New York State Thruway (I-90, exit 54), take State 400 (Aurora Expressway) to the Maple Street exit; follow Maple until the intersection with Main Street; turn right onto Main and take the next right onto Shearer Avenue. The Fillmore House is the second on the right at 24 Shearer.
Admission is charged.

Hours: June through mid-October, Wednesday, Saturday and Sunday afternoons.

Allow forty-five minutes for the tour.

Information: East Aurora Historical Society, 24 Shearer Avenue, East Aurora, NY 14052, 716-652-0167 or 716-652-4228.

Events: On January 7, Millard Fillmore's birthday is celebrated at Tony Rome's Globe Hotel in East Aurora with birthday cake, skits, and historical re-enactments.

If you are staying overnight: Open Gate Motel, 7270 Seneca Street (State 16 and 78), Elma, 716-652-9897; Transit Manor Motor Inn, 2831 Transit Road (on US 20 and State 78, less than a mile north of State 400), Elma, 716-674-7070; Holiday Inn Express, 6700 Transit Road (State 78, just north of I-90, exit 49), Williamsville, 716-634-7500; Lancaster Motor Inn, 6685 Transit Road (just north of I-90, exit 49), Williamsville, 716-634-6560.

When in the area: Downtown Buffalo is just a commuter's drive away. On the waterfront is the Naval and Servicemen's Park (pages 58–63), largest inland military park of its kind in the country. North of downtown are the Buffalo and Erie County Historical Society and the Theodore Roosevelt Inaugural National Historic Site (pages 255–262), Buffalo's legacies from its 1901 world's fair.

Location: The Millard Fillmore birthplace reproduction is in Fillmore Glen State Park on State 38, a mile south of the village of Moravia.

Admission is charged to enter the park but is free to see the cabin.

Hours: Warm-weather months, daily.

Allow ten minutes to see the cabin.

Information: Fillmore Glen State Park, RD 3, Box 26, Moravia, NY 13118, 315-497-0130.

Note: Fillmore Glen State Park is beautiful and offers full park facilities such as camping, swimming, picnicking, hiking, fishing, and in winter, cross-country skiing. Highlights are gorge walking trails that cross a stream on eight bridges.

If you are staying overnight: Camping in Fillmore Glen State Park (57 sites) is available mid-May to mid-October (see address and phone above); Econo-Lodge, US 11 (off I-81, exit 10), McGraw, 607-753-7594; Downes Motel, 10 Church Street (less than a mile south of I-81, exit 11, on US 11), Cortland, 607-756-2856; Comfort Inn, 2½ Locust Street (just east of I-81, exit 11), Cortland, 607-753-7721; Benn Conger Inn (seven-room mansion B&B once home to founder of Smith-Corona), 206 West Cortland Street (off State 222, ten miles west of I-81, exit 12), Groton, 607-898-5817.

When in the area: A little more than twenty miles north in Auburn is the home of another American political figure of the same era, William Seward (pages 213–217), and a twenty-minute drive west of Auburn is Seneca Falls, home of the National Women's Hall of Fame and Women's Rights National Historical Park (pages 133–140). If you are seeking nature and a place to walk in the woods, head southwest to Ithaca and Watkins Glen (pages 81–87).

Location: Forest Lawn Cemetery is at the corner of Delaware and Delavan avenues in Buffalo. Take the New York State Thruway (I-90) to State 38 (exit 51) to State 198; take the Delaware Avenue exit off State 198 and follow south.

Admission is free.

Hours: Year-round, daily.

Information: Forest Lawn Cemetery, 1411 Delaware Avenue, Buffalo, NY 14209, 716-885-1600.

39 Hanford Mills Museum
East Meredith

Stand and look at the trickling creek, just a little burbling stream seemingly more refreshing than rushing. You wonder how it packs its power, power enough to run the massive machines inside the Hanford Mills Museum in East Meredith. But Kortright Creek indeed provides the power to turn the maze of belts and wheels and pulleys inside the mill complex that grew from a single sawmill when much of this area was wilderness to become a rural industrial complex.

The museum incorporates sixteen original buildings, but the central fixture is the first structure, a sawmill turned major manufacturing operation, built about 1846. Numerous additions expanded the mill throughout the nineteenth century, the last one taking place in the early 1900s.

The guided tour takes you downstairs, where in the damp chill you can watch the ten-by-twelve-foot Fitz Steel Overshot waterwheel, turned by the water of Kortright Creek, create the whopping power needed to operate the whirring blur of belts and shafts that makes the machinery upstairs work. After setting your eyes on the entire complex, you may well think that a gushing river and not that tiny creek would have to be the force behind it. (The mill was never shut down even in the coldest months. Because the flume that brings in the water is below the frost line, it doesn't freeze in winter.)

Upstairs, where the air is warmer most of the year, visitors are shown a melange of machines on which demonstrations are offered. Craftspeople can be witnessed at any given time churning out dowels for broom handles, barrel heads, or boxes based on historic Hanford milk crates. Even though this complex is a museum, it is still actively used to produce specialty items. Some machines were built for single purposes that seem trivial, like shaping barrel tops or carving handle holes in milk crates. Then there are the more all-purpose machines: a fifty-inch circular saw, various styles of planers, lathes, a band saw, and two table saws.

Step a few feet away from the woodworking operation and you will be at a point where chaff was separated from grain and grain was ultimately ground. You can look through the window of a grain elevator where grain is placed in a large hopper and stored in bins. There is the chalkboard where shipments of grain were logged in, as well as a wooden shovel; wood was used because a metal shovel could strike a nail and ignite a spark.

The grain mill connects to the sawmill because feed grinding would be a major portion of the business here until the early 1960s. The man who expanded the sawmill was David Josiah Hanford. D.J., as he was known, bought the sawmill in 1860 and built the gristmill in 1869. He passed the business on to his two sons, Will and Horace, in the 1890s, who sold it to three brothers by the appetizing name of Pizza in 1945. The Pizza brothers continued running the complex until 1967.

Though the village of East Meredith was settled ten to twenty years before the mill was constructed, it was Hanford's mill that helped spur on the growth of the community. Additional farms, tradesmen, and small businesses gradually took root around Hanford's operation, and by the turn of the century the village was made up of two general stores, two blacksmiths, a meat market, and a furniture factory, among other businesses. But over the years the mill was the only business able to successfully adapt to the changing times.

By the early twentieth century, when D.J. Hanford's sons were running the show, the combined sawmill and gristmill operation formed just one part of the business. At one time or another, Will and Horace and their employees also produced such novelties as butter-tub covers, cheese and milk boxes, broom handles, and milk crates.

The Hanford family installed an electric dynamo run by waterpower in 1898 and soon generated electricity for both the mill and the village; the Hanfords continued to provide electric service – including even the East Meredith streetlights – until the arrival of the electrical grid in 1926.

It is also believed that the family-run mill was instrumental in bringing telephone service to this remote area and that the Hanfords possibly had the first switchboard. The Hanfords' business became what practically amounted to the heartbeat of the village. They even ran a supply store where locals could buy a grab bag of goods, from a gasoline engine to a washing machine. In time this became the place for neighbors to meet other neighbors and catch up on local gossip.

And then, with the coming of the Ulster and Delaware Railroad in 1900, the mill served yet another purpose. Because the railroad right-of-way ran behind the Hanford property, the Hanfords also maintained the first freight office in East Meredith and continued to do so until the passenger station and depot were completed.

D.J. Hanford had fought for a decade to bring the railroad to the mill, knowing he would need it to expand his business. He died before it arrived, but sons Will and Horace reaped the many benefits it brought. Before the railroad came, goods had to be hauled three to fifteen miles – now they simply needed to be wheeled out the back door and loaded onto boxcars. The mill added more markets from greater distances, and it is believed that the railroad kept the business going well into the twentieth century.

While the sawmill will constitute the major portion of your visit to the Hanford Mills Museum, there are additional buildings on the grounds (either restored or in the process of being restored) worthy of a look, not the least of which is the business office, frozen in a previous time, with its early-twentieth-century adding machine and old Dayton fan.

Location: From the east on I-88, exit 16 (Emmons–West Davenport), take a left heading east toward West Davenport, then take a left onto State 23 (heading east) toward Davenport Center and follow the signs to the museum. From the west on I-88, exit 15 (the third Oneonta exit), take State 23 into Davenport Center and follow the signs. The museum is at the junction of County 10 and 12 in East Meredith, ten miles east of Oneonta and twenty-five miles south of Cooperstown.

Admission is charged.

Hours: May through October, daily.

Allow ninety minutes for the tour.

Information: Hanford Mills Museum, East Meredith, NY 13757, 607-278-5744.

Events: An impressive list includes: May 1, Opening Day; early June, Of Field & Forest, draft horse tilling and planting, gristmill demonstrations, wagon and pony rides, Maypole dancing; July 4, Independence Day Celebration, music, ice-cream making, historic recreations; mid-July, A Gathering of Artisans, traditional craftspeople demonstrate and sell their wares; early August, Lumberjack Festival, log rolling, ax throwing, pole climbing, and other traditional lumberjack competitions; mid-September, Antique Engine Jamboree, engines on view, antique cars, barbecue; late September, Hearth & Harvest, hands-on fall activities like canning, spinning, weaving, quilting, and chair caning with local craftspeople; Columbus Day weekend, similar special events scheduled.

Note: Picnic tables are on the grounds.

If you are staying overnight: Super 8 Motel, State 23 (I-88, exit 15, then a quarter mile east), Oneonta, 607-432-9505; Holiday Inn, State 23 (I-88, exit 15, then a mile east), Oneonta, 607-433-2250; Cathedral Farms Country Inn, State 205 (just north of junction with State 23), Oneonta, 607-432-7483.

When in the area: Cooperstown, home of the National Baseball Hall of Fame (pages 173–177) and the Farmers' Museum (pages 178–183), is twenty-five miles north.

The American Trotter

Winter

40 Walt Whitman Land
Huntington Station

It may be hard to comprehend that Walt Whitman, "The Good Gray Poet," was born on Long Island until you realize that this was the Long Island of 1819, long before Levittown. This was the Long Island of farms and fishermen and endless acres of emptiness. This was the Long Island Whitman referred to by its Native American tag, "fish-shape Paumanok."

> Two boats with nets lying off the sea-beach, quite still,
> Ten fishermen waiting—they discover a thick school of
> mossbonkers—they drop the join'd seine—ends in the water,
> The boats separate and row off, each on its rounding course
> to the beach, enclosing the mossbonkers,
> The net is drawn in by a windlass by those who stop ashore,
> Some of the fishermen lounge in their boats, others stand
> ankle-deep in the water, pois'd on strong legs,
> The boats partly drawn up, the water slapping against them,
> Strew'd on the sand in heaps and windrows, well out from the
> water, the green back'd spotted mossbonkers.

—Walt Whitman
A Paumanok Picture
1881

It may also be difficult to picture Walt Whitman as a child, since his common image is one of a pale old man with flowing white hair and a rumpled white beard. But like all of us, he started out as a baby.

Whitman's birthplace, in the West Hills section of Huntington, stands in an area of commercial businesses and has served a variety of purposes over a dozen and a half decades: farmhouse, boardinghouse, small restaurant, private residence. There was a danger in the 1930s that the landmark would be converted into a roadhouse. It was in 1952 that the house opened to the public. Today it is a New York State Historic Site.

The cozy home where Whitman first saw the world's wonders that would inspire him for most of the nineteenth century was built sometime between 1810 and 1819 by his father, Walt Whitman Sr., a carpenter. Walt Jr. was born on the first floor in the borning room, a bedroom typically found in Long Island farmhouses of the day, close to the kitchen and designed for the birthing of babies. Walt was one of four children born here, and the dark blue and white bedspread stretched across the canopy bed was handwoven by a nineteenth-century Whitman in-law. When not used for its intended purpose, the borning room was a guest bedroom, occupied by a visiting aunt or other relative.

Walt Whitman Sr. was part of a long-standing Long Island family. The first mention of the Whitman family in this part of the island was in the records of a 1668 town meeting. The poet's mother was of Dutch descent, and there is a mixture of English and Dutch features in the little home. English bone china is seen in a cabinet, while in the parlor and borning room are mantels with convex curved shelves, a common New York Dutch treatment. And one can't help noticing the two Dutch doors.

The oldest room is the dining room, also part kitchen, and is furnished with period cooking utensils, including a cheese slicer, a tin spit, and a livestock knife with a serrated edge, perfect for cutting meat. Pewter plates and practical jugs sit on the hutch, and the floorboards here are original, as are the house's hand-carved beams.

> *The log at the wood-pile, the axe supported by it,*
> *The sylvan hut, the vine over the doorway, the space clear'd*
> *for a garden . . .*
> *The sentiment of the huge timbers of old-fashion'd houses and*
> *barns . . .*
>
> — Walt Whitman
> *Song of the Broad-Axe*
> 1856, 1881

The two rooms on the upper floor have been set aside as a museum room and library/gift shop. Along with a collection of reference books in the library is a well-made video in which tales of Whitman's life are told and his poetry is read as scenes of modern-day landscapes and events are shown. His most famous poem is heard as images of the assassinations of Lincoln, John Kennedy, Robert Kennedy, and Martin Luther King are seen.

> *O Captain! my captain! our fearful trip is done,*
> *The ship has weather'd every rack, the prize we sought is won,*
> *The port is near, the bells I hear, the people all exulting,*
> *While follow eyes the steady keel, the vessel grim and daring;*
> *But O heart! heart! heart!*
>   *O the bleeding drops of red*
>   *Where on the deck my captain lies,*
>   *Fallen cold and dead.*
>
> — Walt Whitman
> *O Captain! My Captain!*
> 1865–66, 1871

Whitman was a fervent Lincoln admirer and wrote *O Captain! My Captain!* as part of a group of poems titled *Memories of President Lincoln*. Included is the famous *When Lilacs Last in the Dooryard Bloom'd*.

It is in the upstairs museum room that you read of Whitman's Civil War activity. As he scanned a casualty list one day in December 1862, Whitman learned that his younger brother George was one of the many casualties at Fredericksburg. He rushed to the battle site to find his brother, who had suffered only a slight wound. But as he trekked among the wounded, the middle-aged poet found his own mission for the war.

Whitman moved to Washington to serve as a volunteer nurse, or wound-dresser. An exhibit says that over the next three years Whitman made over 600 visits, aiding 80,000 to 100,000 sick and wounded soldiers in military hospitals around the nation's capital. It was commonplace to find the bearded poet sitting at the side of a wounded army man's bed, writing a letter home for him.

A sight in camp in the daybreak gray and dim,
As from my tent I emerge so early sleepless,
As slow I walk in the cool, fresh air the path near by the
hospital tent,
Three forms I see on stretchers lying, brought out there
untended lying,
Over each the blanket spread, ample brownish woolen blanket,
Gray and heavy blanket, folding, covering all.

—Walt Whitman
A Sight in Camp in the Daybreak Gray and Dim
1865, 1867

As with many artists' work, Whitman's poems, revered as classics today, were ignored and derided by his contemporaries.

His poetry, says the narrator in the video, was as revolutionary as his appearance. Abandoning rhyme for free verse, Whitman was viewed in his own words as "worse than a failure" by his countrymen. He thought nothing of writing about love and sex in stuffy Victorian America.

One of Whitman's contemporaries wrote, "Who is this arrogant young man who proclaims himself the Poet of the time, and who roots like a pig among a rotten garbage of licentious thoughts?"

In 1865, Whitman was fired as a clerk in the United States Department of the Interior after the secretary found *Leaves of Grass* to be vulgar.

> *This is the female form,*
> *A divine nimbus exhales from it from head to foot,*
> *It attracts with fierce undeniable attraction,*
> *I am drawn by its breath as if I were no more than a helpless vapor, all falls aside but myself and it . . .*
> *Hair, bosom, hips, bend of legs, negligent falling hands all diffused, mine too diffused,*
> *Ebb stung by the flow and flow stung by the ebb, love-flesh swelling and deliciously aching . . .*
>
> — Walt Whitman
> *I Sing the Body Electric*
> 1855, 1881

However, Whitman's *Leaves of Grass,* his ever-changing epic volume containing much of his work, was highly regarded by admirers of literature in other countries, and his poetry found a place in world literature long before it found one in the United States.

Walt Whitman died in 1892 and is buried in Camden, New Jersey, where he lived in his later years. But Long Island is forever regarded as Whitman land. At age four, he moved with his family to Brooklyn, only to return eastward at age sixteen. For the next several decades he lived in places like Huntington, Hempstead, Smithtown, and Babylon, as well as Brooklyn, teaching school and publishing newspapers. Whitman's weekly, *The Long-Islander,* is still published today. One of his schoolmaster's desks has a permanent home on the second floor of the birthplace, while one of the homes where he lived while teaching school is on the grounds of Old Bethpage Village (pages 52–57), known as the Conklin House. Whitman made his last visit to Huntington in 1882, to relive old memories and see friends.

Location: Walt Whitman House State Historic Site is on 246 Old Walt Whitman Road in Huntington Station. Take the Long Island Expressway (I-495), exit 49N, north 1.8 miles on State 110, then left onto Old Walt Whitman Road to the birthplace on the right. From the Northern State Parkway, exit 40N, head north one mile on State 110 to Old Walt Whitman Road. From the Jericho Turnpike, take State 110 south half a mile, then bear right onto Old Walt Whitman Road to the birthplace on the right.

Admission is free, donations accepted.

Hours: Year-round, Wednesday through Friday afternoon, Saturday and Sunday, morning and afternoon.

Allow half an hour to tour the home, another hour to walk the historic Whitman district (see note below).

Information: Walt Whitman House State Historic Site, 246 Old Walt Whitman Road, Huntington Station, NY 11746, 516-427-5240.

Events: Late May or early June, Birthplace Celebration and Poetry Festival, period music, Whitman walk, poet-in-residence, and poetry readings (past poets-in-residence have included

Allen Ginsberg, Sharon Olds, and Adrienne Rich); year-round, lecture series and open poetry readings.

Note: An eight-page brochure outlining a walking tour of the Walt Whitman historic district is for sale at the house for a nominal price. The tour takes visitors past ancestral Whitman homes (one dating to the late seventeenth century) and the family burying ground. The brochure also lists other nearby Whitman-related sites, such as Jayne's Hill (400-foot-high hill that Whitman climbed and wrote about), schoolhouses where Whitman taught, and the office of *The Long-Islander,* the newspaper Whitman founded.

Researchers are welcome to use the Whitman House library. Picnicking is available at the site.

If you are staying overnight: Howard Johnson Motor Lodge, 270 West Jericho Turnpike (State 25), Huntington Station, 516-421-3900; Ramada Inn, 8030 Jericho Turnpike (State 25), Woodbury, 516-921-8500; Holiday Inn, 215 Sunnyside Boulevard (I-495, exit 46), Plainview, 516-349-7400. Please note that lodging is extremely expensive on Long Island.

When in the area: To the south is the re-created nineteenth-century Old Bethpage Village Restoration (pages 52–57), which includes the Conklin House, the Smithtown house where Whitman lived while a teacher. To the southeast are the best works of nature and man at Old Westbury Gardens (pages 74–80). Nearby are Sagamore Hill National Historic Site (pages 263–269) and the Vanderbilt Museum and planetarium (pages 9–13).

41 On Wall Street Today
Manhattan

Fix your mind on the image of an anthill on a patch of your lawn on a hot, parched, summer day and you will be prepared for a view of the trading floor from the visitors gallery at the New York Stock Exchange. Standing high above the floor where all the action takes place, you will at first find it hard to follow the mesmerizing movements in the human anthill below. But a visit to the stock exchange is well arranged so that you get to the visitors gallery as the last stop on your journey into the heartbeat of the nation's economy.

It is here that stock trading information flows to the trading floor, then out to the 10,000 institutional funds and 7,000 brokerage offices that minute by minute check the pulse of this dynamic organism.

Prior to stepping into the gallery, you will see a slide presentation, scan wall and push-button displays, and listen to a brief but efficient primer on the basic technique of reading that tape that flows like an endless stream of dots and numbers, telling you how your favorite stock is doing.

So even if you think Dow Jones and the Industrials was a mid-sixties rock group, don't hesitate to step inside the pillared building at 20 Broad Street. You won't leave with the expertise of a Louis Rukeyser, but you will exit with considerably more knowledge than you had when you came in.

The history of the trader's mecca, known familiarly as Wall Street, had its beginnings on a pleasant May day in 1792 when George Washington was in his first term as president and the new country was still crawling.

At the time, securities such as bales of cotton and casks of sugar were bought and sold at auctions through competitive bidding. The two dozen traders and brokers most involved in the securities market met on May 17, 1792, under an old buttonwood tree in the middle of that busy district, near 70 Wall Street, with the intention of preventing a monopoly of sales by the auctioneers.

They agreed to avoid public auctions, to collect a minimum commission on all sales of public stock, and to "give preference to each other" in their negotiations. This eventually would become known as "the Buttonwood Agreement."

They continued to meet by the buttonwood tree. And when chilly air moved in toward the end of the year, they gathered in the cozy confines of the Tontine Coffee House at the corner of Wall and Water streets. Said a visitor from Sweden in the early 1790s, "In the neighborhood of the Tontine all public auctions are held. Large packages, bundles, and barrels cover the sidewalks." And this is how it all started.

Further quotations, some more insightful than others, accompany more facts in this fascinating exhibit on the stock exchange's background.

Could women ever find a place in the world of economics? The exhibit shows that in 1899 a financial writer named John McKenzie said, "Women make poor speculators. When thrown upon their own resources they are comparatively helpless. Excelling in certain lines, they are forced to take back seats in speculation. Without the assistance of a man, a woman on Wall Street is like a ship without a rudder." It took decades to prove McKenzie incorrect. The first woman was not admitted to the trading floor until 1967.

In "Your Questions Answered" you will find at the touch of a button easily comprehensible explanations of all those terms you always felt were too obvious to ask about.

Select a question like "What is meant by bulls and bears?"

The answer will appear: "Bulls believe stock prices will rise. Bears say they will decline."

Or this one: "What is meant by price-earnings ratio?"

On the floor at the New York Stock Exchange

Answer: "It is the price of a share of stock divided by earnings per share for a 12-month period. It is a convenient way to compare stocks of varying prices and earnings."

And there's this one: "What are the major market indicators?"

By the time you leave, you'll know that the answer is the New York Stock Exchange, the Dow Jones Industrial Average (which is composed of thirty of the most widely held industrial common stock companies), and Standard and Poor's index of 500 stocks.

And you will be well on your way to accomplishing perhaps the most challenging feat here, learning that elusive technique that many otherwise intelligent human beings can't seem to master: reading a stock table.

There are two ways to learn. First, there is a wall display explaining it all in language for the layperson. There is also a regularly scheduled twelve-minute talk by a New York Stock Exchange staff member, who uses terms that are easy to understand. Those already familiar with the stock table can spend the time at any of three computer terminals, checking on the latest reports of their stocks.

The tour ends with a guide to viewing the trading floor. Learning that all stock exchange employees on the floor are dressed in distinct colors identifying their duties will help you to see some semblance of order in what seems to the uninitiated to be the epitome of disorderliness.

Because of space limitations, only a certain number of people are allowed in the visitors gallery at one time, so you will likely have to wait a few minutes before entering. New York Stock Exchange spokespersons say that the longest wait is usually fifteen minutes and rarely more than half an hour.

There is undeniable excitement in seeing the trading floor for the first time, similar to the experience of first laying eyes on famous Washington landmarks like the Capitol or the White

House or any other locale you see almost every night on TV. Switch on the network news the evening after your visit and as you hear the anchorperson say, "Today on Wall Street, the Dow Jones Industrials were . . ." you won't be able to help feeling a bit of a thrill knowing you were right there.

When you look down onto the floor, you'll see masses of people, mostly men, rushing from telephones to counters and back again amid an ocean of discarded paperwork covering the floor. Relax if you can't recall all you heard during the earlier talk. A taped explanation about six minutes long plays automatically. Watch the people in green jackets–they are supervisors. Those with orange shoulder straps on blue jackets are messengers, while brokers have oval or square numbers on their jackets.

Reporters wear dark blue jackets; their job is to report trade on computer cards and insert it into light-sensitive machines to distribute it. In years past, when tickers were used, information was put in pneumatic tubes and transported from sending to receiving stations. A model of a classic but now obsolete brass and oak trading post is on display just outside the visitors gallery entrance.

The original old posts are now relics in museums and universities across the country; one is in the New York State Museum in Albany. They have gone the way of the stock ticker, which hasn't been seen here for nearly three decades. Transmission of stock and quote data from the floor has been fully automated since the 1960s.

Perhaps New York City is so often associated with its more modern diversions–Broadway, Rockefeller Center, the Metropolitan Museum of Art–that Americans tend not to think about its colonial history. Yet one of the country's most important

242

colonial historic sites is just a quick walk from the New York Stock Exchange.

It was on the site of Federal Hall National Memorial, on the corner of Wall and Nassau streets, that George Washington was inaugurated as the first President of the United States. This occurrence alone makes this place noteworthy. A bronze statue of Washington on the steps of this building depicts him lifting his hand from the Bible immediately after taking the oath of office on April 30, 1789.

However, it was also here that one of the landmark trials in colonial America was held. In a case that inspired our fore-fathers to adopt the cherished liberty of freedom of the press, John Peter Zenger was found not guilty of "seditious libel" against Royal Governor William Cosby. Zenger's attorney claimed that the biting critical songs attacking Cosby that Zenger printed were truthful criticism of the government and therefore could not rightly be considered libelous. The jury agreed.

This spot was the scene of other momentous acts, specifical-ly the Stamp Act and various acts of Congress. The Stamp Act Congress met here in 1765 to formally protest the hated taxing scheme and as a result adopted the Declaration of Rights and Grievances, stating that the English in the colonies had the same rights as those in England and could not be taxed without their consent. Twenty-four years later, the first United States Congress under the Constitution met here and ratified the first ten amend-ments to the Constitution, the Bill of Rights.

All those illustrious events happened on this spot, but not in the Greek Revival building sitting there today. This is the third structure to occupy the site. First built as a customs house, it later served as a subtreasury from 1862 to 1920. After serving as a home for various government agencies, the structure was pronounced a national memorial in 1955, administered by the National Park Service.

Dioramas inside present scale models of the first presidential inauguration. One depicts the inaugural parade from Washington's home on Cherry Street near the Brooklyn Bridge to Federal Hall. Another presents a view of the inauguration from the Federal Hall balcony with flags hanging from windows and bunting on the pillars. Changing exhibits fill other galleries inside.

The most memorable feature of the building is the massive rotunda, sixty feet in diameter with twenty-seven-foot-high Corinthian columns. When this was a customs house, a big round desk occupied the rotunda center. Today you will likely find a classical pianist, an operatic tenor, or a gospel choir here as a part of regularly scheduled lunchtime concerts.

Location: The New York Stock Exchange visitors center is at 20 Broad Street, near the intersection with Wall Street.

Admission is free.

Hours: Year-round, weekdays, except for most holidays.

Allow forty-five minutes to an hour and a half depending on your interest and the time you visit.

Information: New York Stock Exchange, 11 Wall Street, New York, NY 10005, 212-656-5166.

Note: As with most attractions, summer and school vacations are traditionally the busiest times here. If you make your trip during those periods, plan to come before 11:30 A.M., or expect a short wait.

Location: Federal Hall National Memorial is at 26 Wall Street on the corner of Wall and Nassau streets.

Admission is free.

Hours: Year-round, weekdays including Washington's Birthday and July 4, but closed other major holidays.

Allow thirty minutes to an hour.

Information: Federal Hall National Memorial, 26 Wall Street, New York, NY 10005, 212-264-8711.

Events: Washington's Birthday and July 4, holiday programs usually featuring colonial music, films, and other entertainment; April 30, costumed re-enactment of George Washington's inauguration; weekly midday concerts are scheduled regularly.

Note: Federal Hall National Memorial has a significant film library relating to George Washington and colonial America, and films can be shown on request. The staff prefers to receive such requests at least three days in advance.

If you are staying overnight: Get information on conventional lodging and tour packages from the New York City Convention and Visitors Bureau, 2 Columbus Circle, New York, NY 10019, 212-397-8222 (seven days a week). For information on alternative lodging, contact any of these bed and breakfast agencies: Bed, Breakfast, & Books, 35 West 92nd Street, New York, NY 10025, 212-865-8740; City Lights Bed & Breakfast, P.O. Box 20355, Cherokee Station, New York, NY 10028, 212-737-7049; New World Bed & Breakfast, 150 Fifth Avenue, Suite 711, New York, NY 10011, 212-675-5600; Urban Ventures, 38 West 32nd Street, Suite 1412, New York, NY 10001, 212-594-5650.

When in the area: An exciting place to unwind and grab a bite to eat is South Street Seaport (pages 304–310). Boats leave from Battery Park for the Statue of Liberty and Ellis Island (pages 295–303), while up around Gramercy Park is a site relating to another great president: the birthplace of Theodore Roosevelt (pages 263–269).

42 New York State Museum
Albany

. . . with all the opulence and splendor of this city, there is very little good breeding to be found . . . they talk loud, very fast, and all together.
    —John Adams, 1774, on New York City

Reading Adams's words in the New York State Museum in Albany may lead one to think that some things never change. Yet a little farther along you see a diorama of a wilderness setting that includes a timber rattler in repose. The locale is not the Adirondacks but upper Manhattan 300 years ago.

Things have changed, immensely so, and the New York State Museum chronicles the changes brought by both people and nature. The museum, one of the best of its type we have seen in any state, shows visitors, via life-size dioramas, films, video exhibits, transplanted antique vehicles, and reconstructed building interiors, the "intricate relationship between human beings and the environment."

You see this in many massive displays, not just those one would expect, such as prehistoric hunters tracking a wolverine, but also urban scenes, including a 1930-ish barbershop from Manhattan's upper west side and a 1920s Texaco gas station with a hand-cranked gasoline pump, the kind everyone's grandfather remembers.

The museum is divided into three huge halls focusing on different aspects of the state: the New York metropolis, the Adirondack wilderness, and Native Peoples of New York.

Wander through each hall and you will be accompanied by music peculiar to each region. In the metropolis, Liza Minnelli's "New York, New York" sets the tone; in the Adirondack region, it's the songs of the birds and the rushing water of mountain streams. The songs of the city, however, can also be heard in

Chinese, Spanish, Yiddish, or Italian. New York City is a city of neighborhoods, as one exhibit explicitly points out. It is here that you see the Hispanic depression-era barbershop. Prices in the 1930s were 80 cents for a haircut and 40 cents for a shave. The prices fell to 30 and 20 cents respectively after 1937.

There is also 24 Mott Street in Chinatown, home of the Tuck High Company, which sold foods, dry goods, spices, and utensils. Then there is the turn-of-the-century sweatshop with five garment workers and an infant crowded into a rat trap of a room. As untold refugees fled Europe, the companion commentary reads, Americans were making a habit of wearing machine-sewn clothing. The sweatshop was the result.

Another depicted neighborhood belongs to Big Bird and Oscar the Grouch. The brownstone set from Sesame Street is fully replicated, complete with Oscar poking his head out of a steel garbage can. Hard to believe that this so recognizable TV set is made of nothing but papier-mâché, canvas, wood, and paint.

Continue wandering through this maze of the re-created metropolis. The stock market trading post from the thirties, the Broadway-area tableau from the day when *Showboat* was the biggest thing to hit the stage, and the 1940 subway car will educate as well as ring nostalgic. And you didn't have to be alive in 1940 to appreciate it today.

The metropolis exhibit isn't limited to man-made effects. Keeping in tune with the museum's theme, you see that nature won't let go of the city. Check out the model of a vacant lot where house finches, English sparrows, a brown snake, common plantains, and dandelions make their home.

There is another neighborhood here, one that opened in 1992 but dates back 400 years to upstate's Mohawk Valley. You pass through a Mohawk Iroquois village palisade—a surrounding wall made of vertically set poles or posts—and enter a Native American village, circa 1600.

The focus of the village is the bark-covered and sapling-framed longhouse, standing sixty feet long, nineteen feet high, and twenty feet wide. Inside the longhouse visitors see a group of nineteen life-size Iroquois figures modeled from contemporary Mohawk children, adolescents, and adults, as well as historic photographs. You can hear the clan mother, in reality an elder Mohawk woman storyteller, narrating ancient tales in English to her extended family.

Some of today's upstate residents may be surprised to find that New York City is a magical spot for bird-watchers. The Big Apple is located along the Atlantic Flyway, a major north-south bird migration route, and thousands of species are found in Central and Van Cortlandt parks every year; photos of birds that fall victim to urban air conditioners show that many don't make it out of the city.

Maybe they should stop instead in the Adirondacks, New York State's purest wilderness. The Adirondack rocks were formed deep below the earth's surface over 1,000 million years ago. But even here, the presence of people has taken its toll on native animal life, most significantly in the last 200 years.

As in the metropolis hall, life-size dioramas in the Adirondacks section show all aspects of people and their effect on the environment. One presents two men trying to cooperate with nature in the crudest form of early wilderness camping. They have set up camp in a basic shelter of wood and bark—no Coleman canvas tents here. Another diorama shows a tangled log-jam on the upper Hudson River, a common occurrence when lumber companies commenced their log drives during the gushing snow melt of early spring.

The diorama dominated by the ponderous moose is a paean to animals that people have driven from the Adirondacks. The moose, whose meat became meals and whose hide went for snowshoe webbing and moccasins, was gone by the 1860s. The elk vanished by the 1830s, the wolverine by the 1840s, and the lynx by the 1890s.

About that time many parts of the Adirondacks were rapidly becoming havens for New Yorkers with leisure time on their minds. The circa 1900 wagon, locally called a mountain taxi, was typical of those that carried passengers and their luggage from the railroad station to hotels.

But other city residents came due to orders from their doctors. Patients afflicted with tuberculosis were often given this prescription for rest and recuperation: the clean air, pristine water, and tranquility of the Adirondacks.

The model of the 'Rondack combination couch and chair, displayed on a common resort deck surrounded by a birchwood fence, was a frequent sight around the turn of the century. An accompanying advertisement proclaims the 'Rondack "highly endorsed by leading physicians for tuberculosis patients and convalescents."

Museum visitors can journey even farther into the state's past. A diorama of Ice Age hunters, the state's first residents, highlights a representation of the Hudson Valley tens of thousands of years ago. A mastodon and her calf stand in a frigid setting of glaciated terrain; Syracuse in January never looked colder.

There are in addition many smaller exhibits on topics like state gems, state birds, old fire-fighting equipment, and a group of Holocaust refugees who prior to being relocated were interned in Oswego on Lake Ontario during one of the state's coldest winters. All these exhibits are worth seeking out.

Location: The New York State Museum is in the Cultural Education Center in Empire State Plaza in downtown Albany. From I-87 southbound, take I-90 east to I-787 south to US 20 west (Madison Avenue) to the museum. From I-87 northbound, take

Interstate 787 north (exit 23) to US 20 west (Madison Avenue) to the museum. From I-90 westbound, take the Albany/Troy exit and bear left onto I-787 south, then exit at US 20 west (Madison Avenue) to the museum. From I-90 eastbound, take I-787 south to US 20 west (Madison Avenue) to the museum. Parking is available at the museum visitors lot off Madison Avenue, at lots on the corners of Madison and Pearl streets and Madison and Philip streets, and in the Empire State Plaza underground garage.

Admission is free. Parking is free on weekends.

Hours: Year-round, daily.

Allow two to three hours.

Information: New York State Museum, Cultural Education Center, State Education Department, Empire State Plaza, Albany, NY 12230, 518-474-5877 or 518-474-5842.

Events: Films, temporary exhibitions, and programs are scheduled regularly.

If you are staying overnight: Albany Marriott, 189 Wolf Road (I-87, exit 4), 518-458-8444; Red Roof Inn, 188 Wolf Road (I-87, exit 4), 518-459-1971; Motel 6, 100 Watervliet Avenue (I-90, exit 5), 518-438-7447; Tom Sawyer Motor Inn, 1444 Western Avenue (US 20, just east of I-87), 518-438-3594.

When in the area: Schuyler Mansion State Historic Site (pages 251–254) is also in Albany. The attractions of Saratoga Springs are just half an hour away, while within half an hour's drive south are Martin Van Buren's house in Kinderhook (pages 42–46), the American Museum of Fire Fighting (pages 33–36) in Hudson, and Olana, the home of artist Frederic Church (pages 195–200) south of Hudson.

43 Schuyler Mansion State Historic Site
Albany

William Schuyler both worked and relaxed at home, a mansion high on a bluff in an isolated part of Albany. When he took in the view outside his home, his eyes were soothed by vast acres of pastureland that included the property of the nearby Dutch church.

The church, boxy and with an angled roof, was far more typical of Schuyler's surroundings than was his Georgian-style mansion. As late as 1789, Albany still resembled a cozy medieval Dutch town. The reason why Schuyler chose to build his home in the Georgian style is unclear, but it is thought that he may have been inspired by other similar buildings already existing in the colonies; Philipse Manor Hall State Historic Site in Yonkers is a prime example. Whatever the reason, Schuyler Mansion was an anomaly in Albany in its day.

On the other hand, the chief occupant of the house fit perfectly in this elegant version of home sweet home. Philip Schuyler was an aristocrat, a member of a family that had been in the colonies for a century, and a patriot who had entertained the likes of George Washington, Benjamin Franklin, Benedict Arnold, and Alexander Hamilton during the American Revolution.

But Schuyler's ardor toward the colonists' cause was never as fervent as that of his more famous guests. In the tense years prior to the firing of the shots at Concord and Lexington, Schuyler was a moderate, opposed to the radicals who fiercely defied England. When fighting broke out, Maj. Gen. Schuyler was put in command of the Northern Department of the Continental Army, but his patriotism was questioned when he was accused of abandoning Fort Ticonderoga.

He was later cleared of charges of neglect of duty and once more took an active role in the war. Following the signing of the Treaty of Paris, he became a well-known statesman, serving in the New York State and United States senates as well as holding other noteworthy positions.

It was in Schuyler's mansion that Gen. John Burgoyne and his staff were simultaneous guests and prisoners. Following Burgoyne's defeat at the Battle of Saratoga in October 1777, he and his aides-de-camp were sequestered here for ten days.

The home has a romantic history too. Two famous weddings took place here. Family friend Alexander Hamilton married Schuyler's daughter, Elizabeth, in December 1780. Then in 1858, Caroline McIntosh, widow of a later owner of the mansion, married former president Millard Fillmore.

Keep these stories of the mansion in mind when you go through it and what could be just another old mansion tour will come to life with the ghosts of the Schuylers, Hamiltons, Burgoynes, and Fillmores.

The elaborate formal parlor where Elizabeth Schuyler and Alexander Hamilton married is typically Georgian. Much of the furniture is Hepplewhite in style, and the chairs are pushed against the walls as was the custom at the time; they were brought out to the center of the floor only when needed. There's a portrait of the groom, Hamilton, and a pianoforte, circa 1810, complete with sixty-eight keys, far short of today's standard eighty-eight. Letting in light are massive windows, each with twenty-four panes – extravagant, considering that glass was taxed in Schuyler's day.

The room believed to be the one where Burgoyne was sequestered is the southeast bedchamber upstairs. The bed is covered by a vivid and colorful bed curtain in the chinoiserie style of Chinese intricacy. The colors of the room – seen in paint and elegant reproduction flocked wallpaper – are documented to the 1790s. This room most reflects Schuyler's social standing as one of Albany's upper crust, since less fortunate eighteenth-century residents would never have been able to afford such lively decor.

It is known through his letters that Schuyler had gout as well as other ailments. It is also known that he was bled many times, since Schuyler claimed to feel better following a good bleeding. In addition, bad blood was believed in Schuyler's day to be at the root of many maladies. On a table in the bedroom is a typical blood-letting instrument, and a spring-loaded lancet, used for the same purpose, is on display in the Schuyler Mansion visitors center.

Rare though they were in Schuyler's day there was a dining room in the mansion and it is reproduced here. The ball-and-claw-foot dining room table is set formally and symmetrically with oyster shells on the plates. Receipts show that oysters were one of Schuyler's favorite foods; he bought them by the barrel.

The mansion is also unusual in that it is believed to have had a detached kitchen, common in the South but rare in the Northeast, where torrid summer heat was less of a problem. In addition, evidence indicates that there was a detached smoke-house, used to flavor and preserve meat, and a separate icehouse to refrigerate foods. The nearby Hudson River produced much food in the form of fresh bass, sturgeon, and other fish, making for sumptuous suppers that needed to be kept cool for mealtime.

Location: Schuyler Mansion State Historic Site is at 32 Catherine Street, two blocks west of South Pearl Street, in Albany. From I-787 north, take the Port of Albany exit and follow signs for State 32N; turn left onto Rensselaer Street (which becomes Morton Avenue), then left onto Clinton Street and right onto Catherine Street. Mansion parking is on the left. From I-787 south, take the Madison Avenue/Port of Albany exit, turn left onto Green Street, right onto Rensselaer Street (becomes Morton Avenue), and follow above directions.

Admission is free.

Hours: April through October, Wednesday through Saturday and Sunday afternoon; rest of year by appointment.

Allow twenty to thirty minutes to see the visitors center and an hour for the house tour.

Information: Schuyler Mansion State Historic Site, 32 Catherine Street, Albany, NY 12202, 508-434-0834.

Events: May, Farm Day, farm animals and demonstrations such as flax processing, wool spinning, and blacksmithing; December, Christmas Open House, colonial crafts, music, and holiday greens (but no Christmas tree since there was none in Schuyler's day).

Note: Parking is available in a lot at the rear of the mansion.

If you are staying overnight: Albany Marriott, 189 Wolf Road (I-87, exit 4), 518-458-8444; Red Roof Inn, 188 Wolf Road (I-87, exit 4), 518-459-1971; Motel 6, 100 Watervliet Avenue (I-90, exit 5), 518-438-7447; Tom Sawyer Motor Inn, 1444 Western Avenue (US 20, just east of I-87), 518-438-3594.

When in the area: The New York State Museum (pages 246–250) is close by in Governor Nelson A. Rockefeller Empire State Plaza in downtown Albany. President Martin Van Buren's home, Lindenwald, is half an hour south in Kinderhook, while half an hour north is everyone's favorite resort, Saratoga Springs, home to the Canfield Casino (pages 270–274) and the National Racing Museum and Hall of Fame (pages 275–278). East of the town of Saratoga Springs is Saratoga National Historic Park (pages 47–51), site of the Battle of Saratoga in the Revolutionary War, while to the north is Grant Cottage State Historic Site (pages 201–206), where the dying president spent his last days.

44 Remnants of a World's Fair
Buffalo

Back in the days before theme parks and living-history villages, when a world's fair really meant something, Buffalo hosted the Pan-American Exposition. The year was 1901 and this was a major world's fair. The world came to Buffalo that year, and neither the city nor Erie County nor the United States would ever be the same.

Electricity was a new thing, and when the spectacular Electric Tower was illuminated in all its glory, the eight million visitors, most of whom journeyed to Buffalo by train, gasped in amazement. This marvel of man couldn't have happened just anywhere; all the electricity came from power generated from nearby Niagara Falls.

There was a dual purpose for the "Pan." On the one hand it was a display of the wonders of technological advancement. On the other it was a celebration of the nations of the Western Hemisphere and the cooperation and trade that existed among them, with an emphasis on American dominance. This was the period just before the building of the Panama Canal, and Americans were rolling in waves of superpatriotism.

Two important buildings with connections to this glorious world's fair still stand in their original locations. One is the fair's former New York state building, with its 3,900-pound bronze doors and eleven relief sculptures, constructed specifically for the event. The other is the Ansley Wilcox Mansion, located closer to downtown, where Theodore Roosevelt took the oath of office as President of the United States on September 14, 1901.

A little over a week before the day Roosevelt took the oath, the people of Buffalo were excitedly awaiting the visit of President William McKinley to the "Pan." On September 5, McKinley made an anti-isolationist and anti-tariff speech at the fair. On the morning of September 6, the president took a side trip to

Niagara Falls. His afternoon schedule placed him in the world's fair's Temple of Music, where he was to attend a public reception.

Before speaking, McKinley decided to spend some time shaking hands with the public. In the crowd was a young anarchist named Leon F. Czolgosz. When McKinley offered his hand, Czolgosz shot the president twice with a gun hidden in a handkerchief. McKinley lingered for eight days, dying at 2:15 A.M. on September 14.

Vice President Theodore Roosevelt was in Vermont on September 6 and rushed to Buffalo after hearing of the shooting. Following surgery doctors seemed so confident of McKinley's recovery that on September 10 Roosevelt left Buffalo and joined his family on a planned hiking trip in the Adirondacks. On September 13, Roosevelt trekked to the top of Mount Marcy and while descending the mountain spotted a man running ferociously toward him.

Roosevelt later recalled, "There wasn't a thought in my mind but that the president would live and I was perfectly happy until I saw the runner coming. I had had a bully tramp and was looking forward to dinner with the interest only an appetite worked up in the woods gives you. When I saw the runner I instinctively knew he had bad news, the worst news in the world."

Roosevelt actually became president at 2:15 A.M. on September 14 while in a buggy en route to a train in the Adirondacks. But he wasn't officially sworn in until 1:30 that afternoon while standing in borrowed clothing at a pie-crust table in the library of the home of a friend, the dignified and gray-haired philanthropist Ansley Wilcox, where most of McKinley's cabinet was waiting.

Today, a transparent window wall permits a full view into the library, which looks just as it did when the attention of the nation was focused on this house. The filled bookcases, gas chandeliers, gas lamp, and Windsor rocker are original, as is the historic pie-crust table.

As you examine this showcase of late Victorian prosperity your guide will offer an account of the unusual inauguration. Because of the solemnity of the occasion, and because he did not want to appear to be dramatizing the unfortunate event, Roosevelt refused an official escort to the house and ordered that no photographs be taken during the swearing in. However, a photographer was permitted to take pictures after the ceremony and these proved helpful in restoring the house to its original appearance.

Teddy Roosevelt recited the oath of office in a calm voice and immediately afterward requested that McKinley's cabinet members all stay at their posts. Later that day he attempted a walk down Delaware Avenue, but the crowds forced him back inside the mansion. A little over a week later, TR wrote to his friend Henry Cabot Lodge, "It is a dreadful thing to come into the presidency this way; but it would be a far worse thing to be morbid about it."

Theodore Roosevelt wasn't the only president to be a guest in this house. Wilcox hosted TR's successor, William Howard Taft, nine years later in the dark oak morning room, where the Wilcox family typically gathered after breakfast while servants were cleaning the rest of the house. Wilcox also used this room as his den, and it was on his desk that Roosevelt composed his first presidential proclamation.

Mrs. Wilcox's upstairs bedroom was her private getaway. The sewing baskets and tables are evocative of her love of knitting and embroidering, common activities for wealthy women of the day. The dining room downstairs, full of glitter with its silver, crystal, and hanging chandelier, is set for a formal meal. Just about all meals were eaten here, since few upper-crust families of the late Victorian era ever ate a casual meal in the kitchen.

To learn more about this day that changed American history, step into the parlor, now a small museum devoted to the assassination of McKinley and the inauguration of Roosevelt. The exhibits range from the grisly to the warm. There is the handkerchief Leon Czolgosz used to cover up his handgun and samples of teddy bears sold by Sears & Roebuck during the Roosevelt administration.

The other standing relic from the world's fair, the majestic Pan-American Building that housed the New York state pavilion, today is home to the Buffalo and Erie County Historical Society museum.

History elsewhere might be dry facts and artifacts, but not here. Expect to examine Howdy Doody drinking glasses and political humorist Mark Russell's bow tie; expect to pump out energy while riding a stationary bicycle and listen to radio jingles from the days of Harry Truman.

"Bflo. Made!" is the name of a major exhibit consisting of several galleries that opened in 1992. Just about everything produced in Buffalo from the 1840s to the 1980s—from the Pierce Arrow to Wildroot hair tonic to Buffalo chicken wings is represented.

What young baby boomer drinking chocolate milk out of a Howdy Doody glass in 1953 ever thought it would be in a museum? But the glasses were premiums given away by Welch's Grape Jelly, product of a plant in metropolitan Buffalo and of grapes grown in Niagara County.

The same goes for the boxes of Cheerios and Wheaties, produced by a Buffalo branch of General Mills, or the packages of Wildroot, brainchild of two Buffalo barbers who worked out of the Iroquois Hotel. Sales of this alcohol-free cream oil zoomed during World War II, when alcohol, along with so many other materials and resources, was in short supply.

Following the war, Sattler's Department Store at 998 Broadway saturated the radio air waves with its advertising, and there were few western New Yorkers who couldn't recite the "one stop wonder store" jingle by heart. You can hear the 1947 version here.

Many may have heard the jingle while resting in a Barca-Lounger, the reclining chair made in Buffalo and also on view, circa 1950. Today they might relax in their loungers and watch Mark Russell's specials on PBS. Buffalo native Russell's felt hat and press card represent his popularity among the politically savvy. Push a button and listen to Russell skewer Oliver North and Leona Helmsley in a segment of a past show.

Not all Buffalo's claims to productive fame date to the last few generations. George Pierce founded his automobile company in 1896, and a Pierce Motorette from the year 1901 – appropriately enough – is displayed alongside a Pierce-Arrow hood ornament, a Pierce-Arrow advertising poster, and a Pierce-Arrow tire gauge. The Pierce-Arrow was the epitome of the luxury car until, like many businesses, it became a victim of the Great Depression. The company was forced to liquidate its assets in 1938.

Yes, there is also a tribute to Buffalo's gustatory contribution to the world. Buffalo chicken wings have made menus across the nation. Witness those displayed here.

The building's raison d'etre is also represented. A permanent exhibit on the Pan-Am Exposition was replaced in 1994 to make room for the current "Neighbors" exhibit, focusing on Buffalo's many ethnic groups and neighborhoods. But the world's fair has always been a source of interest, and temporary exhibits will focus on the fair periodically. You might see Leon Czolgosz's handcuffs, world's fair admission tickets, and the guide book to the fair, "Around the Tank with Uncle Hank," narrated by the fictional Uncle Hank.

It was a time when technological progress was speeding along—the incubator was introduced at the fair—but social progress was still in the dark ages. A photo of "Naughty Pleasures on the Midway" highlights a topless "Hawaiian beauty" in chains, and there are tickets for a plantation tour hosted by three "cullud gemmen."

Then step to the lower level for a trip back even further in time. The turn-of-the-century and 1870s streets are filled with life-size storefronts from actual Buffalo businesses, including Adam, Meldrum & Co. and the Buffalo Savings Bank. The toys in the window of Barnum's Variety Store, a Buffalo landmark from 1854 to 1938, are relics from the days of our grandparents' grandparents; there is a china tea set, a doll's sleigh, a checkers set, and trains. The man who was president just before Barnum's store opened was Buffalo's Millard Fillmore, and his carriage is here, too.

Location: Theodore Roosevelt Inaugural National Historic Site is at 641 Delaware Avenue, Buffalo. From I-90 (New York State Thruway), take State 33 (Kensington Expressway) to State 198 (Scajaquada Expressway); take the Delaware Avenue exit and head south to the site on the left. See "Note" below for parking specifics.

Admission is charged.

Hours: April through December, Monday through Friday and Saturday and Sunday afternoons; closed Sunday January through March.

Allow forty-five minutes to an hour.

Information: Theodore Roosevelt Inaugural National Historic Site, 641 Delaware Avenue, Buffalo, NY 14202, 716-884-0095.

Events: Mid-August, Teddy Bear Picnic, stories and activities for kids and their bears. First full week in December, Victorian Christmas, presentations and lectures.

Note: You can park on the street or in a special lot for site visitors in the back of the mansion on Franklin Street, across from 547 Franklin. To reach the lot, heading south take a left onto Allen Street (just past the site) and left onto Franklin. Heading north, take a right onto Allen, then left onto Franklin.

Special guided and self-guided architectural walking tours of historic Buffalo neighborhoods are sponsored by Theodore Roosevelt Inaugural National Historic Site; call site for more information.

Location: The Buffalo and Erie County Historical Society is at 25 Nottingham Court, just off Elmwood Avenue, in Buffalo. Follow directions above onto State 198 (Scajaquada Expressway); take "History Museum" exit onto Elmwood Avenue heading north, then right onto Nottingham Court. There is a sizable parking lot. By bus, take Metro Bus #20/Elmwood Avenue.

Admission is charged.

Hours: Year-round, Tuesday through Saturday and Sunday afternoon.

Allow two hours.

Information: Buffalo and Erie County Historical Society, 25 Nottingham Court, Buffalo, NY 14216, 716-873-9644.

Events: Summer, Lakeside Luncheon Series, speakers and lunch; Summer Series for Kids, tours, activities, and crafts; August or September, Pan-Am Day, films, walking tours, lectures, exhibits, entertainment; October, Heirloom Day, genealogy workshop; December, Stars of the Season Songfest, holiday concert.

Note: Films of President McKinley and the Pan-American Exposition can be viewed. Contact museum for information.

If you are staying overnight: Best Western Downtown, 510 Delaware Avenue (State 384), Buffalo, 716-886-8333; Holiday

Inn-Downtown, 620 Delaware Avenue (State 384), Buffalo, 716-886-2121; University Manor Motel, 3612 Main Street (State 5), Buffalo, 716-837-3344; Lancaster Motor Inn, 6685 Transit Road (State 78, just north of I-90, exit 49), Williamsville, 716-634-6560; Motel 6, 4400 Maple Road (I-290, exit 5B), Amherst, 716-834-2231.

When in the area: Naval and Servicemen's Park, with its submarine, navy ships, aircraft, and other military exhibits (pages 58–63), is downtown while the wonders of Niagara Falls (pages 150–155) are just north. You can also learn about another side of the much maligned President Millard Fillmore, who lived and is buried in Buffalo, at his home in suburban East Aurora to the southeast (pages 218–224).

45 In Search of Theodore Roosevelt
Manhattan and Oyster Bay

It wasn't like Theodore Roosevelt to get his exercise in an easy way, like on a putting green. Roosevelt took friends and visiting dignitaries on point-to-point hikes on which they had to go over, above, or through, but never around, any obstacle in their way.

French ambassador Jean-Jules Jusserand was forced to swim naked across a stream too deep to ford, and British ambassador Sir Mortimer Durand once became stuck in a wooded mass of roots and hedges. British diplomat and friend Cecil Spring Rice once responded to these treks by sighing, "You must always remember that the president is about six."

TR wouldn't have been hurt by that comment. He welcomed the chance to take his six children on point-to-point hikes near his home, Sagamore Hill, in Oyster Bay on Long Island. In part, he enjoyed the hikes because he was finally getting a chance to be a child. His own youth was spent as a sickly asthmatic in a New York City brownstone.

The original building was razed in 1916, but three years later a private group bought the property at 28 East 20th Street near Gramercy Park and reconstructed it. The birthplace and Sagamore Hill are both National Park Service sites today.

About 40 percent of the furnishings inside the 20th Street house are original pieces. Another 20 percent came from other Roosevelt family members. An adjoining building, on the lot where Teedie's Uncle Robert lived, is a museum that through personal belongings, photos, and political cartoons tells Theodore Roosevelt's story.

And what a story. Known as Teedie to his family, the sick and frail child was so weak he couldn't even attend school away from home. Some of his earliest memories were of his father carrying him in his arms trying to help him breathe.

As a young boy, Teedie became an avid reader, craving books on nature and history and dreaming of the open outdoors. He chose a hobby, taxidermy, that a housebound boy could enjoy, and he called his collection of trophies the Roosevelt Museum of Natural History.

He gradually improved his physical condition inspired by the words of his father, "You have the mind but you haven't got the body. To do all you can with your mind, you must make your body match it." So Teedie began to work out regularly in a gymnasium his father had installed in the house's back piazza.

When Theodore Roosevelt was born, his birthplace was on a quiet residential street, something hard to believe when you approach the house today. But when you enter the house, the noise of the city is locked outside and the world of Teedie Roosevelt, the child, surrounds you.

The black horsehair chairs that he recalled scratching his young legs surround the dining room table. Young people touring the house can relate to such childhood annoyances, but adults are more interested in the furniture style, characterized by guide Kathryn Gross as "modified Gothic Revival." The china rose pattern prompted Kathryn to tell us the literal translation of the family name: "field of roses."

Since the dining room runs the width of the house it affords visitors some perspective on its narrow frame. In nineteenth-century New York City, there were rows and rows of similar brownstones, and in most, as here, the parlor was the most elegant room. This one is decorated in blue in the then-fashionable Rococo Revival style, and the ceiling sports a glass chandelier. Later in life, the president recalled that he once absconded with a glass prism that had fallen from the chandelier; perhaps, Kathryn Gross suggested, the nearsighted boy was mesmerized by the colors of the rainbow reflecting off it.

Theodore came into this world in a room just like the

reconstructed master bedroom one flight up. The rosewood and satinwood bedroom set is original and was purchased by the Roosevelt family in the 1850s for the exorbitant price of $3,000. Next to it is the nursery with its crib, sleigh bed, rockers, and a tiny chair used by Teedie to sit in front of the fireplace. Who

Teddy Roosevelt's study complete with hunting trophies, Oyster Bay

would know that years later he would sit in a much bigger chair in the Oval Office?

Theodore Roosevelt became president on September 14, 1901, after the assassination of William McKinley. (See pages 255–258.) While he was president, his Long Island home, Sagamore Hill, became known as the Summer White House.

Visitors to Sagamore Hill can see the acres of woodlands where TR led his guests and children on point-to-point hikes. Look past the trees that have grown since the turn of the century and Long Island Sound comes into view. It was on these waters that the president would row his young ones to a faraway stretch of beach for an overnight camping trip.

Sit on Sagamore Hill's peaceful piazza and you can view the outdoors as the Roosevelts did. On this piazza Roosevelt received his nominations for governor of New York, for vice president, and for president of the United States. It was here that he often spoke to groups like woman suffragists, servicemen, and Boy Scouts.

Politicking on a more personal note was reserved for the library, the first room seen inside Sagamore Hill. Ambassadors from two warring countries, Russia and Japan, met with TR in this room and came out agreeing on a treaty ending the war. The treaty was signed a month later in New Hampshire and earned the president the Nobel Peace Prize.

The silver candlestick on TR's library desk symbolizes the presidential peacemaker—it was used to supply the wax that sealed the treaty. The animal trophies throughout the room, including three mountain lion skins, bear witness to the Roosevelt endorsement of the strenuous life.

It is hard to escape in Sagamore Hill TR's love of the wild and rugged. The hirsute head of an African cape buffalo stares

blankly in the entrance hall, while in the North Room (a cavernous thirty-by-forty-foot reception area looking more like a hunting lodge) are elephant tusks and antelope and buffalo heads.
Roosevelt's Rough Rider sword, hat, and revolver hang on an
improvisatory pair of antlers turned hat rack.

First Lady Edith Roosevelt took it all in stride. Spotting her
husband as he rushed indoors with a profusely bleeding scalp
cut, she urged, "Theodore, I wish you would do your bleeding in
the bathroom. You will ruin every rug in the house."

Edith's personal hideaway was the downstairs drawing room,
brighter and softer than the library and the North Room, and
she received her guests by the rosewood desk. But even her
room has a polar bear rug given by Arctic explorer Adm. Robert
Peary.

The Roosevelts' six children also left their marks in Sagamore Hill, but their legacies are relegated to the second floor
with its nursery, bedrooms, and red bathroom. A full-time resident in the nursery today is an original teddy bear, dreamed up
by a shrewd toymaker after TR refused to shoot an old bear in
Mississippi that was brought and placed before him for his
hunting pleasure. Cartoonist Clifford Berryman immortalized
the event in ink on paper shortly afterward, and before long, the
teddy bear, an American institution, was born.

Location: Theodore Roosevelt Birthplace National Historic Site
is at 28 East 20th Street near Gramercy Park in Manhattan. The
closest subway stops via the IRT and BMT are at 23rd and 14th
streets.

Admission is charged.

Hours: Year-round, Wednesday through Sunday.

Allow an hour to take the guided tour and see the museum.

Information: Theodore Roosevelt Birthplace National Historic

Site, 28 East 20th Street, New York, NY 10003, 212-260-1616. *Events:* Music concerts, Saturday afternoons throughout the year. *Note:* A brochure, "Following Teddy's Footsteps," detailing a self-guided walking tour through the historic Gramercy Park area is available. The birthplace also maintains an excellent library of films and videotapes about Theodore Roosevelt and will show them on request.

If you are staying overnight: Get information on conventional lodging and tour packages from the New York City Convention and Visitors Bureau, 2 Columbus Circle, New York, NY 10019, 212-397-8222 (seven days a week). For information on alternative lodging, contact any of these bed and breakfast agencies: Bed, Breakfast, & Books, 35 West 92nd Street, New York, NY 10025, 212-865-8740; City Lights Bed & Breakfast, P.O. Box 20355, Cherokee Station, New York, NY 10028, 212-737-7049; New World Bed & Breakfast, 150 Fifth Avenue, Suite 711, New York, NY 10011, 212-675-5600; Urban Ventures, 38 West 32nd Street, Suite 1412, New York, NY 10001, 212-594-5650.

When in the area: In lower Manhattan are the food, shops, and ships of South Street Seaport (pages 304–310) along with the New York Stock Exchange and Federal Hall National Memorial (pages 238–245), which marks the site where George Washington was inaugurated as first president of the United States. A ferry ride off Battery Park are the Statue of Liberty National Monument and Ellis Island (pages 295–303).

Location: Sagamore Hill National Historic Site is on Cove Neck Road in Oyster Bay. From the Long Island Expressway (I-495), exit 41, take State 106 north into Oyster Bay; turn right at the third traffic light onto East Main Street, and about three miles east of town turn left onto Cove Neck Road to Sagamore Hill. *Admission* is charged.

Hours: Year-round, daily.

Allow an hour and a half to tour the home and walk the grounds.
Information: Sagamore Hill National Historic Site, Cove Neck Road, Box 304, Oyster Bay, NY 11771, 516-922-4447.
Note: If you have visited Sagamore Hill in the past, you will notice that the house, once yellow and red, is now painted gray. This accurately represents the house's color when Theodore Roosevelt was president. Theodore Roosevelt is buried in Youngs Memorial Cemetery near Sagamore Hill, where he died at the age of sixty in 1919. To further explore TR's life, plan a visit to Theodore Roosevelt Inaugural National Historic Site in Buffalo (pages 255–262). This is the home where TR was suddenly sworn in as president following the assassination of President William McKinley.
If you are staying overnight: Howard Johnson Motor Lodge, 270 West Jericho Turnpike (State 25), Huntington Station, 516-421-3900; Ramada Inn, 8030 Jericho Turnpike (State 25), Woodbury, 516-921-8500; Holiday Inn, 215 Sunnyside Boulevard (I-495, exit 46), Plainview, 516-349-7400. Please note that lodging is extremely expensive on Long Island.
When in the area: Head west along State 25A for a drive of twenty minutes or so to the Vanderbilt Museum (pages 9–13), a Spanish Revival mansion, natural history museum, and planetarium in Centerport. Further south is Old Bethpage Village Restoration (pages 52–57), a re-created village and journey into nineteenth-century Long Island.

46 The Canfield Casino
Saratoga Springs

For decades, the biggest tourist attraction in Saratoga Springs was called Morrissey's Elegant Hell. People from all parts of New York, the Midwest, and the South – especially the South – came to partake of the delights of this three-story gambling casino facing Congress Park in the center of town.

Despite its sordid nickname the casino operated with the full knowledge of the good people of Saratoga Springs. Sure, Deity-inspired reformers like Anthony Comstock spoke ill of Morrissey's Hell, and Comstock even tried to raid it once, but the den of roulette wheels and playing cards was permitted to flourish.

And why not? The gaming trade brought in money, lots of it, and these mid-Victorian-era years are seen as Saratoga's glory years. Fabled hotels like the Grand Union and Congress Hall were built, and the city drew big-name entertainers like Victor Herbert and Chauncey Olcott. For those whose wagering preferences ran toward horses, gambling at the racetrack rivaled that at Morrissey's casino. And the health-conscious made their regular pilgrimages to take the natural baths.

How little has changed. Casino gambling is, of course, illegal here, but every August they are still off and running at Saratoga Racetrack. Singers continue to come and belt out their best, Herbert and Olcott being replaced by the likes of Tina Turner and the Moody Blues. The baths are ever popular for the health-conscious and hedonistic alike. The striking Victorian homes yesterday's visitors promenaded past continue to line Broadway and Union Street.

And you can still enter Morrissey's Elegant Hell and set your eyes on dice and a roulette table. Most every town larger than a football field maintains a historical society museum, but few can claim that theirs is in a gambling casino. Today John Morrissey's monument to nineteenth-century decadence belongs to the Historical Society of Saratoga Springs and the building is home to three separate historical museums, although where one ends and the other picks up is an invisible line and doesn't really matter to most visitors. Few towns have access to such a large and lavish building. Enter the Italianate-style structure and you can still see the large domed windows and brass chandeliers that greeted gamblers a hundred years ago when they came to play, never realizing they were making history.

The first people to make special trips to this corner of the state came for the curative waters, and it did not take long for the waters to be exploited. In the days of primeval medical knowledge, long before any government regulations, every unscrupulous opportunist sold bottled spring water. One brochure in the historical society's collection, dated 1885, challenges a fake healing business, reading, "The Story of a Disreputable Transaction. A Fraud Exposed!" In the spirit of reform that swept the country during and following Theodore Roosevelt's years in the White House, the state of New York took control of more than 160 springs in 1911 and created the spa reservation to preserve them.

In time those who ventured far from home to take the Saratoga waters wanted social activities to occupy their time, and innkeepers obliged by adding frills like billiard tables and musical instruments. The arrival of the railroad increased accessibility and with it came more people, followed by bigger hotels and more frills. And even more.

In the nineteenth-century casino room is a roulette table like the one Morrissey employed here, seven Indian clubs the part-time boxer used for training, and his old desk filled with pigeonholes and drawers; look closely and you can see that the set of drawers on the right is actually a safe. John Morrissey ran an honest casino, and his rules were few and to the point: no gambling on Sunday, no women in gaming rooms, no Saratogans in gaming rooms, and no credit.

If admiring Saratoga's abundant Victorian homes makes you curious for a peek inside, step up to the museum's third floor, where period rooms recreate Pine Grove, the Victorian home of a prominent local family. Standing out in the Pine Grove parlor is the Haines piano, inlaid with mother-of-pearl, that came into the family as a wedding gift, while a velvet love seat rests on wall-to-wall carpeting, a Victorian-era status symbol.

Down the hall a bedroom is filled with furnishings of an earlier time: an Empire sleigh bed, a Duncan Phyfe window bench, and a Hepplewhite washstand. Compare it to the typical heavy Victorian bedroom next door. Most notable is the "Saratoga trunk," known as a "camelback trunk," for its rounded top; these were immensely popular in the late 1800s and were hated by hotel porters because they couldn't be stacked one atop the other.

Temporary exhibits fill a gallery on the second floor. The current one, "Honorable Work, 1870–1970," focuses on African-Americans in Saratoga in the nineteenth and early twentieth centuries. Many came to work in the hotels and spas; a reproduced classified ad from 1904 reads, "Wanted. Two waitresses. Colored preferred. Also dishwasher."

Of course, many blacks were patrons, too, and were permitted to use the same baths as whites but were relegated to separate sections. Then there is a cartoon from the British magazine *Puck,* from 1910. Incredibly bigoted in nature, even for the time, it features stereotypical cartoons of Jews and blacks bringing money to a waiting Uncle Sam at the entrance to Saratoga.

When did the casino stop serving its intended purpose? Local objections forced gambling to cease in 1907, and Richard Canfield, a man known as the "Prince of Gamblers," who succeeded Morrissey as owner, sold the casino to the city in 1911.

Gambling returned to Saratoga Springs in the 1920s, but was allowed only in lake houses outside the city limits. It was permanently halted following Senate hearings in 1951 on gambling and organized crime.

Should you be visiting on one of those warm and welcoming upstate summer days, plan to take a walk through Congress Park, in front of the casino. Congress Spring, the one that started Saratoga on the road to resort fame, is under a Greek Revival pavilion, and sculptor Daniel Chester French's *Spirit of Life* never fails to impress. (French sculpted the *Seated Lincoln* in the Lincoln Memorial in Washington, D.C., and the *Minute Man* at the Old North Bridge in Concord, Massachusetts, among many other notable works.)

Location: To reach Saratoga Springs from the south, take the Northway (I-87), exit 13N, onto US 9, which becomes Broadway, the main thoroughfare in the city. Or you can take exit 14 onto Union Avenue into downtown. Congress Park is off Broadway in the center of Saratoga Springs, opposite Congress Street.

Admission is charged.

Hours: June through October, Monday, Tuesday, Thursday, Friday, Saturday; Wednesday and Sunday, afternoons only. November through May, Wednesday through Sunday, afternoons only.

Allow forty-five minutes to an hour and a half to see the museum, half an hour for the park.

Information: Historical Society of Saratoga Springs, P.O. Box 216, Saratoga Springs, NY 12866, 518-584-6920.

Events: August, antique show.

Note: There are no guided tours in the museum. The main portion of the museum is on the second and third floors. A small but quality book and craft shop and the Ann Grey Gallery, which hosts changing local art and history exhibits, are on the first floor.

If you are staying overnight: Saratoga Motel, 440 Church Street, Saratoga Springs, 518-584-0920; The Springs Motel, 165 Broadway, Saratoga Springs, 518-584-6336; The Turf and Spa Motel, 140 Broadway, Saratoga Springs, 518-584-2550 or 800-972-1229; Landmark Motor Inn, US 9 (one mile north of I-87, exit 17N), Glens Falls, 518-793-3441 or 800-688-8283.

There are dozens of bed and breakfasts in Saratoga Springs and the vicinity. The following are in the city itself: Blue Moon Bed & Breakfast, 119 Nelson Avenue, Saratoga Springs, 518-583-4905; Six Sisters Bed & Breakfast, 149 Union Avenue, Saratoga Springs, 518-583-1173; Saratoga Bed & Breakfast, 434 Church Street, Saratoga Springs, 518-584-0920. For a more complete list of B&Bs contact the Saratoga County Chamber of Commerce, 494 Broadway, Suite #212, Saratoga Springs, NY 12866, 518-584-3255. Note that lodging rates during racing season are extremely high. It's not unusual for a room that rents for $50 in winter to rent for over $100 in August. You will find more reasonable rates at that time in surrounding towns like Glens Falls to the north.

When in the area: The National Museum of Racing and Hall of Fame (pages 275–278) pays tribute to Saratoga's other claim to recreational fame, while the area's claim to history, Saratoga National Historical Park (pages 47–51) is nearby. A short drive north brings you to the top of Mount McGregor and the Grant Cottage State Historic Site (pages 201–206), the Victorian mountain home where President Grant retreated to write his memoirs while dying of cancer.

47 National Museum of Racing
Saratoga Springs

One of the two best places to horse around in New York State is—where else?—Saratoga Springs. The National Museum of Racing and Hall of Fame is to thoroughbred racing what Cooperstown is to baseball. Jockeys, trainers, and horses are all enshrined here, but the museum, with its life-size three-dimensional displays and video terminals, will hold the interest even of those who don't know Secretariat from Mr. Ed.

Summer may be when the action is, but winter is the best time to see Saratoga without the crowds and excessive lodging costs. Designed in the shape of a racetrack, this museum showcases a starting gate at the beginning (as you read about racing in colonial America) and a winner's circle at the end. In between are lessons on odds making, an examination of what makes horses run so fast, and re-creations of a barn on the backstretch at Santa Anita in California and a paddock at Hialeah in Florida.

In the Santa Anita barn, a groom tends to the finer points of primping her horse's face; a purple blanket labeled "Breeder's Cup" is draped over a rail. In the background, another horse poking his head through a barn window waits for his turn to be groomed. As you study this tableau you are invited to pick up a headset and listen to some of America's top trainers like Jonathan Sheppard, Jack Van Berg, and Wayne Lukas reveal the secrets of their profession.

The paddock setting is vintage 1930s Hialeah near Miami. Against a backdrop of palm trees, a jockey sits astride his horse twenty minutes before post time, listening to the owner, garbed in straw hat and sharp sport jacket, giving some tips while the trainer looks on. Headsets here permit you to listen to jockeys like Angel Cordero and Eddie Arcaro discuss the rigors of riding.

Once he is at the track, the jockey's life is a regulated one. As soon as he arrives his movements are limited to the jockey's room. In a re-creation of a cozy such room, a mannequin representing Angel Cordero in silks and cap sits in front of a mirror among the accoutrements of his trade. Not until he walks to the paddock does the jockey have any contact with the crowd. And soon they're off and running.

Tribute is paid to the horse as well as the human. The racehorse is an English product, developed when native running horses were bred with Arab stallions. Of the over 100,000 thoroughbred foals born yearly, each can be traced back in the direct male line to one of just three Arab stallions: Ben Brush, Domino, or Fair Play. A display utilizing fiber optics and a push button illuminates the sire line of any of ten sires, including Secretariat, Prince John, Seattle Slew, and Northern Dancer, listed on a panel.

Fiber optics also plays a role in exhibits helping visitors compare a horse's skeleton to that of a human; parts of each are lit up as a voice-over on tape discusses them. As you sample a videotape, the voice of Dr. George Pratt, based at the Massachusetts Institute of Technology and a leading expert on thoroughbreds, discusses the horse's motion. The horse's rump goes down as he takes off at the starting gate, Pratt explains, just as a car's bottom does when you step on the accelerator. Out of the gate a champion racer will reach over forty miles per hour in two and a half seconds. "So," explains Pratt, "the horse that walks around, eats grass, looks at the view, and gives every appearance of tranquility was, in fact, designed by God to explode."

The honorees in the actual hall of fame for American thoroughbred racing are immortalized by metal plaques that list the person's or horse's statistics and offer a thumbnail biography. To be eligible for membership in the hall of fame, a horse must be retired. While it is all right for the humans to still be active, they must have sufficient years of experience.

The hall of fame plaques sit on the walls of an auditorium

where an eighteen-minute multimedia presentation on aspects of thoroughbred racing is shown regularly. In the same room are a kaleidoscopic arrangement of jockeys' silks and heat-activated video terminals that let you punch up the history and racing highlights of any horse, jockey, or trainer. We selected Citation and saw a grainy vintage clip of Eddie Arcaro on his back charging across the turf many years ago.

Finally, the museum tips its jockey's hat to its hometown. An exhibit called "Saratoga: Queen of Spas" boasts a full-scale replica of portions of the front desk and verandah of the classic United States Hotel, a hallmark of Saratoga in the Gilded Age. Stained glass is the rule as a mannequin dressed as a proper Victorian young lady, parasol in hand, sits waiting for a male friend, perhaps, while the mustachioed clerk glances her way. This scene was enacted many times in the heyday of Saratoga in the late 1800s.

Location: To reach Saratoga Springs, take the Northway (I-87), exit 14, onto Union Avenue. The museum is at the corner of Union Avenue and Ludlow Street.

Admission is charged.

Hours: Year-round, daily, afternoons only on Sunday except during racing season, when it is open Sunday mornings too.

Allow one to two hours.

Information: National Museum of Racing and Hall of Fame, Union Avenue, Saratoga Springs, NY 12866, 518-584-0400.

Events: Early August, Induction ceremonies.

If you are staying overnight: Saratoga Motel, 440 Church Street, Saratoga Springs, 518-584-0920; The Springs Motel, 165 Broadway, Saratoga Springs, 518-584-6336; The Turf and Spa Motel, 140 Broadway, Saratoga Springs, 518-584-2550 or 800-972-1229; Landmark Motor Inn, US 9 (one mile north of I-87, exit 17N), Glens Falls, 518-793-3441 or 800-688-8283.

There are dozens of bed and breakfasts in Saratoga Springs and the vicinity. The following are in the city itself: Blue Moon Bed & Breakfast, 119 Nelson Avenue, Saratoga Springs, 518-583-4905; Six Sisters Bed & Breakfast, 149 Union Avenue, Saratoga Springs, 518-583-1173; Saratoga Bed & Breakfast, 434 Church Street, Saratoga Springs, 518-584-0920. For a more complete list of B&Bs contact the Saratoga County Chamber of Commerce, 494 Broadway, Suite #212, Saratoga Springs, NY 12866, 518-584-3255. Note that lodging rates during racing season are extremely high. It's not unusual for a room that rents for $50 in winter to rent for over $100 in August. You will find more reasonable rates at that time in surrounding towns like Glens Falls to the north.

When in the area: Canfield Casino (pages 270–274) pays tribute to the wealth and splendor of Victorian Saratoga and faces Congress Park downtown. The region's Revolutionary-era heritage is preserved at Saratoga National Historical Park (pages 47–51), site of the famous colonists' victory. High on a hill a short drive north is Grant Cottage State Historic Site, President Ulysses S. Grant's last place of residence (pages 201–206).

48 Hall of Fame of the Trotter
Goshen

For some who visit the Hall of Fame of the Trotter, the draw is the art, especially the abundant collection of Currier and Ives lithographs, shown twice a year.

Others, especially those with kids in tow, are here to see the horses.

And of course, there are those who have followed the sport of harness racing for years.

But many just want to get away from the city for a day and have found no better escape than the village of Goshen, population 4,900, on the fringes of the Catskill Mountains. These are the people to whom the names of Howard Beissinger, Robert Farrington, and Max Hempt may well be members of an accounting firm in Milwaukee. These day-trippers know as much about harness racing as they do about Australian rules football. Mention Lindy's Pride and they will think of an airplane that crossed the Atlantic in 1927.

But you don't have to be a harness-racing aficionado to enjoy a visit to the Hall of Fame of the Trotter at the Trotting Horse Museum. Although it is just an hour and a quarter's drive from the cavernous Meadowlands racetrack in East Rutherford, New Jersey (site of the Hambletonian, the sport's premier race), it may as well be a million light-years away.

This is truly small-town America, and it was here, in 1838, that trotters first raced on a stretch of land now known as Historic Track. In front of Historic Track was the Good Time Stable, a Tudor-style building with genuine half-timbering and angled rooflines. Ultimately the stable would become the Hall of Fame of the Trotter, and Historic Track would be the first – and thus far the only – sporting site to be designated a Registered National Historic Landmark.

Despite the museum's historical significance, the people at

the hall of fame recognize that the rest of the world is not as familiar with harness racing as they are with baseball and football. Step inside and you can read about the basics in various displays.

Most important is the distinction between trotters and pacers. Both are standardbred horses, as opposed to thoroughbreds, and are raced with a driver (not a jockey) in a two-wheeled vehicle called a sulky. Trotters move with a diagonal gait, their left front and right rear legs moving in unison. Pacers go with left front and left rear in tandem. One thing standardbreds don't do is run. Any horse caught running, called going "off-stride," must return to the specified gait or be disqualified.

That in mind, head to the gallery called the Living Hall of Fame, where the dozen or so persons still alive who have contributed greatly to the sport of trotting are enshrined. Or step inside the Peter D. Haughton Room of Immortals, named for a young driver whose career was cut short in an automobile accident, where more than 100 men and women and more than 130 horses are immortalized. The names, like those of Beissinger, Farrington, and Hempt mentioned earlier, will mean nothing to many visitors, but each is accompanied by a capsule summary of his or her accomplishments.

Unlike the plaques or medallions seen in many other sports halls of fame, each honoree is immortalized by a miniature statue crafted by Beverly Lopez, a Weston, Connecticut, artisan who collaborated on such projects as the United States buffalo nickel and the statue of George Patton at West Point.

The statuette of trainer and driver Howard Beissinger, for example, freezes a typical moment in his career: Beissinger, sitting on a fence post with a sandwich in one hand, a cup in the other, and a sponge, tape, and brush at his feet. Max Hempt, a driver, horse farm owner and executive, is dressed in a tie and jacket and sits at an office desk, cigar in hand. Driver Robert Farrington stands at an outdoor faucet, waiting for a red bucket to be filled. Each is worth a study for the detail and expression alone.

You will likely admire the Currier and Ives prints, presented for six-week stretches twice yearly, in summer and during the holiday season. The rest of the time that space is occupied by the works of local artists, all for sale.

The building's original stables have been cleverly transformed into galleries showcasing aspects of the sport from horse ownership to what the well-dressed horse wears. Be prepared to shell out at least $900 a month for grooming and training alone if you want to own a trotter.

Ready for some trivia? In one gallery discussing horse colors, we learned what illustrious American composer Stephen Foster was singing about in his immortal "Camptown Races." When Foster sang, "I'll bet my money on the bob-tail mare," he was referring to Flora Temple, a champion trotter of the day and a bay horse. The term "bay horse" refers to her color, somewhere between reddish tan and rich mahogany brown, a common shade for harness racing horses in that day. You'll recall the line, "Somebody bet on the bay."

The bay continued to dominate harness racing well into the twentieth century, so says the exhibit. A study in 1966 uncovered the following details: a total of 53 percent of trotters were bays, while the next most common color, at 25 percent, was brown. Of the 25,347 horses in the study, only four were pinto. Now that, truly, is a horse of a different color.

Location: The Hall of Fame of the Trotter is at 240 Main Street in Goshen. From I-84, take exit 121 onto State 17 west, then take exit 124B onto State 207 east; head straight through the traffic lights to the museum on the right. From the New York State Thruway (I-87), take exit 16 onto State 17 west and follow the directions above.

Admission is charged.

Hours: Year-round, daily; afternoons only on Sunday.

Allow at least forty-five minutes if you are a casual visitor. Those who would like to pore over the many exhibits should allow up to an hour and a half while trotter buffs should plan half a day.

Information: Hall of Fame of the Trotter, P.O. Box 590, 240 Main Street, Goshen, NY 10924, 914-294-6330.

Events: Early July, Hall of Fame Day, induction ceremonies, distinguished guests; mid-December, Classic Choral Society's Christmas Concert; educational series throughout the year.

Note: Films on harness racing are shown daily during race season. The museum gift shop is a utopia for those interested in either the sport or fine reproductions of Currier and Ives lithographs. For information on the racing program at the adjacent park, contact Historic Track, Box 192, Goshen, NY 10924, 914-294-5333.

If you are staying overnight: Super 8 Lodge, 563 Route 211 East (just north of I-84, exit 4W, and just east of State 17, exit 120), Middletown, 914-692-5828; Holiday Inn, Crystal Run Road (just north of State 17, exit 122), Middletown, 914-343-1474; Days Inn, US 6 and State 17M (just south of I-84, exit 3E), New Hampton, 914-374-2411; Dobbin's Stagecoach Inn (1740 stagecoach inn with four rooms), Maplewood Terrace and Main Street (next to village hall), Goshen, 914-294-5526.

When in the area: The recreation-minded will find nature hikes and stellar views at Bear Mountain and Harriman State Parks (pages 169–172), about twenty miles east. The history and heritage inherent to West Point (pages 163–168) is just north of Bear Mountain.

49 Corning Glass Center
Corning

When Prince Charles and Lady Di married in 1981, they didn't receive any Corningware as a wedding gift. They are probably the only couple in the world that didn't. Or so it seems. Whether the lack of such gifts led to the downfall of the fairy-tale marriage may be a question for the ages. A question more easily answered is the extent of the Corning Glass Center, which exhibits tons more than Corningware. Visit and you will be witness to one of the most complete museum complexes anywhere devoted to one theme.

It is a place where glassworkers with catlike patience speak in their own cryptic tongue, where the museum maintains twice as many pieces as there are people in Corning, and where you will see specimens of glass stronger than Schwarzenegger's fist. To make things easier for visitors, the glass center is divided into three parts: the Corning Museum of Glass, the Hall of Science, and the Steuben Glass Factory.

A videotape introduces you to the factory by offering an overview of the glassmaking process. Sit near the front benches to best hear the presentation, since the background noise of machinery is deafening–despite the glass partition separating workers from onlookers.

Corning Glass spokespersons proudly point out that the Steuben Factory is one of the few still making handcrafted glass. It is also a place where workers speak a curious language; watch the shop working at a glory hole with the gaffer putting the final touches on a piece of glass before it is placed in a lehr and afterwards sent to the finishing lines.

Translated from glassmakers' lingo into English, it means this: watch a small group working at a reheating oven with the master glassblower putting the final touches on a piece of glass before it is placed in an annealing oven and afterwards sent to the line where it will be ground and polished.

Some of the Steuben glass is engraved, and you will be able to see engravers plying their trade close up. Extraordinary patience is needed to engrave Steuben glass. Besides the responsibility of performing an exacting job, the engravers execute it with countless visitors literally looking over their shoulders. Although we can't imagine taking a job that permits outsiders to watch us at work, the Steuben workers expect it. Study them as they engrave the most complex designs on crystal using rotating copper wheels.

Humanity has been working with and decorating glass for thousands of years, and we have been using it even longer. At the Corning Museum of Glass, you can take a look at the items made by the Steuben workers' counterparts more than 3,000 years ago. Glass vessels made in Mesopotamia (present-day Iraq) by coating a clay-and-animal-dung core with molten glass are some of the oldest pieces here. They have been dated to 1400 B.C.

The museum boasts more than 24,000 objects, and many visitors are overwhelmed once they set eyes on the massive collection. Casual visitors tend to study the first few galleries and then suffer from what one museum director elsewhere calls "visual indigestion," seeing too much of a good thing at one stretch.

As you tour the museum keep in mind that it is arranged with a time tunnel effect. You start off with ancient and Islamic glass, such as an 800-year-old perfume bottle engraved with images of animals. A magnifying glass lets you look closely— how many different animals can you find?

Gradually, you approach the Middle Ages and the Renaissance, with Venetian goblets and German flasks, before reaching colonial America and the modern world. There is a handy time line comparing glass developments with major historical events.

You see three English goblets coupled with the year 1776, when John Hancock was putting his John Hancock on the Declaration of Independence in Philadelphia. When the Erie Canal was completed in 1824, mass production of American tableware was fully underway, thanks to the development of mechanical pressing. Two ornately patterned compotes, probably made in Sandwich, Massachusetts, an early glass manufacturing center, illustrate the infant days of mechanization.

Save time for the detailed collections near the museum's end, such as the dazzling display featuring hundreds of paperweights. Encased in glass are likenesses of everything from the purple finch to the quizzical face of Ulysses S. Grant.

You will probably wear a quizzical expression too when you step inside the Hall of Science and Industry and see glass accomplish some pretty remarkable feats. It is almost as if glass is a star performer at a carnival sideshow where the barker might lure you inside with tempting teasers such as, "See a glass pipe as strong as a hammer. See a slab of glass withstand a bath in corrosive acids. See the world's largest lightbulb, a total of 75,000 watts of pure power. See a man take rods of glass and transform them into shapes of animals as easily as if he was bending rubber." If you have never seen demonstrations of this caliber before, you will be truly amazed and surprised.

Location: From New York City and the east, take the Southern Tier Expressway (State 17) to the Cedar Street exit in Corning and follow it to the Corning Glass Center. From the New York State Thruway (I-90), take exit 41 or 42 and follow State 414 (or State 14 to State 414 in Watkins Glen) into Corning. At the end of State 414 take a left onto Pulteney Street, then the next right onto Centerway; the glass center is on the right.
Admission is charged.

Hours: Year-round, daily.

Allow two to three hours.

Information: Corning Glass Center, Corning, NY 14831, 607-974-8271.

Events: Special exhibits are scheduled annually. When we last attended, there was one focusing on glass from the Roman Empire, including glassware from the collections of museums as disparate as the Romanisch-Germanisches Museum in Cologne, West Germany, and the J. Paul Getty Museum in Malibu, California.

Note: Glassware in all forms is sold in several different shops in the complex. The Artist Gallery Shop sells glassware from a number of domestic and international glass firms. The World Glass Shop offers works by contemporary glass artists. The Consumer Shop has various Corning products, including closeouts and discontinued items. The Gift Shop stocks glass jewelry and Corning sunglasses as well as T-shirts and traditional gifts. The Steuben Shop sells items of fine crystal.

In summer a free double-decker bus takes visitors from the parking lot to the glass center and other sites in town. Many visitors enjoy following a visit to the glass center with a walk down Market Street in downtown Corning. The street has been refurbished to present a turn-of-the-century appearance, with dozens of specialty and gift shops, eateries and outlets. The shops carry everything from glass (naturally) to quality Christmas ornaments to ceramics.

If you are staying overnight: Corning Hilton Inn, State 17 (east of town), Corning, 607-962-5000; Stiles Motel, State 415 (State 17, exit 2, then half a mile west), Painted Post, 607-962-5221; White Birch (B&B), 69 East First Street, Corning, 607-962-6355; Rosewood Inn, 134 East First Street, Corning, 607-962-3253.

When in the area: The recreation of the Finger Lakes region (pages 81–87) is just to the north, as is Hammondsport, home of Bully Hill Vineyards (pages 156–161), one of the best places in the state to come drink the wine.

50 International Museum of Photography
Rochester

If you recall the advertising slogan "You press the button, we do the rest," you are probably older than you care to admit. You are also familiar with "The Father of Amateur Photography," the man who made it possible for any person, no matter how clumsy with machinery, no matter how unskilled an artist, to take family and vacation pictures with the ease of, well . . . pushing a button.

Rochester's George Eastman did not invent the camera. Professionals had been using cameras years before Eastman first saw the light of day in 1858. But the key word is "professionals." The process of taking photographs was lengthy and awkward and involved massive equipment, fragile and cumbersome glass plates, and serious know-how. The average American citizen did not take photographs until Eastman developed his first Kodak camera in 1888.

The International Museum of Photography at the George Eastman House first opened to the public in 1949 but underwent a massive face-lift in the late 1980s, unveiling its new climate-controlled wing in January 1989. Just five years earlier the museum trustees voted to donate the extensive museum collection, wasting away in poor storage conditions in the eighty-year-old mansion, to the Smithsonian Institution in Washington, D.C. The people of Rochester, not thrilled about losing a valuable cultural asset and tourist magnet, banded together, and with the help of a $17 million challenge grant from Eastman Kodak the new wing was built.

In effect Eastman's mansion and the photography museum are two different attractions connected by a passageway, and each could serve as a site on its own, with the house reflecting the man and the museum a camera onto the world of photography. The expansive gardens, also part of the face-lift, might be viewed as an additional attraction.

Like many people, Eastman was a person of contradictions. He loved making money and spending it on himself, but he also loved giving it away, donating over $100 million to philanthropic causes during his life. He fit the stereotype of the man's man who went on hunting expeditions around the world and played billiards in a smoke-filled upstairs room replete with raccoon and bear skins. But he also loved flowers and was a skilled horticulturist.

He loved the company of women, yet never married. His mother was to be his sole companion during his later adult years, and he built the Colonial Revival mansion with the intention of her sharing it with him. But Maria Kilbourn Eastman lived here only two years before dying at age eighty-two. From then on George Eastman lived alone.

Still, he never lacked for female friends, four of whom were married women he often lunched with and called the lobster quartette after one of their favorite meals. It was common to see Eastman taking them clothes shopping and buying outfits they admired. As a horticulturist (the gardens have been restored in the manner in which Eastman kept them), he would give each woman an orchid corsage when they visited.

Eastman talked with them about subjects that he couldn't discuss with his male friends, ranging from birth control to suicide. It wasn't idle talk. Eastman committed suicide in his bedroom at age seventy-eight, shooting himself in the heart with an automatic Lugar. In poor health, Eastman left a suicide note that read, "My work is done. Why wait?"

And so the rooms in his mansion reflect the many aspects of his character. Designed just after the turn of the century with beaux-arts glitter by Gilded Age architects McKim, Mead and

White, the house retains tons of original furnishings and, thanks to period photographs, is very accurate historically.

The living room and the light and spacious conservatory represent the public George Eastman, the philanthropist who held concerts here for friends and workers at his company. Both rooms are liberally decked with greenery, representative of Eastman's love of plants, while the original Steinway piano and music stand in the living room recall Eastman's fondness for music. Concerts are regularly scheduled in the living room today, an echo of Eastman's offerings. The vast and open living room has been painstakingly refurbished to look as it did in Eastman's day, from the American Empire-style furniture to the ceiling's cast plaster moldings representing the four seasons.

The fiberglass elephant head with the jutting tusks mounted over large glass windows represents not the Grand Old Party but Eastman's grand old hobby. Photographs show that Eastman had mounted in the same location the head of an elephant he had bagged in Africa while hunting in 1928. Eastman's taxidermists were so impressed with his catch that they made a mold of it to cast a copy for promotion purposes. When the mansion was refurbished in 1989, the same mold was used to make the replica you see today.

Wild game aside, the most noteworthy item in the conservatory is an Aeolian pipe organ, restored and still played at public concerts here. The organ console and organist are concealed from view by a tiered bank of potted plants, but the sounds escape up to the oculus, an oval-shaped piece of tinted glass embedded in the roof, which works like an echo chamber.

The Little Library, paneled, orderly, and reminiscent of colonial design, joins the billiard room as tributes to the private George Washington Eastman. The library was built as a reception room, fashionable around the time the house was built but not so by 1927, when Eastman converted it into its current use as a book repository. His original texts still sit on the shelves, and subject matter ranges from biographies of Frederick Douglass and Booker T. Washington to poetry to early dentistry. As a boy Eastman saw his mother's teeth pulled out for health reasons while she sat at the kitchen table; because of his witnessing her agony, dental schools became one of his favorite charities.

Unlike many of the wealthy of his day, Eastman hated antiques and decorated his home in what were the most modern furnishings. The Atwater Kent radio and Edison cylinder Victrola in the billiard room were state-of-the-art when the entrepreneur used this room to read and relax by himself. Be sure to notice the stained glass roundels in the windows, each representing a different form of transportation: tin Lizzie, horse and carriage, canal boat, hot-air balloon, bicycle, and steamship.

Prior to the 1980s restoration the second story was used mainly as a photo gallery. Today Eastman's second-floor bedroom is the restoration gallery, where photos documenting the massive refurbishment are displayed. In another upstairs room is a display telling Eastman's own Horatio Alger story.

But his lasting legacy is in the museum section of the property. As you might guess, it is filled with cameras of all kinds from all periods, and lots of them are Kodak products. Interestingly, the name of the company is nothing but a nonsense word. Eastman wanted a name for his company that could not be translated into another language. He liked the letter *K*, some say because of his closest female relatives, sister Kate and mother Maria Kilbourn Eastman. So he took the letter *K* and threw in the middle letters.

One docent said, "In France it's Kodak, in Russia it's Kodak, in any language it's Kodak," acknowledging that Eastman got his wish.

291

The introductory video, "The Lengthened Shadow of a Man," presents a photograph Eastman took of a village in Africa called "Kodok," cementing the image of a company name pronounceable in any language.

The museum is both a study in photography development and a trip down memory lane as you remember your first Brownie (which Eastman named after a fictional character in a children's story) or your first Instamatic. You will probably also recognize a non-Kodak product, the Polaroid Swinger, dated 1964, as modern in its day as Eastman's Atwater Kent radio.

In 1839, the acme of photo technology was the invention of Louis Jacques Daguerre, the world's first commercial camera, and one is on view, along with the first box of Eastman's Gelative Dry Plates, dating from 1880. Several exhibits showcase how cumbersome the early processes were; witness the early specimens of silver, glass, paper, and chemical bottles.

Specialty and novelty cameras aren't a twentieth-century development, and the detective camera, in the shape of a gun, is proof. It was produced in 1883. Compare it to the dime-a-dozen children's and novelty cameras from a later period that take the forms of Mickey Mouse, Snoopy, and a can of Budweiser beer. There is also the Coquette, the petite camera, circa 1930, that was packaged with lipstick holder and compact, especially for women.

Eastman's first camera, the one he invented in 1888, is here. It was a bulky contraption, and America's first amateur photographers paid $25 for a fresh-from-the-factory camera complete with a roll of film with 100 exposures. When it came time for developing, the camera owner sent the entire camera with film to Kodak, who returned it with developed photographs and a fresh roll of 100 exposures. A century of progress is evidenced by the first public installations of both an Associated Press Leaf

Picture desk and a photo CD demonstrating the most recent advances in imaging technology.

Location: The International Museum of Photography at the George Eastman House is at 900 East Avenue in Buffalo. Westbound from the New York State Thruway (I-90), take exit 45 to I-490 west. Eastbound from I-90, take exit 47 to I-490 east. From I-490, take exit 19; turn right onto Culver Road, then left onto East Avenue, and follow it three blocks to the mansion on the right.

Admission is charged.

Hours: Year-round, Tuesday through Saturday and Sunday afternoons.

Allow two to three hours.

Information: International Museum of Photography at the George Eastman House, 900 East Avenue, Rochester, NY 14607, 716-271-3361.

Note: Guided tours of both the house and the museum are offered twice daily, once in the morning and once in early afternoon, at no extra charge. Otherwise, you tour the house on your own. In addition, films from the museum's collection are shown four times weekly at the museum's adjacent Dryden Theater. Vending machines are in the museum's Studio Cafe. Plans are to turn it into a working café where hot and cold foods will be served.

If you are staying overnight: Days Inn–Downtown Rochester, 384 East Avenue, Rochester, 716-325-5010; Holiday Inn–Genesee Plaza, 120 East Main Street, Rochester, 716-546-6400; Red Roof Inn, 4820 West Henrietta Road (State 15 at I-90, exit 46), West Henrietta, 716-359-1100; Dartmouth House (B&B, four rooms, one suite), 215 Dartmouth Street, Rochester, 716-271-7872; 428 Mt. Vernon (seven-room B&B), 428 Mt. Vernon Avenue,

Rochester, 716-271-0792; Adventures in Bed & Breakfasts, P.O. Box 567, Geneseo, NY 14454, 800-724-1932 or 716-243-5540, for bed and breakfast listings in Genesee Country area.

When in the area: A visit to the nineteenth century is on tap at the multibuilding Genesee Country Museum (pages 207–212), a re-created village nearby in Mumford. To the south is a classic mansion and gardens, Sonnenberg Gardens (pages 107–112) in Canandaigua.

51 Statue of Liberty and Ellis Island
New York Harbor

The Lady on Liberty Island certainly needs no more publicity, and neither does Ellis Island. Attendance in the months following the reopening of the statue in the summer of 1986 reached 20,000 visitors a day, more than some attractions draw in a year. Attendance has leveled off but still reaches over a million a year.

National Park Service personnel say the best information we can give you about the Statue of Liberty and Ellis Island is advice on the most efficient ways to spend your time so lengthy waits don't force you to miss attractions you had your heart set on seeing.

1. Plan your visit in the winter, when crowds are at their thinnest. You will get more individual attention from rangers, and free guided tours inside the Statue of Liberty museum and on Ellis Island are offered mainly in the off-season. After mid-March, tours are rarely offered due to unmanageable numbers. (Bear in mind that, like most of the federal government, the National Park Service is cutting costs and tours could be scrapped at any time.)

2. Make the statue your first sightseeing stop and come as early as possible. We rode a 10:30 A.M. ferry from Battery Park on the Saturday of a winter holiday weekend and there were few other tourists on board. By the time we were nearing the end of our visit about 2 P.M., there was a one-hour wait to climb to the statue's crown and a sizable wait to enter the statue museum.

3. Take the New Jersey ferry if possible. Many people don't even realize that there is a ferry from New Jersey to the Statue of Liberty and Ellis Island. There are significantly fewer people on it, you can avoid the hassle of Manhattan, and there is free parking at the terminal. The ferry leaves from Liberty State Park in Jersey City, reached by taking exit 14B off the New Jersey

Turnpike extension. (Please note that both ferries stop at both Liberty and Ellis islands.)

4. If your main desire at the statue is to climb to the crown, think twice about it and then think again. One ranger says, "The worst thing the average visitor can do is go to the crown."

Why? The view is often disappointing. From the crown you get a view of Brooklyn and little else. Most people, we were told, spend about twenty seconds in the crown.

The alternative is to take the elevator to the top of the pedestal, not as high as the crown but complete with an unencumbered 360-degree view that includes the skyscrapers of lower Manhattan.

If you are dying to climb to the crown just to say you did, make it your first stop once inside the statue and make sure you have strong leg muscles. There is no elevator and no connection between the stairway leading to the crown and the elevator that stops at the pedestal. You must walk 354 steps each way. If you have a heart condition, forget the climb. The climb down will be more taxing than the one up, and your calves are likely to feel like Welch's Grape Jelly by the time you reach bottom.

5. Allow a full day to see both the Statue of Liberty and Ellis Island, including time to park your car and forty minutes total aboard either ferry. In summer and on weekends and holidays, expect to wait for the ferry or admission to the statue and Ellis Island. If you don't have to wait, then your visit will be that much more pleasant.

6. Allow time to see the museum inside the Statue of Liberty. It opened with the refurbished statue in 1986 and is located on two floors. The bottom level is devoted to the statue, its history, construction, image, and symbolism. The upper level focuses on immigration. The best way to see the museum is to take a guided tour through either or both levels, then walk

through later at your leisure. (Again, guided tours are limited mostly to the winter months.)

By now, most everyone is familiar with the basic story of the Statue of Liberty and Ellis Island. You probably know that the statue was a gift from France and was largely the work of Frédéric Auguste Bartholdi. It is made of copper, and its torch symbolizes liberty lighting the world. Ellis Island, you're probably aware, was the gateway to America and a Babel of confusion, fears, and dreams for immigrants from all nations.

The museums present both these sites in human terms. Consider, for example, that Bartholdi's model for the statue's face was his mother. Compare the full-scale reproduction of the famous face to that of Mrs. Bartholdi. Our guide said that visitors have claimed that Mrs. Bartholdi resembles a host of celebrities from George Washington to Elvis Presley.

It wasn't pure altruism that compelled France to give the gift to the United States. There were political motives. Bartholdi said that the idea for the statue came from his friend and compatriot Edouard de Laboulaye, a French scholar and outspoken opponent of the ruling French Second Empire. Laboulaye had cited the United States as a model of liberty, independence, and anti-monarchial government. The gift of this statue to the United States government underlined these feelings. Bartholdi's name for his creation, "Liberty Enlightening the World," said Laboulaye follower Henri Martin, is "a sublime phrase which sums up the progress of modern times."

The best-known symbol of the statue today is the poem by Emma Lazarus including the lines "Give me your tired, your poor, Your huddled masses yearning to breathe free." Most visitors are in for a couple of surprises when they encounter the poem. The first is that these famous words are not found at the work's beginning. There are nine lines in the fourteen-line poem

Visit the Statue of Liberty and the Ellis Island Museum

preceding them, as you can see for yourself when you read it on its original bronze plaque, displayed indoors. Yes, indoors. The poem was never displayed outdoors, and prior to its current spot in the museum it was on an interior pedestal wall.

More words, these on the back of postcards, can be read in an ingenious display celebrating the statue's exploitation in pop culture. A mountainous display of postcards has been arranged so that the yellow colors in the cards form the statue's likeness; walk behind it and you see another image of the statue made from postcards, this one in blue.

Look closer and you see the many forms in which this allegorical figure has been portrayed. One postcard has her waiting for a subway train. Another shows Miss Liberty buried in sand up to her crown as in the final scene of *Planet of the Apes*. Others present her face replaced by famous ones like that of Ronald Reagan and the *Mona Lisa*.

Use of the statue's form by other pop culture creators can be seen on videotape, including a *Mad* magazine foldout featuring Ms. Liberty as a bra-burning feminist and the cover of Supertramp's 1979 best-selling "Breakfast in America" album, depicting her as a waitress in a coffee shop, raising high a tray of breakfast goodies.

Her more sublime meaning is explored in the gallery devoted to the history of immigration in the United States. A Jewish kiddush cup from Czarist Russia is near a photograph of a sea of humanity packed into Manhattan's lower east side around the turn of the century. A model of a steamer similar to those that transported Irish immigrants sits not far from a warning from the anti-immigrant American Party (also known as the Know-Nothing Party) of the 1850s advising others to watch out for "the Satanic Plot and Artful Crimes of Popery."

But the overall mood of the gallery is upbeat, as is that of the refurbished Ellis Island. An introductory film, absolutely moving, sets the feeling. Emigrants who left Russia, Italy, Poland, Denmark, Greece, and Ireland, among other countries, were tossed and rolled about for three months on fetid ships filled with the odors of vomit and sweat, the cries of screeching babies, and the moans of the sick, and finally arrived in the United States. In the film, a naturalized American recalls his arrival at Ellis Island, saying that he was initially scared of the police in America, not realizing that they were there to help, not brutalize, people. Things were just not to be like they were in Europe.

Today's visitors enter Ellis Island in the same manner that their ancestors did, through the main front doors, into the baggage room, where period suitcases and trunks of wicker and wood sit stacked atop each other, and then proceed upstairs to the yawning Registry Room, the great hall with the multipaned semicircular windows that offer views of lower Manhattan and the Statue of Liberty. A few original benches remain, and there is an authentic official's desk, a nondescript little furnishing, but intimidating to the newly arrived immigrant.

A posted commentary by the desk reads, "Nearly every day, for over two decades (1900-24), the Registry Room was filled with new arrivals waiting to be inspected and registered by Immigration Service officers. On many days, over 5,000 people would file through this space. For most immigrants this great hall epitomized Ellis Island. Here they encountered the complex demands of the immigration laws and an American bureaucracy that could either grant or withhold permission to land in the United States."

Nothing was as feared as the medical exam. As the mass of humanity passed by their posts, Public Health Service doctors watched to see who limped or sniffled or coughed. Illnesses that were reason for possible deportation included cholera, favus, epilepsy, tuberculosis, and trachoma—especially trachoma, a contagious eye infection that could lead to blindness or death. Doctors checked for trachoma by turning a person's eyelid inside out with a buttonhook and looking for swelling of the inner eyelid, and such a buttonhook is on view. Appropriately, trachoma was cured by a Japanese immigrant to America.

Abbreviations for ailments were written in blue chalk on the arrivals' clothing: "K" for kidney problems, "H" for heart problems, "E" for eye illnesses, and "X" for mental illness. Those suspected of mental illness were given intelligence tests. Those who didn't pass were deported.

Though many believe that high percentages of immigrants were deported, the fact is that 98 percent of all who arrived at Ellis Island were admitted. However, with 5,000 to 7,000 people arriving per day during the island's peak years, 2 percent equaled 3,000 to 4,000 persons a month. Ellis Island became known by two names: for most it was the "Island of Hope"; for the rest, it was the "Island of Tears."

Detainees stayed in dormitories and one has been re-created. Beds hang by chains, one atop another, with mesh or canvas mattresses, and each is equipped with a blanket. It resembles an enlisted men's sleeping quarters on a battleship, and there is a trio of no-frills sinks attached to a wall.

Other side rooms depict aspects of immigrant life. In one there are postcards of steamships that carried immigrants across the Atlantic and old black-and-white films of immigrants arriving at the ferry slip. All the while you can listen to songs of the new Americans who came when the century was young.

Tin Pan Alley and mass immigration married to produce some unforgettable (and many foreseeable) songs, evidenced by the wall of sheet music in another side room. Posted is the music to such songs as "My Pretty Colleen," "Chinatown," "My Brodda Sylvest," "Hello Wisconsin," "Jake the Yiddasha Ball Player," "I Love a Lassie," and "Land of Spaghetti."

"Treasures from Home" is an exhibit filled with ruffled clothing, Bibles, ornamented shoes, faded photos, wooden toys, and elaborate candelabrums brought to America by folks like the "Jensen family from Denmark" and the "Jue family from China." Be sure also to take a few minutes to see "Silent Voices," an exhibit dedicated to the Ellis Island years after it was closed but before it was restored, those decades when the building sat vacant at the mercy of looters, wind, and rats. Chairs, typewriters, huge cooking pots, a cash register, pipes, and more, sit piled up, dusty and crusty and decrepit. The exhibit affords an idea of the job the restorers had in front of them when they took on their tedious task in the mid-1980s.

Outside Ellis Island is the Wall of Honor, a 950-foot-long seawall topped with copper plaques engraved with about 200,000 names of immigrants who came to America, though not necessarily through Ellis Island. To raise funds for the restoration, the Statue of Liberty–Ellis Island Foundation offered to inscribe the name of any immigrant for a donation of $100. The response was an avalanche of donations, with people like Barbara Bush and Lee Iacocca sending money to have their ancestors' names inscribed. My family did too; look for Reuben and Eva Zimmerman Schuminsky on panel 375 and David and Lena Goldstein Struman on panel 406.

Regardless of how cynical you have become about life and politics, it's hard not to swell with pride at Ellis Island, as you admire a tribute to this melting pot, the likes of which are found nowhere else on the globe.

Location: The Statue of Liberty is on Liberty Island, next to Ellis Island, in New York Harbor. Both are reached by ferries from

Battery Park in Manhattan and from Liberty State Park in Jersey City, New Jersey.

Admission is free for the statue and Ellis Island but charged for either ferry ride.

Allow a full day to see both and from three to five hours for the Statue of Liberty and museum and three to four hours for Ellis Island. Expect to wait half an hour to a few hours to enter the Statue of Liberty anytime except the dead of winter. (And even then!)

Information: Statue of Liberty National Monument, Liberty Island, New York, NY 10004, 212-363-3200 for basic recorded information, 212-363-8340 to speak with a human. For information on the Manhattan ferry: 212-269-5755; on Liberty State Park: 201-915-3400; on the New Jersey ferry: 201-435-9499.

If you are staying overnight: Get information on conventional lodging and tour packages from the New York City Convention and Visitors Bureau, 2 Columbus Circle, New York, NY 10019, 212-397-8222 (seven days a week). For information on alternative lodging, contact any of these bed and breakfast agencies: Bed, Breakfast, & Books, 35 West 92nd Street, New York, NY 10025, 212-865-8740; City Lights Bed & Breakfast, P.O. Box 20355, Cherokee Station, New York, NY 10028, 212-737-7049; New World Bed & Breakfast, 150 Fifth Avenue, Suite 711, New York, NY 10011, 212-675-5600; Urban Ventures, 38 West 32nd Street, Suite 1412, New York, NY 10001, 212-594-5650.

When in the area: Another full day of sightseeing, as well as shopping, can be spent at South Street Seaport (pages 304–310). On weekdays, consider a stop at the New York Stock Exchange and Federal Hall National Memorial (pages 238–245). A short subway ride away is Theodore Roosevelt's birthplace (pages 263–269).

52 South Street Seaport
Manhattan

Read the following letters home from a hypothetical visitor to lower Manhattan's South Street Seaport and see if you can tell what's wrong with them.

Letter #1
Dear Folks,

My three-day weekend in New York City has finally arrived and I'm spending my first day at South Street Seaport. So far I've seen the two levels at Fulton Marketplace and have sampled a Greek gyro, a south Philly cheesesteak sandwich, a potato knish, and for dessert, a helping of gourmet chocolate. I will see the rest of Manhattan over the next two days, but I'm off to see more of South Street Seaport today. There's just one problem—I keep hearing about the South Street Seaport Museum, but I haven't found it anywhere.

Letter #2
Greetings from Gotham,

It's a day later but I'm still at South Street Seaport. There is so much I haven't done yet. I walked through lots of specialty shops in different buildings and it seems that I bought something in each. I'm coming home with, among other things, a pith helmet, a plush penguin, and some computerized gadget to measure how much in debt I am. Pigged out at a couple of bakeries for breakfast, had an Irish coffee at an old-fashioned Irish pub, a pastrami on rye for lunch, and a shrimp roll for a mid-afternoon snack. Tonight it's Italian or Cajun or maybe down-home barbecued ribs. Toured a couple of grand old ships docked here. Still haven't found the museum yet.

Letter #3

Hail from the Big Apple,

Let me get right to the core of the matter. I'm back at South Street Seaport. My three-day weekend is almost over and I still haven't seen it all. I glanced in all the shops, but I would have loved more time – barely got the chance to browse through the gourmet kitchenware, marine brass store, and cat menagerie. Got a suntan on a noontime harbor cruise. Wolfed down a tostada, a slice of New York pizza, a dish of sweet-and-sour chicken and fried rice, a falafel, and a hot fudge sundae with real ice cream and a ton of toppings. (I was going to watch the calories, but hey, you only live once.)

Saw a printer's shop from the 1870s and an exhibition about Norwegian immigrants. The rest of Manhattan will have to wait for another trip, but not until I have seen the rest of what's here – the other ships, the exhibitions, and the food; there's so much I haven't sampled. Oh yes – I never found the South Street Seaport Museum. That will have to wait too.

Now, pick one answer from the list below and tell us what's wrong with these letters.

1. No one can really spend three days at South Street Seaport and not be bored.
2. No one eats a Greek gyro together with a potato knish.
3. No one who eats Mexican, Chinese, Italian, and Middle Eastern food in one day has enough room left over for a hot fudge sundae with a ton of toppings.
4. No one could walk around South Street Seaport for three days and still miss the museum.

Let's go over the answers.

1. Yes, one could. Whether one wants to bypass the rest of Manhattan is another thing. But spending a trio of days at South Street Seaport can be done without great difficulty. You've got a complex of shopping and dining malls, historic ships and boats, museum galleries and exhibition buildings, guided historic tours and harbor excursions.

2. Incorrect. I did it myself.

3. I did this too. (Oink!)

4. Correct. If you don't understand what you're looking for, you could easily miss the museum. If you ask for help, you will get an enigmatic answer. The conversation usually sounds like this.

Q–But where's the museum?

A–All over the seaport.

The South Street Museum is called "a museum without walls." It's an alternative concept. There are several museum galleries and displays. But instead of being housed under one roof, they are in numerous buildings throughout the entire complex. Yet the museum is not just indoors. Vintage ships and boats docked at the waterfront are also part of the South Street Seaport Museum. So is a reconstructed nineteenth-century printer's office and a diverse handful of first-class museum shops.

Many, including those who work and live in Manhattan, have discovered South Street Seaport to be one of the Big Apple's biggest plums. They have discovered that midtown is not the only place to amble down the streets alternately window shopping, dining, and picking up a bit of culture on the side.

However, the museum hardly represents all that one can see and do here. Harbor cruises are an inviting option. The Semi-Circle Line Cruise, run by the famous Circle Line, will take you around lower Manhattan and back, offering views of the World

Trade Center, the Statue of Liberty, Ellis Island, Wall Street, the Chrysler Building, and the Empire State Building.

There is the century-old schooner *Pioneer,* on which you can literally sail off into the sunset. And there is New York Unearthed, an actual museum program but located a five- to ten-minute walk from the Seaport at 17 State Street and Battery Park. Here remnants of New York's past are on view, artifacts excavated from beneath the city's streets, and you can watch archaeologists in action in a glass-enclosed laboratory.

And for those who admit that when the going gets tough, the tough go shopping—and eating—there are over 120 stores and eateries in the five-building complex. They extend from the common—Mexican food and fashions—to the exotic—MGM film memorabilia and pickles of every kind. Our letter writer discussed only a fraction of what exists.

There is a purpose behind all this food, frolic, and fun, and much of it is historic. New York City was first settled near the point where the seaport sits, and the city grew from there. When the Erie Canal opened in 1825, the city became connected to the Midwest by way of water. Products made and grown in the country's heartland were shipped and unloaded here. Thanks to its harbor New York City flourished. South Street Seaport—the museum, the buildings, the food, and the merchandise—is a tribute to more than three centuries of commerce by way of water.

The South Street seaport suffered a long period of decline after steam power replaced sail power and the city's ports shifted from downtown to Manhattan's west side. But in the 1970s a revitalization program was put into effect with much credit going to the Rouse Company, developers extraordinaire, responsible for similar urban centers like Faneuil Hall Marketplace in Boston and Harborplace in Baltimore. (And don't be surprised if you see some of the same stores here that you have seen at other Rouse complexes.) As is the case in these other Rouse projects, automobile traffic is banned through the seaport center.

If you have only one day and want to make the most of South Street Seaport, you may want to follow this example. Here is what we did in six and a half hours.

Hours 1 and 2: Explored Fulton Market, which is filled with food stalls, and Museum Block, with its food and retail emporia, from top to bottom. Had lunch for two composed of selections from five different food sellers (including the noted combination gyro and knish plate).

Hour 3 and first half of hour 4: Took ninety-minute Semi-Circle cruise around lower Manhattan.

Hour 4 (second half) and 5: Walked to waterfront, enjoying views of Brooklyn Bridge and harbor. Took guided tours of two ships, the *Peking* (a four-masted bark built in Germany in 1911) and the *Ambrose* (a lightship built in 1907). You can walk around each boat on your own in certain seasons, but the tour affords one deeper understanding. On the *Peking* men raised the anchor by hand. On the *Ambrose* it was lifted by hydraulic means. Meals on the *Peking* usually consisted of a chunk of hardtack, often accompanied by roaches and bugs.

Hours 6 and 7: Went on a browsing expedition through Pier 17 Pavilion, all three levels of it. Saw stores specializing in candles, stuffed animals, safari clothing, German cutlery, designer sunglasses, hats, leather, perfumes, handmade pottery, movie mementoes, and exotic chocolates. And more.

We left after six and a half hours with a real understanding for what South Street Seaport is all about. But you can design your own day. And don't miss the museum!

Location: South Street Seaport is roughly surrounded by Water,

John, and Beekman streets and the East River. By car from the east side, take FDR Drive's Brooklyn Bridge and Civic Center exit, which will take you onto Water/Pearl streets three blocks north of the seaport area. From the west side, take Fulton Street or drive around the tip of Manhattan through the Battery underpass to South Street. From Brooklyn, the Brooklyn Bridge, Manhattan Bridge, and Brooklyn Battery Tunnel all provide access to lower Manhattan. From New Jersey, take the Holland Tunnel. The following subway lines stop at either Fulton Street and Broadway or Fulton and Nassau streets: 7th Avenue IRT line (2 or 3); Lexington Avenue IRT line (4 or 5); 8th Avenue IND line (A or CC); IND and BMT lines (J, M, or RR). The M15 bus lines along Water Street make several stops near South Street Seaport. Other bus lines, including M9, M10, M101, and M102, also provide access to the seaport.

Admission is charged to most museum properties, including all ships and guided tours. Admission is also charged for the harbor sails and excursions. Admission is free to all shopping and dining complexes.

Hours: Year-round, daily.

Allow one hour for a guided museum tour of any of the ships and an hour and a half for the Semi-Circle Line cruise. One can spend as little as half an hour at South Street Seaport to grab a quick bite to eat or days to see everything and take a harbor cruise. To get a sufficient taste of South Street Seaport, allow a minimum of four hours, preferably about six.

Information: South Street Seaport Museum, 207 Front Street, New York, NY 10038, 212-669-9400. South Street Seaport, 19 Fulton Street, New York, NY 10038, 212-732-7678. Harbor Tours on the Circle Line, 212-563-3200. The schooner *Pioneer,* 212-669-9417.

Events: There is something going on nearly all the time. A partial list includes: late winter, Jazz Festival, free local performers and big name paid concerts; September, Street Performer Festival, jugglers, mimes, comedians, puppeteers, musicians; late October, Pumpkin Festival, pumpkin-flavored food, pumpkin sculpture competition, hay rides, folk concerts, children's activities; late November and December, Chorus Tree, a huge "living" Christmas tree of singers performing Chanukah and Christmas songs, seasonal decorations, appearance by Santa Claus.

Note: The best place to get museum tickets and information is the visitors center at 12 Fulton Street or the Pier 16 ticket booth.

If you are staying overnight: Get information on conventional lodging and tour packages from the New York City Convention and Visitors Bureau, 2 Columbus Circle, New York, NY 10019, 212-397-8222 (seven days a week). For information on alternative lodging, contact any of these bed and breakfast agencies: Bed, Breakfast, & Books, 35 West 92nd Street, New York, NY 10025, 212-865-8740; City Lights Bed & Breakfast, P.O. Box 20355, Cherokee Station, New York, NY 10028, 212-737-7049; New World Bed & Breakfast, 150 Fifth Avenue, Suite 711, New York, NY 10011, 212-675-5600; Urban Ventures, 38 West 32nd Street, Suite 1412, New York, NY 10001, 212-594-5650.

When in the area: Within walking distance are the New York Stock Exchange and Federal Hall National Memorial (pages 238–245). Near Gramercy Park is the birthplace of Theodore Roosevelt (pages 263–269). And in the harbor, accessible by boats leaving from Battery Park, are the Statue of Liberty and Ellis Island (pages 295–303).

Index

Other titles in the 52 Weekends series:

52 Michigan Weekends
52 New York Weekends
52 Wisconsin Weekends

Spring 1995
52 Illinois Weekends

Fall 1995
52 Florida Weekends
52 Iowa Weekends
52 New Jersey Weekends

All books are $9.95 at bookstores
Or order directly from the publisher (add $3.00 shipping and
handling for direct orders):

Country Roads Press
P.O. Box 286
Castine, Maine 04421
Toll-free phone number: **800-729-9179**